from Darren Kong
Dec. 1993

ACCENTS
OF THE
ORIENT

EASTERN INFLUENCE
ON WESTERN COOKING

SUSAN GRODNICK

Published by HPBooks, a division of Price Stern Sloan, Inc.
360 North La Cienega Boulevard, Los Angeles, California 90048

ACCENTS
OF THE
ORIENT

EASTERN INFLUENCE
ON WESTERN COOKING

SUSAN GRODNICK

PHOTOGRAPHY BY TERI SANDISON

HPBooks
a division of
PRICE STERN SLOAN
Los Angeles

DEDICATION

For Scott

ACKNOWLEDGEMENTS

Without Chris Tomasino and Sam Mitnick, there would be no book. My heartfelt thanks to both of them for believing in it.

My thanks also to my husband, Scott Grodnick, for his encouragement, suggestions, and loving critiques as well as his patience in tasting almost everything.

Thanks to Elaine Woodard and Jeanette Egan of HP for their help.

A special thanks to Becky LaBrum for her painstaking copy editing and intelligent suggestions.

Thanks also to Susan Poskanzer and Pam Older for letting me use their printers. It made finishing the book much easier.

CREDITS

Photography and styling by Teri Sandison, Los Angeles
Food Styling by Norman W. Stewart
Tableware from the following Los Angeles galleries: New Stone Age (213) 658-5969, By Design (213) 652-9230, Wild Blue (213) 939-8434, Tesoro (213) 391-7292, Lynne Deutch (213) 658-8737, FreeHand (213) 655-2607, Country Floors Tiles (213) 657-0510.

CONTENTS

Spiced Pecans / Curried Guacamole / Crab Fritters / Fried Won Tons with Salsa / Egg Rolls with Potato-Onion Filling / Cheese Tempura / Pearl Balls / Chinese Pizza / Pumpernickel Shrimp Toasts / Chinese Mushrooms Stuffed with Crabmeat / Stuffed Grape Leaves / Oysters with Ginger-Wasabi Sauce / Steamed Cucumbers Stuffed with Crabmeat / Mackerel Seviche / Mackerel Sushi / Paper-Wrapped Chicken with Salami / Sesame Chicken in Phyllo / Seafood Salad with Miso Sauce / Smoked Trout Mousse / Pork and Crab Terrine / Shrimp Quenelles with Ginger-Wasabi Sauce

Cold Vegetable Soup / Vichyssoise with Coconut Milk / Cream of Oriental Mushroom Soup / Thai Black Bean Soup / Hot and Sour Chicken Noodle Soup / Chicken Minestrone / Hearty Vegetable Soup / Curried Split Pea and Sausage Soup / Lentil Soup with Oriental Eggplant / Fennel Fish Soup / Dashi / Clam Chowder / Agnolotti Soup

Stir-Fried Chicken Enchiladas / Lemon Chicken / Chicken Breast with Nori / Soy-Roasted Chicken / Thai Pie / Crunchy Chicken Salad / Chicken and Sun-Dried Tomato Salad with Ginger Vinaigrette / Fried Chicken / Steamed Chicken Rolls / Coconut Milk Chicken / Baked Chicken Wings / Sautéed Chicken Livers / Roast Chicken with Cilantro and Lime / Cornish Game Hens with Tamarind Marinade / Duck Breasts with Black Bean Sauce / Kung Pao Turkey with Pumpkin Seeds

Sushi Salad, page 144

INTRODUCTION

One day as I was rummaging through my cabinets looking for ingredients for a lamb marinade, I came across a jar of sambal oelek. I used it instead of pepper, and the lamb was a big hit. The success of that experiment inspired me to take a serious look at the contents of my kitchen cabinets. I was amazed to see how many things I had accumulated, many of them purchased to make one dish, then forgotten. Most of these ingredients were far more versatile than I had realized. There was a large bottle of *nuoc nam*, Vietnamese fish sauce, used in almost every Vietnamese dish. It smelled awful in the bottle but added a delicate perfume to my salmon papillotes. Glutinous rice, which gets incredibly sticky, made a fabulous filling for batter-fried poblano chilies. Miso and sake brushed on lamb cubes gave them a beautiful brown crust. Fermented black beans spooned into lentil soup added saltiness in a new way.

Trying to add an Oriental ingredient to each Western dish became a game for me. It turned out to be so easy that I looked the other way, adding Western touches to dishes from the East. Tortillas, for instance, make great wrappers for mo-shu vegetables. Mashed potatoes and onions are excellent in egg roll skins; curly rotelle is better than straight egg noodles with thick sesame sauce.

At the same time, I was eating out in new restaurants, often run by Americans. I began to notice more and more Oriental foods—ginger, soba, miso, snow peas, water chestnuts, oyster sauce—turning up in all kinds of dishes, from pasta and pizzas to poached fish and roasts. These dishes weren't "authentic" anything; they were just delicious. They were the essence of the melting pot, combining ingredients and techniques from various cultures to create a different, American cuisine.

The idea is not new. Ethnic groups have been changing the way Americans eat for centuries. What is new is the direction of the inspiration. For years, serious cooks looked to Europe for guidance about what was sophisticated and chic, which meant, in turn, what was considered good. A *pot au feu* was worthy of company, but a New England boiled dinner was family fare; chocolate mousse was thought to be better than chocolate pudding; and many believed that only the French could make fine wine. The pendulum has swung now. Restaurants and food aficionados are extolling the virtues of American cooks and ingredients. At the same time, Americans no longer feel the need to slavishly recreate the foods of any particular cuisines, even native ones. Instead, they look to use the best of what each has to offer.

As immigration from the Orient has increased, so have the newcomers' demands for foods rarely seen here before—and American cooks have benefited. The proliferation of health food stores has helped, too. Many Oriental ingredients, like nori, soba, and egg roll skins, are staples of those shops. Some foods have become so popular they are even sold in supermarkets. It is not unusual to see a section devoted to water chestnuts, sesame oil, dried Chinese mushrooms, and, of course, soy sauce. Many markets today carry fresh ginger and daikon. Some sell snow peas and shiitake mushrooms. It's a wonderful sight for the cook.

I am especially drawn to Asian foods, relishing their unusual textures and flavors. This book reflects my interest, taking ingredients and dishes from the West—North and South America and Europe—and combining them with those from Asia—China, Japan, Indonesia, Vietnam, Korea, Thailand, the Philippines. In some cases, traditional dishes are simply seasoned differently; for example, a marinade may use soy sauce and sesame oil instead of salt and olive oil. Certain dishes, like Italian focaccia, use a Western technique. Others, like won tons served with salsa, are more Oriental. Some are as unusual as Thai chicken curry baked in a pot pie.

The more I cook, the more I discover how versatile Oriental foods are and how easily they adapt to other ingredients and combine with other dishes. Slices of sweet and sour lotus root are a delicious surprise in a mixed green salad. Polenta makes a great base for braised ribs with fermented black bean sauce. Soba, somen, and other Oriental noodles are a nice change from spaghetti and fettuccine.

There are a few basic differences between many of my recipes and those served in the Orient. First, I use less oil for stir-frying and skip the deep-frying often called for. To those of us who think of Asian food as especially healthful, it's surprising how often the traditional recipes specify deep-frying meat or fish before stir-frying it. I still deep-fry egg rolls and certain appetizers, but I avoid this technique in most dishes. I also use less sugar. The Japanese in particular have a national sweet tooth, although they don't eat the rich desserts we do. Their basic flavoring is sweet and salty—but not too highly seasoned. I use some sugar in Japanese-inspired dishes, but not enough to be authentic; and because I do like it hot and full of flavor, I go heavy on the wasabi and generally increase the seasonings. On the other hand, most dishes inspired by Thailand are greatly toned down to allow American taste buds to survive.

A major difference between Americans and the rest of the world is the amount of meat and other protein we eat. The small chicken that serves six to eight in France may be considered barely enough for three here. In Asia, the meat or poultry, almost always cut into small pieces, is a small proportion of the meal. I compromise in my recipes: I allow far more protein per person than is typical in other countries, but also respond to my own family and friends, who are eating less meat even if they aren't vegetarians. Americans who consider a half-pound hamburger a snack will be disappointed by these recipes. If the added vegetables aren't enough to satisfy you or your family, make double or plan to serve fewer people than I recommend. Recipes for pork chops, braised brisket, and cut-up chickens usually allow for more typically American portions.

As much as I like to cook, I don't like to plan days ahead for a meal. I generally start dinner about an hour before I serve it. Therefore, I make dishes with simple sauces, rather than those that need to simmer for hours. There are exceptions, of course, but you'll find that most of the recipes in this book are quick to do and that a lot of the work can be completed ahead. I hate to do much cooking once company arrives.

Although I don't say it in each recipe, cooks should always taste a dish before it is done. Since none of these recipes is meant to be authentic, feel free to adapt each one to your needs, changing ingredients depending upon your preferences and what's available, altering the seasoning to your own taste. I hope you use this book as an introduction to the wealth of Oriental ingredients, from fresh ginger, daikon, and Chinese cabbage to a range of sauces and seasonings, making them a part of your everyday cooking.

As much as I try to write clear, detailed recipes, cooking is not an exact science, especially when it comes to cooking times. One stove's high heat is another's medium-high, and the results will be different in different pans or in the same pan on different days when the fish is fresher or the onions more watery. Fortunately, it doesn't matter all that much. Keep an eye on the food and use your common sense. If something doesn't seem done, cook it longer. If it's cooking too fast, lower the heat.

I have been asked about the distance the grill rack should be from the coals. It depends on the grill. I have an indoor grill with a rack resting directly on the coals, and an outdoor one with a rack that's usually about 3 inches above the coals. I don't find that the cooking times vary much. When I broil, the rack is usually 3 inches below the heat source—but the food is closer than that, since the distance depends on the thickness of the food. I never let food broil unattended, so I can see how things are going and make adjustments as needed.

In the end, if the food tastes good, it is a success. If you cook it faster or slower or play with the ingredients, it doesn't matter to those who eat the finished dish.

Ingredients

Many of the recipes in this book call for ingredients you may not normally use, though you can probably find most of them if you live in a city or town with an Oriental population. Some, like soy sauce, bamboo shoots, water chestnuts, and tofu, are standard supermarket items. Others—soba and adzuki beans, for example—are sold in specialty markets and health food stores. Items you cannot find in your area can be purchased by mail order (see page 205). Fortunately, most of these ingredients have a fairly long shelf life, so you needn't feel compelled to use them all up in a frenzy.

Adzuki Beans (azuki beans, *sasage mame*)

In Japan, these small dried red beans with white tips are cooked with rice or made into a sweet bean-paste stuffing for cakes. Their slightly sweet flavor adds interest to salads and other dishes. Stored in an airtight container, they will keep for months at room temperature.

Bamboo Shoots

If you are lucky enough to buy bamboo shoots fresh, you'll find them at their peak in winter and early spring. Canned bamboo shoots are available all year. Once you open the can, rinse the shoots; place them in a jar, cover them with fresh water, and refrigerate, covered. If you change the water every few days, the shoots will keep for a week or two.

Bean Curd. *See* Tofu.

Bean Paste, Chinese

Although related to miso, this paste of fermented soybeans, flour, and salt is sold in cans, either as a smooth puree or in a chunky form with some whole beans. Transferred to a covered jar, it will keep for years in the refrigerator.

Bean Sprouts

Both mung beans and soybeans are used for bean sprouts; mung sprouts are greener and more delicate-tasting than the yellow soy sprouts. If they are fresh when you buy them, the sprouts will keep for several days in plastic bags in the refrigerator. You can easily sprout your own beans: dampen them, then place them in a jar, cover with cheese-cloth, and store in a cool place for several days. Commercial sprouters are also available.

Bean Threads. *See* Noodles, Cellophane.

Black Beans. *See* Fermented Black Beans.

Bonito Flakes (*katsuobushi*)

Transparent, papery flakes of dried bonito fish are an essential ingredient in dashi, the basic Japanese stock. In the United States, bonito flakes are usually sold in cellophane packages divided into smaller (1.5-gram) packets. Store the flakes out of direct sunlight and try to use them within 6 months.

Cabbage, Chinese (napa cabbage)

There are several different kinds of Chinese cabbage, and the terminology can be confusing. The cabbage I used in these recipes has compact, pale green, oval heads. The leaves are broad, tender-textured, and curly at the edges. Kept wrapped in damp paper towels in an open plastic bag, Chinese cabbage will last for a week or so.

Chilies, Bird's Eye

These incredibly hot little chilies belong to the cherry pepper family. They are round, usually red, and about 1/2 inch in diameter.

Chilies, Dried Red

These 2-inch-long red chilies are sold in cellophane packages. Stored in a covered jar out of direct sunlight, they will last for years. They are *very* hot—if you use the chilies whole in cooked dishes, do not eat them. In some recipes, they are ground together with other seasonings, so the flavor is tempered.

Chilies, Jalapeño

Small, hot jalapeño chilies, originally from Mexico, are gaining in popularity throughout the United States. Fresh jalapeños are about 1-1/2 inches long; they should be plump and smooth-skinned. If you cannot find them, substitute serrano or another hot chili.

A fresh chili's heat is concentrated in the ribs and the seeds, so I usually remove them both. After preparing hot chilies, wash your hands (or rubber gloves, if you wore them) and your cutting board thoroughly; if any of the hot oils come in contact with your nose, lips, or eyes, they'll sting and burn.

Cilantro (Chinese parsley, fresh coriander)

Popular in Southwestern as well as Oriental cooking, this green, flat-leafed herb looks like Italian parsley but is paler, with more finely cut leaves. The flavor is distinct and aromatic, not to everyone's taste. If you buy cilantro with the roots still attached, place it in a glass of water in the refrigerator; it will keep for several days. If the roots have been removed, wrap the leaves in a damp towel and refrigerate.

If cilantro leaves are not available, buy coriander seeds and plant them in pots or in the garden. The leaves that grow from them may not look like the cilantro sold in markets, but they have the same flavor.

Coconut Milk

Not dairy milk at all, this liquid comes from the meat of a coconut. It is sold canned or frozen (leftover canned milk can be frozen, if you like). When you shop, make sure you buy the right product; unsweetened coconut milk is quite different from the sweetened coconut cream used to make tropical drinks.

To make your own coconut milk, combine 2 cups unsweetened shredded coconut (preferably fresh, but dried will do) and about 2 cups very hot water in a food processor. Process until pulpy. Pour through a fine sieve or cheesecloth, pressing firmly to extract all liquid from the solids.

Corn, Baby

Whole, 2- to 3-inch-long ears of corn on the cob are available in 15-ounce cans. You can eat them plain, use them as crudités, or add them to salads and stir-fried dishes. To firm them, soak for about 30 minutes in ice water before using. If you don't use the entire can, place the leftovers in a container and cover with fresh water; store, covered, in the refrigerator. If you change the water every few days, the corn will last for at least a week.

Frozen baby corn has recently come onto the market, but distribution is so limited that I haven't tried it.

Curry Paste, Thai Red

This oil-based mixture includes chilies as well as other curry spices. It comes in plastic containers and will keep in the refrigerator for months. If you want to make your own, see the recipe on page 189.

Curry Powder

Although many Oriental dishes are curried, they are not made with the ubiquitous powder Westerners think of as curry; each dish features a particular blend of spices. While many of these spices are components of the commercial powder, it's still best to use the spices called for in the recipe.

Daikon (Chinese turnip)

Much larger and more delicate-tasting than the familiar red radish, daikon has transparent white skin and an elongated shape. A single root may weigh several pounds. Daikon can be eaten raw, simmered in soup, braised with meat, or deep-fried. It will keep for several days in the refrigerator.

Eggplant, Oriental

Much smaller than our eggplants—just 4 to 6 ounces each—the long, skinny Oriental varieties also have paler purple skin and fewer seeds.

Choose smooth-skinned eggplants and use them within 2 days of purchase.

Egg Roll Skins

The traditional dough used to wrap egg rolls comes in 2 varieties. The square, opaque Cantonese wrappers are thicker than the round, transparent Shanghai variety, often called spring roll wrappers. Both will keep in the refrigerator for about a week and in the freezer for several months.

Fermented Black Beans (Chinese black beans, salted black beans)

One of my favorite flavorings, these little black beans are soybeans that have been preserved in brine, then dried. They add lots of salty flavor to many dishes. Stored in an airtight jar, they will keep indefinitely.

Fish Sauce

Sauce made from salted, fermented fish is as ubiquitous in Southeast Asian cuisines as soy sauce is in Japanese and Chinese cooking. Each nation has a different name for the sauce—it is called *nuoc nam* in Vietnam, *nam pla* in Thailand, *patis* in the Philippines, *tuk trey* in Cambodia, *ngan-pya-ye* in Burma. Different fish sauces do vary slightly, but they are still interchangeable in the recipes in this book. Don't be put off by the smell. To Westerners, it seems very strong—but the odor dissipates upon cooking, and the flavor fish sauce imparts to a dish is really quite mild. Bottled fish sauce will keep for years.

Five-spice Powder

The five spices ground together and used as a Chinese seasoning are usually star anise, cloves, cinnamon, Szechuan peppercorns, and fennel seeds. Keep five-spice powder in a cool, dry place. Like any spice, it will begin to lose its flavor after a few months.

Galangal (*lengkuas*)

Like ginger, galangal is a rhizome. In the United States, it is sold dried, as either powder (*laos*) or slices. Keep it in a cool, dry place.

Garlic

Garlic is popular in the Orient. It is said to prolong life and strengthen the body. When buying garlic, choose firm, dry heads. The cloves must be peeled before they are sliced or minced. To loosen the papery peel, hit the clove with the side of a broad knife.

Ginger

Fresh ginger, now widely available, is a rhizome—a thickened underground stem. Most of what we see is called "mature"; it has a thick beige skin and a yellowish interior. In the spring, Chinese markets may carry a much paler, thinner-skinned variety with pink tips, used to make pickled ginger. This young gingerroot is much more delicate in flavor than the mature type and can be used as a garnish.

1. Mung beans, 2. Shiitake mushrooms, 3. Mint, 4. Fresh lemon grass, 5. Star anise, 6. Baby corn, 7. Coconut, 8. Cellophane noodles (bean threads), 9. Bamboo shoots, 10. Adzuki beans, 11. Lotus root, 12. Chiles (mixed), 13. Straw mushrooms, 14. Dried Chinese mushrooms, 15. Dried tiger lily buds, 16. Tree ears, 17. Szechuan peppercorns, 18. Cilantro, 19. Gingerroot, 20. Snow peas, 21. Shiso leaf, 22. Pickled ginger, 23. Udon, 24. Buckwheat soba, 25. Somen, 26. Daikon (grated), 27. Enoki mushrooms, 28. Oyster mushrooms, 29. Suehiromaki (rolled seaweed), 30. Daikon sprouts, 31. Dried lemon grass

The highest-quality gingerroot comes from Hawaii and is so labeled, but any fresh gingerroot should be firm and moist, not withered. If you can only get gingerroot occasionally, store the extra unpeeled root in a pot of clean sand; or peel it, cover it with rice wine, and store it in a jar in the refrigerator.

When a recipe calls for sliced gingerroot, you may leave the skin on, but gingerroot should be peeled before mincing or grating.

Ginger, Pickled

There are different kinds of pickled ginger, but the one I like best and use in my recipes is pink pickled ginger, *amazu shoga*. It is usually sold in very thin slices in vacuum-sealed cellophane packages. Once the package is opened, place the ginger and its brine in a covered container; it will keep in the refrigerator for months.

Ginger, Stem, in Syrup

Although cooked and softened in sugar syrup, these chunks of ginger retain their tang. They make a wonderful topping for vanilla ice cream. Bottled stem ginger is sold in many supermarkets; the Chinese varieties come in colorful crocks. If refrigerated after opening, stem ginger will last for years.

Ginger Preserves

These piquant preserves with bits of ginger in them are delicious on toast with cream cheese.

Ginger Wine

Actually a currant wine flavored with green ginger, this fortified wine imparts a spicy, fruity flavor. The only brand I know is Stone's, imported from England. A bottle lasts indefinitely.

Green Onions (scallions)

Green onions are a basic ingredient in many Oriental dishes. Although many people use the white part for cooking and save the green tops for a garnish, I use the whole onion for practically everything. Bunches should look fresh, the leaves should be dark green and firm, not dry, yellowed, or slimy. Keep green onions wrapped in moist paper towels in the refrigerator for up to 5 days.

Hijiki

These dried black strands of sea vegetation look almost like black tea. They need braising to bring out their mild, licoricelike flavor. Hijiki is delicious with carrots or other vegetables. It's an excellent source of calcium, too—just 1 tablespoon of dried hijiki has as much calcium as 3 quarts of milk.

Hoisin Sauce

Thick, dark hoisin sauce is made from mashed fermented soybeans, salt, sugar, vinegar, and garlic. If you buy canned sauce, transfer it to a jar or plastic container. It may thicken as it sits; if so, stir in a little water. It will keep indefinitely in the refrigerator.

Katsuobushi. *See* Bonito Flakes.

Konbu

Konbu is the dried Japanese sea vegetation that is used to flavor dashi. It comes in large, brittle strips in cellophane packages. Once the package has been opened, place the remaining konbu in an airtight container.

Kosher Salt

Coarse kosher salt, sold in 3-pound boxes in supermarkets, has a cleaner taste than most table salts and is never flavored with iodine. I also like it for its texture—you can pick it up with your fingers. Because kosher salt is coarse, there's less to a measure, so cut down on the salt in these recipes if you substitute a finer variety.

Kumquats

At their peak from December through March, kumquats add a bright accent to winter menus. The name is Cantonese for "golden orange"—but though they belong to the same botanical family as lemons, limes, and other citrus, these small, sweet-sour fruits are members of a different genus. Fresh kumquats have orange skin that is firm but pliable. They will keep in the refrigerator for up to 2 weeks.

Laos. *See* Galangal.

Lemon Grass (citronella)

A long, woody stalk with the fresh scent of lemon. Asian markets sell it fresh, frozen, or dried; the dried form may be in whole stalks, slices, or fine powder (*sereh*).

Before using dried lemon grass, you'll usually need to soak it in water for 2 hours, unless it's going into a soup. Fresh lemon grass stalks may be used whole in soups. For other uses, cut away the top and the tough outer layers of the stalk and grind the white inner part.

For soups and stews, you can substitute 1 teaspoon of powdered lemon grass for a whole stalk. If lemon grass is not available to you in any form, you can approximate the flavor with grated lemon peel (for each stalk, use the peel from 1 lemon).

Lotus Root

Lotus root comes in various lengths and grows in "chains" of several brown-skinned sections that look something like sausage links. A whole, uncut root is not very pretty—but once it's peeled and sliced crosswise, an attractive pattern of lacy holes is evident. To keep the flesh bright and white, soak the slices in acidulated water. Look for firm, unscarred pieces. Uncut, they will last in the refrigerator for a few days.

Mirin

This sweet, syrupy Japanese rice wine is used only in cooking. It is sold alongside condiments and other Japanese ingredients, not as liquor. It will keep for months in a cool, dry place.

Miso

In Japan, there are as many different miso pastes as there are neighborhoods. Though all are made from soybeans, grain, salt, water, and a fermentation starter, the color varies—some misos are lighter, others darker. Flavors also differ—some types are much saltier—but it is difficult to make generalizations based on color. For this reason, I have only specified light-colored miso where the dark paste would spoil the look of a dish. When you prepare these recipes, feel free to try different brands and adjust the quantities of miso to your liking.

After opening a package of miso, store it in a covered container in the refrigerator. It will keep for months.

Mushrooms

Cloud ears (tree ears) are thin black mushrooms with irregular shapes. When soaked in warm water, they expand greatly and become slightly slimy and chewy. Cut away any tough parts before using.

Dried Chinese mushrooms are quite different in flavor and texture from fresh mushrooms. They are sold whole in bags. The price varies greatly, depending on the quality. Store them in a cool, dry, dark place in a jar or sealed plastic bag. Like cloud ears, they must be soaked before using; the stems, which are too hard to eat, should be cut off and discarded or added to stocks. Dried Chinese mushrooms may be used in place of dried shiitake.

Enoki (enokitake) are white mushrooms that resemble oversized straight pins with round tops. Most readily available in fall and early winter, they are sold, with roots still attached, in small packages. They should be firm and dry. Cut away the roots and use the enoki as a garnish, only slightly cooked. Stored in the refrigerator, they'll keep for a few days.

Shiitake mushrooms, with flat brown caps that curve under slightly at the edges, are the most popular mushrooms in Japan. Until recently, only dried shiitake were sold in the United States, but the mushrooms are now being cultivated in Ore-gon and other states and are becoming increasingly available fresh. They are expensive, but worth the price for their special flavor. They're especially delicious when sautéed or grilled. For most cooked dishes, though, the dried shiitake are marvelous.

Dried shiitake will keep indefinitely if stored in an airtight container at room temperature out of direct sunlight. Soak them until soft before using. Both dried and fresh shiitake have woody, inedible stems that should be cut off and discarded.

Straw mushrooms are unusual-looking, with pointed caps and sturdy stems that bulge at the base. They are available in cans, either peeled or unpeeled. If you have leftover canned mushrooms, drain them, place them in a jar, and cover them with fresh water; then refrigerate, covered. If you change the water every day, the mushrooms will keep for about a week.

Noodles, Cellophane (bean threads)

Made from mung bean starch, these dried white noodles are very thin. The kind I buy are sold in tightly wound little bundles, usually weighing 2 ounces each; eight bundles are wrapped together in a red net bag. Unless you're using the noodles in a soup, soak them in plenty of warm water before using (they'll expand a lot). Soak just until soft—if oversoaked, the noodles will get mushy. The dried noodles will keep for years at room temperature.

Noodles, Chinese Egg

Made with wheat flour and eggs, these are sold in 1-pound packages in the refrigerator or freezer sections of Oriental markets and some well-stocked supermarkets. They vary in thickness; some are as thin as angel hair, others as thick as spaghetti. Chinese noodles are a perfect foil for a range of sauces, from meaty Bolognese to fragrant cream sauces. They will keep for a week in the refrigerator, a few months in the freezer. (Dried egg noodles are also available, but opt for the fresh if you have a choice.)

Nori (purple laver)

These thin sheets of sea vegetation, varying in color from deep blackish green to greenish purple, are used extensively in Japanese kitchens. Nori strips will hold foods onto sushi packages; shreds make pretty garnishes. Nori is sold in packages of 10 or more sheets. Once you open the package, store the nori in an airtight container along with the antimoisture pellets included in the package. You may also keep nori in the freezer for up to 3 months. Some varieties come toasted; if you buy untoasted sheets (or if the sheets have been frozen and defrosted), hold them with tongs briefly over a burner to crisp.

Oyster Sauce

This is a thick, rich concentrate made from oysters, salt, soy sauce, and seasonings. The flavor is sweet and salty. Oyster sauce will keep indefinitely in the refrigerator.

Plum Wine

A Japanese wine made from plums, served as an apéritif on the rocks or with club soda. I use it for a refreshing sorbet (see page 194).

Rice

There are three basic kinds of rice—long-grain, short-grain, and glutinous. Long-grain is the fluffiest of the three; short-grain is stickier than long-grain, and glutinous (also called sweet) is stickier still. Short-grain rice is commonly used in Asia. Glutinous rice is saved for certain special dishes, often sweets. Although rice lasts for months, Oriental cooks don't use any that's over 6 months old.

Rice Sticks (rice vermicelli)

These long, thin, wavy noodles made from rice flour are usually sold in 1-pound packages. When deep-fried, they puff up into a crunchy nest; when soaked or boiled, they become soft, ready to absorb the flavor of any sauce. Kept in a dry place, they will last for months.

Rice Wine, Chinese

Chinese rice wine is the standard cooking wine in China. It has more flavor than Japanese sake. If you can't find Chinese rice wine, use sake or dry vermouth in its place.

Rice Wine, Japanese. *See* Mirin; Sake.

Rice Wine Vinegar. *See* Vinegar.

Sake

Sake—Japanese rice wine—is served as a hot drink to accompany Japanese meals. Because its mild flavor doesn't overpower a dish, I use it extensively in cooking in place of white wine and vermouth. It is usually sold with liquor, not with other Japanese ingredients.

Sambal Oelek

This hot Indonesian relish is made from ground chilies. In its native land, it is usually a condiment, but I use it in marinades and sauces. It is sold in bottles and keeps for a long time.

Sausage, Chinese-Style

Two kinds of Chinese sausage are available—pork and liver. For these recipes, I have used the pork sausages. They are thin and firm, reddish in color and sweet in flavor. Most brands contain MSG, but there are a few without it, and these are the only ones I buy. Wrapped in plastic, Chinese sausages will keep for months in the freezer. They must be steamed to soften before using.

Sereh. *See* Lemon Grass.

Sesame Oil

Because the seeds are toasted before pressing, Oriental sesame oil has a richer flavor and a deeper color than the sesame oils found in health food stores. All the recipes in this book use toasted sesame oil. Due to its strong flavor, it is rarely used alone as a cooking oil; instead, it is often added to marinades or stirred into a dish just before serving. Sesame oil can get rancid with age, so buy it in small quantities and store it in a cool place.

Sesame Oil, Hot

This red oil is made by infusing oil with hot chilies and then straining out the chilies. The best kind is made with Japanese sesame oil. Use it sparingly. Like sesame oil, it will last for months if stored in a cool place.

Sesame Seeds

Sesame seeds may be white or black; each color has its own flavor. I most often use the white seeds. To bring out their flavor, toast them in a dry skillet over medium heat until they begin to brown, shaking the pan often and watching the heat so the seeds don't burn.

Shrimp Paste

Called *kapi* in Thailand, *mam rouc* in Vietnam, *blachan* in Malaysia, and *trasi* in Indonesia, shrimp paste is essential to the Southeast Asian kitchen. It has a strong odor but adds wonderful flavor to dishes without overpowering them. Usually sold in small containers, it will keep for months in the refrigerator.

Snow Peas (sugar peas, Chinese pea pods)

These young, flat pea pods are entirely edible, as the French name, *mange-tout* ("eat-all"), indicates. Look for fresh, firm peas without brown spots. To string them, pull off the stem and bring the string back along the length of the pod. If I cannot find fresh snow peas, I prefer to substitute fresh green beans; frozen snow peas are available, but they have little texture.

Soba

These thin beige noodles are made from buckwheat flour. They are usually sold dried, in 1- to 2-pound packages. I prefer them to whole-wheat pasta and use them in place of spaghetti in all kinds of dishes. They will keep in a cool, dry place for at least 6 months.

Somen

These very thin, dried white noodles are sold in 1-pound cellophane packages; each package usually contains five smaller packets of noodles, each wrapped with a paper ribbon. Somen keep for years if stored in a cool, dry place.

Soy Sauce

All soy sauces are made from soybeans, but there are dozens of different kinds—some Japanese, some Chinese, some American. Color and saltiness vary from one to another. Light soy sauces are paler in color but not less salty (in fact, they are saltier), and are used in soups and fish dishes whose color would be muddied by a dark soy.

Unless otherwise stated, the recipes in this book were tested with Kikkoman, the most readily available brand of Japanese soy sauce. Feel free to substitute other brands, but always taste the final product to be sure the flavor is to your liking.

Star Anise

This interesting seasoning is the seed pod of a tree belonging to the magnolia family. Each aromatic pod is shaped like an eight-pointed star. Star anise has a mild licorice flavor and is typically used in marinades or in dishes that are braised or simmered for a long time to bring out the flavor of the spice. Stored in a jar in a cool, dry place, star anise will keep for months.

Sushi Su. *See* Vinegar.

Szechuan Chili Sauce

Made with fresh red chilies, this spicy sauce is sold in cans. If transferred to a covered jar and refrigerated after opening, it will keep indefinitely.

Szechuan Peppercorns

These reddish-brown, open-husked peppercorns have a sharp, slightly numbing flavor. Before use, they are usually toasted in a dry skillet until they start to smoke, then crushed with the fingers or in a grinder (or they may be crushed before toasting). Szechuan peppercorns will keep for months if stored in a jar in a cool, dry place.

Tamarind Pulp

Tamarind adds a fruity, sour flavor to soups, stews, and other dishes. The fresh pods are rarely seen in the United States; you are more likely to find compact blocks of compressed tamarind pulp. Wrapped in plastic and refrigerated, the pulp will keep for a few months.

Tiger Lily Buds (golden needles)

Long, golden-colored lily buds are sold dry. Before using, soak them until softened and discard the knobby ends. Stored in a covered jar in a cool, dry place, they will last for years.

Tofu (bean curd)

Made from the curds of soybean "milk", tofu is sold in many supermarkets and in produce, health food, and Oriental stores. I always buy it loose, in either soft or firm cakes. The cakes should look fresh; most packages are also stamped with an expiration date. To store tofu, cover it with cold water and refrigerate it. As long as you change the water every day, the tofu will last for up to 5 days.

Tonkatsu Sauce

Traditionally served with the deep-fried pork cutlets called *tonkatsu,* this is a thick, fruity-tasting, tomato-based Japanese sauce. Bottles will last for years.

Tree Ears. *See* Mushrooms, Cloud Ears.

Udon

Thick, white udon noodles are usually sold dried, occasionally fresh. The fresh noodles will last only a day or two, but dried udon keep for years. Some Japanese cooks make their own udon. Elizabeth Andoh has an excellent recipe in her book *At Home with Japanese Cooking* (Knopf, 1980).

Vinegar

Chinese black vinegar. Made from fermented rice, Chinese vinegars tend to be lighter and sweeter than Western types. There are different kinds, but in this book, I have used the dark (black) vinegar, said to taste something like Worcestershire sauce. Most of it is imported from China.

Rice wine vinegar. When recipes call for rice wine vinegar, I mean the Japanese variety. Very light and delicate in flavor, it is the base for *sushi su,* the flavored vinegar used for sushi rice—but *sushi su* and rice wine vinegar are not interchangeable in cooking.

Vinegars come in bottles and will last indefinitely.

Wakame

Another interesting sea vegetation, wakame is sold dry in dark, ribbonlike pieces. Once soaked and softened, the pieces become beautiful pale green, uneven ribbons with a slippery texture—an excellent addition to salads. The dried pieces will last for months if stored in a cool, dark place.

Wasabi Powder

This pale green powder comes from dried, ground wasabi, a horseradishlike root. It is usually brushed on sushi rice or served on the side to add to dipping sauces for sashimi or noodles. Wasabi powder is sold in small containers and will stay fresh for months, even after opening.

Water Chestnuts

These are the starchy tuber of a water plant. They are widely available in cans, but you may sometimes find them fresh in Chinese markets. Fresh water chestnuts can be eaten raw or cooked; before using them, cut off the inedible brown peel with a knife. Unpeeled, they will keep in the refrigerator for about 2 weeks.

To eliminate the metallic taste from canned water chestnuts, drop them briefly into boiling water. Leftovers can be stored, covered with fresh water, in a covered jar in the refrigerator. As long as you change the water every few days, they will last for weeks.

Water Chestnut Powder

Dried water chestnuts are pulverized to make this coarse flour, an interesting coating for fried foods. It is sold in boxes. If well sealed and kept in a cool, dry place, it will last for months.

Won Ton Skins

These smooth dough wrappers, each about 3 inches square, are sold in 1-pound packages. I use them for ravioli and tortellini as well as for won tons. The skins will keep for a week in the refrigerator, or for months in the freezer.

Equipment

Most of the utensils mentioned in this book are fairly standard kitchen equipment, available in any cookware shop. The few items you may not be familiar with are described below.

Ginger Grater

This small metal grater with very sharp teeth will cut through the fibers of an unpeeled knob of gingerroot to give a smooth paste that is much finer than minced ginger.

Otoshi-buta (dropped lid)

These flat wooden or plastic lids with raised handles let you simmer foods in very little liquid without much evaporation. The lids fit inside pots to rest directly on the simmering foods; there is only a small space between the edge of the lid and the sides of the pot.

Suribachi

A suribachi is a Japanese mortar and pestle. The pestle is smooth and wooden, the mortar a ceramic bowl with rough unglazed interior walls. This tool is very handy for grinding sesame and other seeds. The Japanese use it for a number of other tasks, even for creaming butter.

S tarters are first courses and appetizers, the dishes that begin a meal. They can be eaten at the table or offered with drinks before guests are seated. If I am entertaining a small group, I prefer serving at the table—people pay more attention to the food then, and I want my efforts to be appreciated. Friends have learned not to expect anything with their preprandial drinks except at large parties, where I usually allow more time before dinner—providing some leeway for latecomers and giving everyone a chance to mingle.

If you entertain like I do, you will turn to this chapter when you're expecting company or making a special meal. The first dozen or so recipes in the group are the kind you can eat with your fingers (although napkins are necessary); the rest should be eaten at the table.

Serve crisp Fried Won Tons with Salsa, page 26, or warm Steamed Cucumbers Stuffed with Crabmeat, page 35.

STARTERS

Spiced Pecans

Usually served before the meal with drinks, spiced nuts are known throughout the world. In this case, I've taken American pecans and flavored them with Szechuan peppercorns and five-spice powder. They are handy to have around for unexpected company, but in my house they never last that long! If you have the willpower, you can store them in a tightly closed jar for a few weeks.

1 CUP PECAN HALVES OR LARGE PIECES

1 TEASPOON SZECHUAN PEPPERCORNS

1 TEASPOON KOSHER SALT

1/2 TEASPOON FIVE-SPICE POWDER

1/4 CUP SUGAR

■■ Preheat the oven to 350F (175C).

Place the pecans in a bowl and add boiling water to cover. Let soak for 15 minutes, then drain thoroughly. Pat dry.

Toast the peppercorns in a dry skillet over medium heat until they begin to smoke, about 1 minute. Remove from the heat. Place the peppercorns and salt in a spice grinder; pulverize. (Or use a mortar and pestle or suribachi.)

Toss the pecans with the peppercorn mixture, five-spice powder, and sugar. Spread them out in a single layer on a baking sheet and bake in the preheated oven for 10 minutes. Stir to mix, return to the oven and bake 5 minutes longer. Then spread the pecans on a plate and let cool. Break apart any pecans that stick to each other.

Makes 1 cup.

STARTERS

Curried Guacamole

Avocados, native to the Western Hemisphere, are one of my favorite fruits. I love their mild flavor, vibrant color, and buttery texture. Most reliable in flavor and texture is the small Hass variety, with pebbly skin that turns black when the fruit is ripe.

Avocados are, of course, the key ingredient in guacamole, a dip that's probably made in as many different versions as there are cooks. This one uses Oriental curry spices instead of the usual Tex-Mex seasonings. Besides adding flavor, the curry keeps the avocado a nice yellow-green color, preventing it from turning an unattractive dark brown. Serve the dip with drinks and blue corn tortilla chips, with eggs, over hamburgers, or alongside Tortillas with Oriental Beef and Black Beans, page 82.

Although some like smooth guacamole, I prefer it to be chunky. One way to keep the avocados from turning to mush is to chop them with an empty tuna can with both ends removed.

1 TEASPOON CHOPPED GARLIC

1/2 TEASPOON MINCED FRESH
GINGERROOT

1 TEASPOON GROUND TURMERIC

1 TEASPOON GROUND CORIANDER

1 TEASPOON GROUND CUMIN

1/2 TEASPOON GROUND RED
(CAYENNE) PEPPER

1/4 TEASPOON GROUND CINNAMON

1 TEASPOON KOSHER SALT

2 RIPE AVOCADOS, PREFERABLY
HASS

1 MEDIUM (1/4-POUND) TOMATO,
CORED, CHOPPED

2 TABLESPOONS LIME JUICE

2 TABLESPOONS CHOPPED FRESH
CILANTRO LEAVES

▬ Place the garlic, gingerroot, turmeric, coriander, cumin, red pepper, cinnamon, and salt in a bowl. Stir to mix. Halve and pit the avocados. Scrape the flesh from the skin and place it in the bowl; discard the skin. With a knife or an empty can, roughly chop the avocado flesh until it is in small pieces. Add the tomato, lime juice, and cilantro. Mix thoroughly.

Makes about 2 cups.

Crab Fritters

Crab cakes are an all-American treat, especially popular in Maryland and points south. To make this deep-fried version of the dish, I mixed the crab with a little fish sauce and coated the fritters in broken rice sticks. The result is crunchy on the outside, with a smooth interior. Serve hot with sake, beer, or cocktails.

VEGETABLE OIL FOR DEEP-FRYING

4 (1/2-INCH-THICK) SLICES WHITE
BREAD, SOAKED IN WATER,
SQUEEZED DRY

1/2 POUND CRABMEAT, ANY BITS OF
SHELL AND CARTILAGE REMOVED,
ROUGHLY CHOPPED

2 LARGE EGGS

1/4 TEASPOON GROUND RED
(CAYENNE) PEPPER

1/2 TEASPOON DRY MUSTARD

1 TEASPOON FISH SAUCE

1/4 POUND RICE STICKS, BROKEN
INTO PIECES LESS THAN AN INCH
LONG

1 RECIPE MUSTARD DIPPING
SAUCE, PAGE 187

▬ In a medium pot, heat about 4 inches of oil to about 375F (190C) or until a 1-inch bread cube turns golden brown in 50 seconds. Meanwhile, in a bowl, combine the bread, crabmeat, eggs, red pepper, mustard, and fish sauce. Stir to blend completely.

Shape a generous tablespoon of crab mixture into a round. Coat it with some of the rice sticks, then press down to make a slightly flat cake. Repeat with the remaining crab mixture and rice sticks. Drop the cakes, a few at a time, into the hot oil. Cook until crisp and browned all over, about 1 minute. Adjust the heat as needed to keep the temperature of the oil constant. Drain on paper towels. Serve hot with Mustard Dipping Sauce.

Makes about 24 fritters.

Fried Won Tons with Salsa

With my fried won tons, I prefer a nippy fresh salsa to the usual sweet sauce. These are great as a first course or with drinks before dinner—I've served them with everything from frosty margaritas to warm sake.

1/2 POUND UNCOOKED SHRIMP, SHELLED, DEVEINED, ROUGHLY CHOPPED

1/4 POUND GROUND PORK

1 GARLIC CLOVE, MINCED

1 TEASPOON MINCED FRESH GINGERROOT

2 TEASPOONS SOY SAUCE

2 TEASPOONS SAKE

1/2 TEASPOON SESAME OIL

1 LARGE GREEN ONION, MINCED

40 WON TON SKINS (ABOUT 1/2 POUND *TOTAL*)

VEGETABLE OIL FOR DEEP-FRYING

1 RECIPE TOMATO SALSA, PAGE 182

STARTERS

Set the shrimp and pork in a bowl. Stir to blend, then beat in the garlic, gingerroot, soy sauce, sake, sesame oil, and green onion. Set aside.

Most won ton skins have cornstarch between them, primarily adhering to 1 side. Set a won ton skin, cornstarch side down, on your work surface, placing the skin on the diagonal so it points toward you. Brush any remaining cornstarch from the skin. Place a scant teaspoon of filling on the skin just above the center; with your finger, rub water around the edges. Fold the skin up over the filling to form a triangle. Fold the top point of the triangle down again over the filling, then bring the 2 side points together. Seal them with a drop of water. Set aside. Repeat until all the filling has been used.

Cook the won tons when you are ready to serve. In a pot, heat at least 3 inches of vegetable oil to about 375F (190C). To test the temperature of the oil, break off a piece of won ton dough and drop it into the oil; it should drop to the bottom briefly, then rise to the top. If it sits on the bottom, the oil isn't hot enough. If it doesn't go down, the oil is too hot.

Add the won tons, a few at a time, to the hot oil. Do not crowd them; they should fit easily in a single layer on top of the oil. Cook until well browned and crisp, 3 to 4 minutes. Adjust the heat as needed to keep the temperature of the oil constant. With a slotted spoon, remove the won tons to a plate lined with paper towels. Lightly pat off the excess oil. If you make the won tons ahead, keep them hot in a low oven.

Serve hot with the salsa for dipping.

Makes about 40 won tons.

NOTE: You can freeze uncooked filled won tons. Cook them frozen; they will take about a minute longer than fresh won tons.

Egg Rolls with Potato-Onion Filling

My favorite knishes have a mashed-potato filling made with plenty of sautéed onions and black pepper. This same mixture is delicious when wrapped in egg roll skins and deep-fried. Serve small rolls with drinks. The large ones, served whole or halved, are perfect with hamburgers.

1/2 CUP VEGETABLE OIL

1 POUND ONIONS, SLICED

1-1/2 POUNDS POTATOES, PEELED, BOILED UNTIL VERY SOFT

1 TABLESPOON KOSHER SALT, OR TO TASTE

1/4 TEASPOON FRESHLY GROUND BLACK PEPPER, OR TO TASTE

ABOUT 14 (6-1/2-INCH-SQUARE) EGG ROLL SKINS (ABOUT 1 POUND *TOTAL*)

BEATEN EGG

VEGETABLE OIL FOR DEEP-FRYING

Heat the 1/2 cup oil in a large skillet over medium-high heat. Add the onions and cook until very soft and light brown, about 10 minutes. Then put the onions and potatoes through the small blade of a food grinder. If you do not have a grinder, put the mixture through a food mill; or chop the onions in a food processor, then beat together the onions and potatoes with an electric mixer. (Do not use a food processor to puree the potatoes; they will turn to glue.) Season the potato mixture with the salt and pepper.

To make large egg rolls, use an entire egg roll skin and 1/4 cup filling. To make small egg rolls, cut each skin into 4 equal squares and use 1 tablespoon filling for each.

To fill large or small rolls, set a skin on your work surface, placing it on the diagonal so it points toward you. Place the filling in the center of the skin in a line running from side to side. Leave plenty of room at the ends.

Fold the bottom point of the skin over the filling. Brush the edges with beaten egg. Fold the sides in to meet over the filling. Brush with more egg and roll up, making sure the exposed point is well sealed. Set aside. Repeat to fill the remaining egg roll skins.

In a deep pot, heat 4 inches of oil to 350F (175C) or until a 1-inch bread cube turns golden brown in 65 seconds. Add the egg rolls, a few at a time, and cook until browned on all sides—2 to 3 minutes for the small rolls, 3 to 4 minutes for the large rolls. Adjust the heat as needed to keep the temperature of the oil constant. Drain on paper towels and serve hot.

Makes about 56 small or 14 large egg rolls.

Cheese Tempura

When you want tempura in Japan, you go to a tempura restaurant, sit at the counter, and eat the batter-fried food piece by piece as it comes out of the hot oil. At the best places, the food never has a chance to cool more than enough to keep you from burning your mouth.

Just about anything the Japanese like, from mushrooms to shrimp, may be coated in tempura batter. About the only thing they don't serve this way—because they rarely eat it—is cheese. However, I am sure they would love the taste and texture: the cheese is very soft and runny inside the crisp coating. As is true for all tempura, the cheese version does not improve with age. I recommend serving it to an informal group happy to have drinks in the kitchen and grab each piece as it is done. At the other extreme, cheese tempura is also wonderful at a large cocktail party if you have someone stationed in the kitchen to cook batches to be passed on trays.

Properly made tempura is light, not greasy, and it is quite simple to prepare. Unlike many batters, tempura batter should be used as soon as it is mixed. If you are serving a crowd, it's better to stir up new batches of batter as needed rather than double the recipe.

STARTERS

3/4 TO 1 POUND EDAM OR ANOTHER
    SEMISOFT CHEESE
VEGETABLE OIL FOR DEEP-FRYING
1 LARGE EGG
3/4 CUP ICE WATER
1 CUP ALL-PURPOSE FLOUR

Remove any wax or rind from the cheese. Cut it into fingers about 1/2 by 1/2 by 1-1/2 inches. Refrigerate until ready to use.

In a deep pot or wok, heat 4 inches of oil to 350F (175C). Meanwhile, with a fork or chopsticks, lightly beat the egg. Add the ice water and 1 cup flour and stir just until fairly smooth.

Dust the cheese pieces lightly with flour. Dip them into the batter, a few at a time, making sure all the pieces are well coated; then drop them into the oil. If the temperature of the oil is correct, the cheese should drop to the bottom briefly, then rise to the top. If it sits on the bottom, the oil is not hot enough. If it doesn't go down, the oil is too hot.

Cook the cheese pieces until they are puffy, soft, and light brown, 1 to 2 minutes. As each piece is done, place it briefly on a rack to let any excess oil drip off. (A rack that fits over part of your wok is perfect for this.) Serve immediately. Adjust the heat as needed to keep the temperature of the oil constant.

Makes 10 or more servings.

Pearl Balls

A pearly white coating of glutinous rice gives these delicious appetizer meatballs their name. Serve them on small plates (or just with napkins), as an accompaniment to drinks; or try them as a first course. They're great for a crowd, because you can assemble them ahead and let them steam unattended when your guests arrive. If you have several bamboo steamers, stack them one on top of the other for efficient cooking.

My version of pearl balls uses a traditionally Italian meatball instead of an Asian one—a flavor surprise, since the look is obviously Eastern. Be sure to serve with a spicy sauce like Mustard Dipping Sauce or one of the salsas.

1 CUP UNCOOKED GLUTINOUS RICE

1 THIN SLICE WHITE BREAD, CRUSTS REMOVED

1/4 CUP MILK

1 POUND GROUND BEEF

1 LARGE EGG, LIGHTLY BEATEN

1/4 CUP FINELY CHOPPED ONION

2 TEASPOONS MINCED GARLIC

1 TABLESPOON MINCED PARSLEY

1 TEASPOON DRIED LEAF OREGANO

1/4 CUP FRESHLY GRATED PARMESAN CHEESE (ABOUT 3/4 OUNCE)

1/2 TEASPOON KOSHER SALT

1/8 TEASPOON FRESHLY GROUND BLACK PEPPER

1 RECIPE MUSTARD DIPPING SAUCE, PAGE 187, TOMATO SALSA, PAGE 182, OR RED PEPPER SALSA, PAGE 182

■ Rinse the rice in several changes of cold water until the water runs clear. Place the rice in a bowl, cover generously with cold water, and let soak for 1 hour.

Place the bread in a small bowl and add the milk. Let stand until the bread is completely soggy. Place the beef in a separate bowl and add the egg, onion, garlic, parsley, oregano, cheese, salt, and pepper. Crumble the soggy bread on top; also add any unabsorbed milk. Mix well. Roll the beef mixture into 1-inch balls. You should have about 30.

Drain the rice and spread it on a flat plate or tray. Roll the meatballs, 1 at a time, in the rice, pressing firmly to cover completely with the rice. Place the coated balls on a plate, cover with plastic wrap, and refrigerate for 1 to 24 hours.

When you are ready to cook the pearl balls, line 2 steamer trays with dampened cheesecloth. Arrange the meatballs over the cloth in a single layer, spacing the balls at least 1/2 inch apart.

Bring water to a boil in the bottom of a steamer or wok. Reduce the heat so the water simmers. Set the trays in place over the simmering water, cover, and steam until the rice coating on the meatballs is translucent, about 25 minutes. Serve hot with sauce or salsa.

Makes about 30 pearl balls.

Chinese Pizza

Pizzas are fun to make because there are so few rules. This one has hoisin instead of the usual tomato sauce and Chinese sausage rather than Italian sausage or pepperoni. It's delicious with drinks or for lunch.

1 TEASPOON (ABOUT HALF OF A 1/4-OUNCE PACKAGE) ACTIVE DRY YEAST

1 CUP WARM WATER

1 TEASPOON KOSHER SALT

2-1/2 TO 3 CUPS ALL-PURPOSE FLOUR

1 TABLESPOON SESAME OIL

2 CHINESE-STYLE PORK SAUSAGES (ABOUT 1/4 POUND *TOTAL*)

2 TABLESPOONS VEGETABLE OIL

1/2 CUP CHOPPED GREEN ONIONS

1/2 CUP HOISIN SAUCE

1 RED BELL PEPPER, CORED, SEEDED, CUT INTO THIN STRIPS

In a small bowl, dissolve the yeast in the warm water. Place the salt and 2-1/2 cups flour in a separate bowl (or in the bowl of an electric mixer fitted with a dough hook). Pour in the dissolved yeast and the sesame oil. Stir to mix; continue mixing until the dough holds together. Turn the dough out onto a floured work surface and knead until smooth but still soft, about 5 minutes, adding up to 1/2 cup more flour if needed. Then place the dough in an oiled bowl and turn it over to oil the top. Cover and let rise in a warm place until doubled in bulk, about 1 hour.

Meanwhile, bring water to a boil in the bottom of a steamer or wok. Reduce the heat so the water simmers. Place the sausages on a steamer rack; set the rack in place over the simmering water, cover, and steam until the sausages are softened and the fat becomes translucent, about 15 minutes. Let the sausages cool, then thinly slice them on the diagonal. Set aside.

Heat the vegetable oil in a small pan over high heat. Add the green onions and cook for 1 minute to soften. Set aside.

When the dough is doubled, punch it down and knead briefly. Divide the dough in half.

Roll half the dough out into a circle about 12 inches in diameter. The dough will tend to spring back on itself, so let it rest from time to time as you roll. Place the dough circle on an ungreased baking sheet. Spread 1/4 cup hoisin sauce over the dough, leaving about a 1/3-inch border at the edges. Sprinkle half the green onions on top, then half the sausage slices. Arrange half the bell pepper strips in an attractive pattern on top. Repeat with the remaining dough and topping ingredients to make a second pizza.

Let the pizzas rise 30 minutes. Meanwhile, preheat the oven to 425F (220C). Bake the pizzas in the preheated oven until the crust is crisp, about 20 minutes. Place on a board, cut into wedges, and serve hot.

Makes 2 (12-inch) pizzas.

Pumpernickel Shrimp Toasts

Since shrimp salad tastes wonderful on dark pumpernickel bread, it is perfectly logical that shrimp toast would be just as good made with distinctive pumpernickel as with white bread. Although in many ways a traditional shrimp toast mixture, this one also includes tarragon and Dijon mustard to better complement the bread. Serve these appetizers hot with drinks or Chinese beer.

1/2 POUND UNCOOKED SHRIMP, SHELLED, DEVEINED, HALVED

2 LARGE SLICES FRESH GINGERROOT, QUARTERED

5 WATER CHESTNUTS

1 MEDIUM GREEN ONION, CUT INTO 1-INCH PIECES

1 TEASPOON PACKED FRESH TARRAGON LEAVES OR 1/2 TEASPOON DRIED LEAF TARRAGON

2 TEASPOONS GINGER WINE OR SAKE

1 LARGE EGG

1/2 TEASPOON DIJON MUSTARD

1 TEASPOON KOSHER SALT

PINCH OF FRESHLY GROUND WHITE PEPPER

1 TABLESPOON CORNSTARCH

VEGETABLE OIL FOR DEEP-FRYING

5 (3-1/2-INCH-SQUARE) SLICES PUMPERNICKEL BREAD, EACH CUT INTO 4 TRIANGLES

■ Place the shrimp, gingerroot, water chestnuts, green onion, and tarragon in a food processor. Process, using on-and-off pulses, until finely chopped. Add the wine or sake, egg, mustard, salt, white pepper, and cornstarch. Process until well blended.

In a deep-fat fryer or pot, heat 4 inches of oil to 350F (175C). To test the temperature of the oil, drop a bit of the shrimp filling into the pot; it should drop to the bottom briefly, then rise to the top. If it sits on the bottom, the oil isn't hot enough. If it doesn't go down, the oil is too hot.

Spread a scant tablespoon of the shrimp filling on each bread triangle. Place the triangles, a few at a time, shrimp side down in the hot oil; cook until browned, about 1-1/2 minutes. Turn over and cook for about 1 minute on the other side. Drain on paper towels. Keep the cooked toasts hot in a 300F (150C) oven while you cook the remaining toasts. Adjust the heat as needed to keep the temperature of the oil constant. Serve hot.

Makes 20 shrimp toasts.

Chinese Mushrooms Stuffed with Crabmeat

Stuffed mushrooms are excellent cocktail party food—not too large, but still substantial. Though many recipes call for fresh mushrooms, I prefer the firmer texture and more interesting flavor of the dried Chinese varieties. Before you soak the mushrooms, look them over to make sure the ones you use are about two-bite size, with enough of a curve to hold the filling.

These appetizers are best when freshly made, but you can fill them ahead and bake just before serving.

ABOUT 24 DRIED CHINESE MUSHROOMS (ABOUT 1-1/2 OUNCES *TOTAL*), EACH 1-1/2 TO 2 INCHES IN DIAMETER

1 CUP (ABOUT 5 OUNCES) CRABMEAT, ANY BITS OF SHELL AND CARTILAGE REMOVED, ROUGHLY CHOPPED

1 TABLESPOON MINCED ONION

1 TABLESPOON MINCED FRESH GINGERROOT

1 TEASPOON SOY SAUCE

1 TEASPOON SAKE

1 TEASPOON DIJON MUSTARD

1 LARGE EGG

OLIVE OIL

FINE DRY BREAD CRUMBS

■ Place the mushrooms in a bowl and add boiling water to cover. Let soak for 20 minutes. Drain the mushrooms and squeeze them dry. Cut off and discard the stems, being careful not to damage the sides of the mushrooms.

Preheat the oven to 350F (175C). Meanwhile, in a small bowl, mix the crabmeat, onion, gingerroot, soy sauce, sake, mustard, and egg.

Brush each mushroom cap with a little oil, then fill with some of the crabmeat mixture, mounding it up over the top. Sprinkle some bread crumbs over the crabmeat filling. Arrange the mushrooms on a baking sheet.

Bake in the preheated oven for 10 minutes. Then turn the broiler on high and return the mushrooms to the oven until browned on the top, about 1 minute longer.

Makes about 24 stuffed mushrooms.

Stuffed Grape Leaves

Grape leaves are large and sturdy enough to make excellent wrappers for *dolmades*—bite-sized rolls traditionally filled with rice, pine nuts, currants, and lamb, braised until tender and served cold as an hors d'oeuvre at Greek or Middle Eastern meals. The cooking method is the same here, but I've used a pork filling seasoned with soy sauce and sesame oil. The Greeks usually keep the stuffed leaves immersed in the braising liquid by weighting them with a plate, but a Japanese dropped lid *(otoshi-buta)* is perfect for the job and easier to remove because it has a handle.

Serve stuffed grape leaves at picnics or as part of an assortment of hors d'oeuvres. They make a nice first course when combined with Baked Eggplant Salad, page 137, some crumbly feta, and oil-cured olives.

1 TABLESPOON OLIVE OIL

2 GARLIC CLOVES, MINCED

1/4 CUP CHOPPED GREEN ONIONS

1/2 POUND GROUND PORK

1-1/2 CUPS COOKED SHORT-GRAIN
RICE; OR 1/2 CUP UNCOOKED
RICE, COOKED IN BOILING WATER
FOR 10 MINUTES, DRAINED

1/4 CUP MINCED WATER CHESTNUTS

2 TABLESPOONS SOY SAUCE

1 TABLESPOON PLUS 1 TEASPOON
SESAME OIL

1/4 TEASPOON FRESHLY GROUND
BLACK PEPPER

ABOUT 1 POUND GRAPE LEAVES
PACKED IN BRINE

1-1/2 CUPS WATER

Heat the olive oil in a medium skillet over medium-high heat. Add the garlic and green onions and cook for 1 minute. Add the pork and cook, breaking up the lumps, until the pork is done through, about 5 minutes.

With a slotted spoon, remove the pork mixture to a bowl, leaving any fat in the skillet. Add the rice, water chestnuts, soy sauce, 1 teaspoon sesame oil, and pepper to the skillet; stir to mix. Set aside.

Bring a large pot of water to a boil. Remove the grape leaves from the brine and drop them into the boiling water. Turn off the heat and let the leaves stand for 2 minutes, then drain. Separate the leaves and pat dry.

Line the bottom of a heatproof 3-quart casserole with some of the torn leaves, making a single layer.

Work with 1 grape leaf at a time. Place the leaf, smooth side up, on your work surface. Cut away any stem that is still attached. Take about 1 tablespoon of the pork-rice filling (the exact amount will vary with the size of the leaf) and place it just above the bottom (stem end) of the leaf. Fold the bottom of the leaf up over the filling, then fold the sides in and roll up, keeping the leaf rounded. Place the stuffed leaf, seam side down, in the casserole. Repeat with the remaining leaves and filling, stacking the stuffed rolls in the casserole in fairly even layers. As you work, you will probably come across some torn leaves; patch these with a piece of another leaf so the filling won't fall out.

When all the leaves are stuffed, pour 1-1/2 cups water into the casserole and drizzle the remaining 1 tablespoon sesame oil on top. Place a dropped lid or plate on top of the leaves so it presses down on them. Bring the water to a boil; then reduce the heat, cover the casserole with its own lid, and simmer for 45 minutes. Let cool, then refrigerate until serving time.

Makes 35 to 40 stuffed grape leaves.

Oysters with Ginger-Wasabi Sauce

Oysters on the half shell make a simple, refreshing beginning to a meal. Although I often let the fishman shuck them, sometimes I do it myself. It takes a little practice, but once you get the knack, there is a lot of satisfaction in triumphing over these bivalves. If you shuck them yourself, you will need a short, sturdy knife. Rinse the oysters well to wash away the grit; then find an opening near the hinge, push in your knife, and twist. With luck, the shell will pop open. Run your knife under each oyster to loosen it, trying to keep the liquor in the shell.

After all that work, I usually eat the oysters very simply, with a drop of lemon juice and maybe a bit of ground pepper. Sometimes, however, I like to try dipping sauces such as this one, perfect for sashimi.

1 TEASPOON WASABI POWDER

1/2 TEASPOON WATER

1/2 TEASPOON GRATED FRESH GINGERROOT

2 TABLESPOONS SOY SAUCE

2 TEASPOONS LEMON JUICE

24 OYSTERS ON THE HALF SHELL

In a small bowl, mix together the wasabi powder and water. Cover and let stand for 5 minutes to develop the wasabi's flavor. Then stir in the gingerroot, soy sauce, and lemon juice.

Serve the oysters over cracked ice to keep them cold. Guests can either drizzle some sauce over the oysters or dip them into the sauce.

Makes 4 to 6 servings.

Steamed Cucumbers Stuffed with Crabmeat

As much as I like cucumbers crunchy and raw, I think it a shame that they are almost always relegated to the salad bowl. Something wonderful happens to them when they are cooked until tender and translucent. For this elegant first course, I've stuffed hollowed-out cucumbers with crabmeat delicately seasoned with soy sauce and sake, then steamed them. The pale rounds of cucumber and crab look particularly striking when arranged around a pool of bright tomato sauce on black plates. Continue the meal with Grilled Salmon with Miso, page 111, or Veal with Ginger, page 89.

3 TABLESPOONS UNCOOKED SHORT-GRAIN RICE

4 MEDIUM CUCUMBERS

1 CUP (ABOUT 5 OUNCES) CRABMEAT, ANY BITS OF SHELL AND CARTILAGE REMOVED, ROUGHLY CHOPPED

2 TEASPOONS LIGHT SOY SAUCE

1 TEASPOON SAKE

1/4 TEASPOON HOT-PEPPER SAUCE

2 TABLESPOONS CHOPPED GREEN ONION

2 LARGE EGG YOLKS

2 TEASPOONS LEMON JUICE

2 TEASPOONS UNSALTED BUTTER

1-1/4 POUNDS TOMATOES, PEELED, CORED, SEEDED, CUT INTO 1/4-INCH CUBES

1 TEASPOON KOSHER SALT, OR TO TASTE

FRESHLY GROUND BLACK PEPPER TO TASTE

■■ Bring 1 large and 1 small pot of salted water to a boil. Add the rice to the small pot and cook for 10 minutes. Drain well and set aside.

While the rice is cooking, cut the ends off each cucumber, leaving a 5-inch length of the center part of the cucumber. (Save the ends for salads.) Peel each length. Then, using a small knife, cut away and discard all the seeds, leaving a hollow cylinder. Drop the hollowed cucumbers into the large pot of boiling salted water and cook for 5 minutes. Drain, cool under cold running water, pat dry, and set aside.

In a small bowl, mix the crabmeat with the soy sauce, drained rice, sake, hot-pepper sauce, green onion, egg yolks, and lemon juice. Stuff the crab mixture into the cucumbers, being sure to fill them completely from end to end. It's probably easiest to use your fingers for this.

Bring water to a boil in the bottom of a steamer or wok. Reduce the heat so the water simmers. Arrange the stuffed cucumbers in a single layer on a flat steamer rack. Then set the rack in place over the simmering water, cover, and steam until the filling is done through, about 3 minutes.

While the cucumbers are steaming, melt the butter in a small skillet or saucepan. Add the tomatoes and cook, stirring quickly, until hot and wilted. Season with the salt and pepper. Keep warm.

Remove the cucumbers from the steamer and cut them into even, 1/2-inch-thick rounds. Arrange 5 rounds in a circle on each of 8 salad plates. Spoon some of the tomato sauce in the center of each plate.

Makes 8 servings.

Mackerel Seviche

Seviche is popular in Central and South America, where the fish is "cooked" in lime juice, then tossed with a simple, often spicy, vinaigrette. When I served a classic version to a Japanese friend, he thought it was a Japanese dish, remarking on the texture of the mackerel. For this seviche, I have emphasized the Asian flavor by making the dressing with fish sauce and curry paste. Although the fish is never exposed to heat, the acid in the lime juice reacts chemically with it and changes it just as cooking would.

Seviche is an excellent first course; serve it with bread to soak up the extra dressing. For the main course, try a robust dish like Braised Short Ribs with Rice Sticks, page 92, or Stuffed Breast of Veal, page 90.

1/2 POUND MACKEREL FILLETS, CUT INTO 1/2-INCH PIECES

1/4 CUP LIME JUICE

2 LARGE SLICES FRESH GINGERROOT

2 TABLESPOONS RICE WINE VINEGAR

1 TABLESPOON FISH SAUCE

1 TABLESPOON OLIVE OIL

1/4 TEASPOON RED CURRY PASTE, PAGE 189

2 TABLESPOONS SLICED GREEN ONION

1 SMALL TOMATO, CORED, CUBED

■■■ Place the mackerel in a glass bowl with the lime juice and gingerroot, making sure that the fish is covered with juice. Let the fish macerate for at least 4 hours, turning it over from time to time; it will become opaque and lose its raw look. Then drain the fish, discarding the lime juice and gingerroot.

In a bowl, whisk together the vinegar, fish sauce, oil, and Red Curry Paste. Add the fish, green onion, and tomato. Arrange in a flat serving bowl. Let rest for at least 1 hour before serving.

Makes 4 servings.

Mackerel Sushi

As much as I love sushi made with raw fish, I never serve it at home, because I'm never sure if the fish I buy is fresh enough. I often make vegetable sushi, though, or use fish that has been smoked or, like this mackerel, marinated in lime juice as for seviche. The tang of the fish complements that of the Sushi Rice; the wasabi adds a zingy accent. The dish is good on its own or as part of an assortment of appetizers like Fried Won Tons with Salsa, page 26, Pearl Balls, page 29, and Spiced Pecans, page 24.

I have a handy plastic rice press that shapes the Sushi Rice into neat rounded fingers, each the perfect size for topping with one piece of fish. If you don't have a rice press, do what the sushi chefs do and shape the rice with your wet hands. The results may not be perfectly symmetrical, but your guests will still be impressed.

1/2 POUND MACKEREL FILLETS, CUT INTO 1/2-INCH PIECES

1/4 CUP LIME JUICE

2 LARGE SLICES FRESH GINGERROOT

2 TEASPOONS WASABI POWDER

1 TEASPOON WATER

1 OR 2 SHEETS NORI, IF DESIRED

1 RECIPE SUSHI RICE, PAGE 144

■ Place the mackerel in a glass bowl with the lime juice and gingerroot, making sure that the fish is covered with juice. Let the fish macerate for at least 4 hours, turning it over from time to time; it will become opaque and lose its raw look. Then drain the fish, discarding the lime juice and gingerroot.

In a small bowl, mix together the wasabi powder and water. Cover and let stand for 5 minutes to develop the wasabi's flavor.

If you are using nori, cut it into strips about 1/3 inch wide.

With a sushi press or your wet hands, shape the Sushi Rice into ovals about 1 by 1-1/4 inches. Spread a little wasabi paste on the top of each rice ball, then top with a piece of fish, skin side down. If desired, wrap a strip of nori around the fish and rice to hold the fish in place, bringing the ends of the strip together at the bottom of the rice ball.

If made ahead, cover with plastic wrap and keep at room temperature for up to 3 hours (if your kitchen is not too hot).

Makes about 15 pieces sushi.

Paper-Wrapped Chicken with Salami

Small portions of food wrapped in parchment paper or heavy cellophane and deep-fried are popular all over China. They make a tasty first course, and they're just as good with apéritifs before dinner. The fillings vary widely, although chicken and a vegetable or two are particularly popular. I chose to combine each piece of spicy chicken with a thin slice of Hungarian salami; a few kernels of corn are hidden between the two for a nice contrast. A sprig of flat-leaf parsley makes a pretty decoration on the top of each package. (Deep-frying salami may sound excessive, but the process actually makes it leaner than the precooked meat.)

The paper wrappers can be sealed in different ways, but they're most often folded like an egg roll (or envelope). However, because I find that the packages may not stay sealed that way, I opt for the half-moon shape the French use for papillotes. Whatever your method, be sure the seal is tight, so the package puffs and protects the food inside. Heavy cellophane makes prettier packages than parchment paper, since you can see the foods. Be aware, though, that the usual thin cellophane cannot take the heat.

1/2 POUND BONELESS, SKINLESS CHICKEN BREAST

2 TEASPOONS SAMBAL OELEK

1 TABLESPOON SOY SAUCE

SESAME OIL

12 THIN SLICES HUNGARIAN SALAMI

1/4 CUP CORN KERNELS CUT FROM A COOKED COB; OR 1/4 CUP FROZEN WHOLE-KERNEL CORN, THAWED

12 SPRIGS FLAT-LEAF (ITALIAN) PARSLEY

VEGETABLE OIL FOR DEEP-FRYING

Cut the chicken into 12 even pieces, each about the size of a salami slice. If necessary, put 2 smaller pieces together to make 1 piece. Place the chicken in a small bowl with the sambal and soy sauce. Let marinate for 30 minutes.

Have ready 12 (6-inch-square) pieces of parchment paper. Using your finger, brush each lightly with sesame oil. Arrange 1 piece of parchment on your work surface, placing it on the diagonal so it points toward you. Place a salami slice just below the center line of the paper. Put some corn on top; the cover the corn with a piece of chicken. Arrange a parsley sprig neatly on top so the leaves are flat.

Fold the paper over the filling so you have a triangle. Turn the ends in, folding and twisting them to make a tight seal. Repeat to fill the remaining 11 pieces of parchment. If not cooking the packages immediately, refrigerate them. Bring to room temperature before cooking.

In a deep pot or wok, heat 3 to 4 inches of vegetable oil to 350F (175C) or until a 1-inch bread cube turns golden brown in 65 seconds. Add 2 or 3 packages to the oil and cook for 2 minutes. The packages should be puffed and brown. Drain on paper towels and keep warm until all the packages have been cooked. Adjust the heat as needed to keep the temperature of the oil constant.

Makes 12 packages.

Sesame Chicken in Phyllo

Tissue-thin phyllo pastry, common in Greece and related to the strudel doughs of Hungary and other countries, isn't typical of the Orient—but it makes an excellent wrapper for this sesame-flavored chicken. I like to serve these appetizers at the table with Sweet Mustard Sauce, but if you prefer, make them smaller and serve with drinks, using the sauce for dipping.

1 POUND BONELESS, SKINLESS CHICKEN BREASTS, CUT INTO 1/4-INCH CUBES

2 TABLESPOONS SOY SAUCE

1 TABLESPOON SAKE

1 TABLESPOON SESAME SEEDS, TOASTED IN A DRY SKILLET

1 TABLESPOON PEANUT OIL

ABOUT 1/4 CUP SESAME OIL

1 TABLESPOON MINCED GARLIC

2 TABLESPOONS JULIENNED FRESH GINGERROOT

1/2 CUP SLICED GREEN ONIONS

1 TEASPOON HOT SESAME (CHILI) OIL

1 (10-OUNCE) PACKAGE FROZEN CHOPPED SPINACH, THAWED, SQUEEZED DRY

1 TABLESPOON FRESH THYME LEAVES OR 1 TEASPOON DRIED LEAF THYME

2 LARGE EGGS

10 TO 12 (9- BY 12-INCH) SHEETS PHYLLO PASTRY, THAWED IF FROZEN

SESAME SEEDS

1 RECIPE SWEET MUSTARD SAUCE, PAGE 187

▬ Place the chicken in a bowl with the soy sauce and sake. Let marinate for 1 hour.

Using a suribachi, mortar and pestle, or spice grinder, grind the 1 tablespoon toasted sesame seeds to a fine powder. Set aside.

Heat the peanut oil and 1 tablespoon sesame oil in a large skillet over high heat. Add the garlic and gingerroot and cook for 1 minute. Add the chicken and its marinade and cook until the chicken is opaque throughout, about 3 minutes. Add the green onions and hot sesame oil and cook until the onions begin to wilt, a few seconds longer.

Place the chicken mixture in a bowl and add the spinach, thyme, ground sesame seeds, and eggs. Mix well.

Work with 1 phyllo sheet at a time, keeping the rest covered with a kitchen towel to prevent them from drying out.

Place 1 sheet on your work surface and cut it into 3 strips, each about 4 inches wide. Work with 1 strip at a time. Brush the surface lightly with sesame oil. Place about 2 tablespoons of the chicken mixture near 1 bottom corner of the strip. Fold the opposite bottom corner over the filling to make a triangle. Fold the filled triangle up and over to the side; then continue to fold the strip in this way, as if you were folding a flag. Place the filled triangle on a baking sheet, brush with sesame oil, and sprinkle with sesame seeds.

Repeat until all the filling has been used; arranging the triangles in a single layer on baking sheets. You should have 30 to 36 triangles.

Preheat the oven to 350F (175C). Bake the triangles in the preheated oven until crisp and brown, 20 to 25 minutes.

Arrange all the triangles overlapping on a platter and serve Sweet Mustard Sauce on the side; or place 3 or 4 on each individual salad plate and spoon some sauce in the middle.

Makes 30 to 36 pastries (enough for 8 to 10 first-course servings).

NOTE: If you prefer to serve these another day, freeze them unbaked, placing wax paper between the layers. Bake them frozen; the baking time will be about the same.

Seafood Salad with Miso Sauce

Nuta is a popular Japanese dish of giant clams and green onions served cold in a miso sauce. I've made a more substantial salad using different shellfish and assorted greens. Because it can be prepared ahead, it is an excellent first course for company. Serve it with a buttery Chardonnay or warm sake, then follow with a main course of Duck Breasts with Black Bean Sauce, page 74.

page 74.

4 GREEN ONIONS, CUT INTO 2-INCH PIECES

1/4 POUND (ABOUT 12) UNCOOKED MEDIUM SHRIMP IN THE SHELL

3/4 POUND (ABOUT 12) MUSSELS IN THE SHELL, WELL SCRUBBED

6 CHERRYSTONE CLAMS IN THE SHELL, WELL SCRUBBED

1/2 CUP LIGHT-COLORED MISO

2 TABLESPOONS SAKE

2 TABLESPOONS MIRIN

1/4 CUP LEMON JUICE

3 TABLESPOONS SUGAR

2 TEASPOONS DIJON MUSTARD

2 CUPS ASSORTED GREENS, SUCH AS BIBB LETTUCE, RADICCHIO, WATERCRESS, BELGIAN ENDIVE, AND CHICORY

▬ Bring a pot of water to a boil. Add the green onions and cook for 3 minutes. Remove with a slotted spoon and set aside. Add the shrimp to the same water and return to a boil. Cook until the shrimp turn pink, about 30 seconds. Drain the shrimp and rinse under cold water. Shell the shrimp, devein them, and set them aside with the green onions.

Place the mussels and clams in a heavy pot over medium-high heat. Cover and cook for for 5 minutes. The mussels should begin to open. Remove any open mussels and cook the remaining mussels and clams for 5 minutes longer. By this time, all the mussels and some of the clams should be open. Remove the mussels and any open clams. Cook the remaining clams until all are open, about 5 minutes longer.

Remove the cooked clams and mussels from their shells and set aside with the shrimp and green onions.

In a bowl, whisk together the miso, sake, mirin, lemon juice, sugar, and mustard. Set aside.

When ready to serve, toss the greens together and divide among 4 salad plates. Arrange 1/4 of the seafood-green onion mixture on top of each salad. Stir the miso dressing to blend and drizzle it over the salads.

Makes 4 servings.

Smoked Trout Mousse

Most fish mousses are made with whipping cream, which makes them luscious but incredibly fattening. I found that soft, spongy tofu (as opposed to the very firm type) can be pureed with the fish to make a rich, spreadable dish much like the traditional version—but far lower in fat. In keeping with the cross-cultural spirit, I added ginger and wasabi to the seasonings. I serve the mousse as a spread for firm slices of toast or as a dip for raw vegetables. Stuffed into seeded small tomatoes, it's a nice first course. It is also a good sandwich spread—try it with sliced tomatoes and cucumbers on pumpernickel.

The tofu does not bind the way cream does, so the mousse needs to be stirred just before serving.

2 TEASPOONS WASABI POWDER

2 TEASPOONS WATER

1 (1/2-INCH) CUBE FRESH
  GINGERROOT

1 LARGE GARLIC CLOVE

1 SMALL (2-OUNCE) ONION, CUT
  INTO CHUNKS

1/2 POUND SKINLESS SMOKED
  TROUT FILLET

1/2 POUND VERY SOFT TOFU,
  DRAINED, BROKEN INTO PIECES

1/8 TEASPOON FRESHLY GROUND
  WHITE PEPPER

1/2 CUP FRESH DILL SPRIGS

■ In a small bowl, mix together the wasabi powder and water. Cover and let stand for 5 minutes to develop the wasabi's flavor.

With the food processor running, drop the gingerroot and garlic through the feed tube to mince. Stop the motor and scrape down the sides of the work bowl. Add the onion and process until finely chopped. Add the trout and tofu. Process until smooth and creamy. Add the wasabi paste, white pepper, and dill. Process until the dill is chopped but not pureed. Turn into a bowl; serve at once or refrigerate for up to 12 hours. Stir well before serving.

Makes about 3 cups.

Pork and Crab Terrine

This terrine is a wonderful change from heavy French pâtés. Made with pork and crabmeat and seasoned with a spicy curry paste, it is an excellent beginning to a meal, exciting in flavor but not overwhelming. Arrange the sliced terrine on plates ahead of time, but wait until the last minute to add the sauce.

Follow the terrine with Cornish Game Hens in Tamarind Marinade, page 73, or Lamb Stew, page 79.

1/2 POUND GROUND PORK

1/4 POUND CRABMEAT, ANY BITS OF
  SHELL AND CARTILAGE REMOVED,
  ROUGHLY CHOPPED

2 TABLESPOONS MINCED ONION

1 TABLESPOON RED CURRY PASTE,
  PAGE 189

1 TABLESPOON FISH SAUCE

2 TABLESPOONS CHOPPED FRESH
  CILANTRO LEAVES

2 TABLESPOONS WATER

1 UNPEELED KIRBY (PICKLING)
  CUCUMBER, CUT INTO THIN
  SLICES

1 RECIPE PEANUT SAUCE, PAGE
  187

■ Place the pork, crabmeat, onion, Red Curry Paste, fish sauce, cilantro, and 2 tablespoons water in a bowl. Blend well; then place the mixture in an 8-1/2- by 4-1/2-inch loaf pan (the pan will be only half full).

Bring water to a boil in the bottom of a steamer. Reduce the heat so the water simmers. Place the loaf pan on a steamer rack over the simmering water, cover, and steam for 1 hour. Check the water level from time to time to be sure the water hasn't boiled away. Add more boiling water as needed.

Place the pan on a rack and let cool to room temperature. If not serving immediately, remove the terrine from the pan, wrap it in plastic wrap, and refrigerate for up to a day.

When ready to serve, cut the terrine into 32 thin slices. Overlap 4 slices on each of 8 salad plates; arrange several cucumber slices on each plate. Spoon some Peanut Sauce down the center of the terrine slices.

Makes 8 servings.

Shrimp Quenelles with Ginger-Wasabi Sauce

Quenelles are a classic French preparation: silky smooth ovals of fish and cream, gently poached. Long the sole domain of dedicated chefs, these delicate dumplings became easily accessible to the home cook with the advent of the food processor. I prefer full-flavored shrimp to the usual pike; the addition of fish sauce and ginger makes this version even more interesting. Cilantro leaves add pretty flecks of green to the pale pink seafood.

These make such a rich beginning to the meal that I usually follow them with a light main course such as Steamed Chicken Rolls, page 68.

Steamed Chicken Rolls, page 68.

1/2 POUND UNCOOKED SHRIMP, SHELLED, DEVEINED

1 (ABOUT 1/4- BY 1-INCH) PIECE FRESH GINGERROOT

2 TEASPOONS FISH SAUCE

1 LARGE EGG WHITE

2 TABLESPOONS FRESH CILANTRO LEAVES (PLUS ADDITIONAL LEAVES FOR GARNISH)

2 TABLESPOONS SAKE

1/2 CUP WHIPPING CREAM

GINGER-WASABI SAUCE, SEE PAGE 43

1 TABLESPOON CHOPPED GREEN ONION

Place the shrimp and gingerroot in a food processor. Process until finely chopped. Add the fish sauce, egg white, 2 tablespoons cilantro, sake, and cream. Process until very smooth. Pour into a bowl, cover, and refrigerate for at least 1 hour. Meanwhile, prepare the Ginger-Wasabi Sauce; set aside.

To cook the quenelles, bring a full teakettle to a boil. Meanwhile, lightly rub a 10-inch skillet with butter. Using 2 wet teaspoons, shape the shrimp mixture into ovals. Drop each quenelle into the prepared skillet, leaving a little space between the quenelles. You should have about 20 fairly smooth, egg-shaped ovals.

Gently pour the boiling water into the skillet, directing it into the spaces between the quenelles so they don't dissolve. The water should just cover the quenelles. Place the skillet over medium heat so the water simmers gently. Cook the quenelles, uncovered, for about 3 minutes, then turn the quenelles over and cook, uncovered, until done through, about 2 minutes longer.

With a slotted spoon, remove each quenelle to a plate lined with paper towels.

Stir the green onion into the Ginger-Wasabi Sauce. Spoon about 1 tablespoon sauce on each of 4 salad plates. Arrange about 5 quenelles like petals around the sauce on each plate. Place a few cilantro leaves in the center of each plate.

Makes 4 servings.

GINGER-WASABI SAUCE:

1 TEASPOON WASABI POWDER

1/2 TEASPOON WATER

1 TABLESPOON MINCED FRESH
  GINGERROOT

2 TABLESPOONS MIRIN

2 TABLESPOONS SAKE

2 TABLESPOONS SOY SAUCE

1 TEASPOON RICE WINE VINEGAR

■■ In a small bowl, mix together the wasabi powder and water. Cover and let stand for 5 minutes to develop the wasabi's flavor. Place the gingerroot, mirin, and sake in a small saucepan. Bring to a boil; then reduce the heat and simmer for 2 minutes. Let cool, then strain into a clean bowl. Stir in the wasabi paste, soy sauce, and vinegar.

I love soups of all kinds and always go back for seconds. In the Orient, soup is often served at breakfast—a sensible choice, although unusual for Westerners—but the recipes in this chapter are meant to be served later in the day. Soups like Cold Vegetable Soup and Vichyssoise with Coconut Milk are excellent beginnings to meals. Others, like Lentil Soup with Oriental Eggplant, Hearty Vegetable Soup, and Clam Chowder, are filling enough for a light lunch or supper along with salad and bread.

While it's nice to smell soup simmering on the stove all day, these recipes are fairly quick. In general, they can be made ahead and reheated, although Clam Chowder and Fennel Fish Soup are best if finished just before serving, and Chicken Minestrone thickens considerably as it stands.

Aside from dashi, I have not included recipes for basic stocks. They're simple to make, though. Whenever I cut up whole chickens or bone breasts, I save and freeze the trimmings until I have a bag full. Then I buy a few backs and throw them in a pot along with the thawed trimmings, a couple of carrots, an onion, a few garlic cloves, and any odd vegetables I have around (celery, turnips, sprigs of parsley). I cover it all with cold water and let it simmer for several hours, skimming off foam and fat from time to time. The finished strained stock keeps in the freezer for months. Beef stock is made in the same way, using bones with some meat and not much fat attached. If you want the stock to be dark, brown the bones under the broiler before simmering them. Fish stock, too, starts with bones and trimmings, but it shouldn't simmer very long—about 45 minutes is enough. Roughly chop the vegetables before adding them so they can give off their flavor in the short cooking time. (Dashi is a quick, light substitute for fish stock.)

When making any stock, the one caveat is not to add any salt. The natural sodium in the bones is surprisingly salty in itself, and the saltiness intensifies as the stock simmers. Add salt to taste when you use the stock.

Cold Vegetable Soup, page 45, has fresh cilantro and snow peas as some of the ingredients. Chicken Minestrone, page 51, is enhanced with tamarind pulp and fish sauce.

SOUPS

Cold Vegetable Soup

Although based on the idea of gazpacho, this chilled soup includes bean sprouts, snow peas, and chunks of baby corn, ingredients foreign to the Spanish versions. It is an excellent start to a summer meal; follow it with Grilled Shark, page 114, or Lamb Kabobs with Hoisin, page 78. If you want the snow peas to stay bright green, add them just before serving so they won't be darkened by the acids in the soup.

1/4 POUND SNOW PEAS, STRINGS REMOVED, CUT ON THE DIAGONAL INTO 1/2-INCH STRIPS

1 CUP SOYBEAN SPROUTS

1/2 CUP ROUGHLY CHOPPED GREEN ONIONS

1/4 POUND DAIKON, PEELED, ROUGHLY CHOPPED

1/2 POUND TOMATOES, CORED, ROUGHLY CHOPPED

1/2 CUP FRESH CILANTRO LEAVES

1 (15-OUNCE) CAN BABY CORN, DRAINED, RINSED

2 CUPS TOMATO JUICE

2 TABLESPOONS SOY SAUCE

2 TABLESPOONS RICE WINE VINEGAR

1/4 TEASPOON FRESHLY GROUND BLACK PEPPER

■ Bring a pot of salted water to a boil. Add the snow peas and cook for 1 minute. Remove with a slotted spoon, cool under cold running water, drain well, cover, and refrigerate.

Return the water to a boil. Add the bean sprouts and cook for 30 seconds. Drain well; cool under cold running water. Drain again, roughly chop, and set aside.

Place the green onions, daikon, tomatoes, and cilantro in a food processor. Process until the mixture is fairly smooth. Pour into a large bowl.

Cut each ear of corn in half lengthwise; then cut each half crosswise into thirds. Add to the bowl along with the tomato juice, bean sprouts, soy sauce, vinegar, and pepper.

Cover the soup and refrigerate for at least 1 hour. Just before serving, stir in the snow peas.

Makes 6 servings.

Vichyssoise with Coconut Milk

Despite its French name, vichyssoise was invented in New York. It's a cold, creamy leek and potato soup that makes a filling hot-weather lunch with a small salad of mixed greens and tomatoes. It is also an excellent starter for a meal of Steamed Catfish, page 114, or Grilled Salmon with Miso, page 111. The addition of daikon and the use of coconut milk instead of cream makes this version unusual. Like all cold soups, it offers an advantage for the host—it's best when made ahead and thoroughly chilled.

1/4 CUP (4 TABLESPOONS) UNSALTED BUTTER

1 TEASPOON MINCED FRESH GINGERROOT

1 TEASPOON MINCED GARLIC

1 POUND LEEKS, WELL WASHED, GREEN TOPS CUT OFF, WHITE PARTS SLICED

1/3 CUP SLICED GREEN ONIONS (WHITE PART ONLY)

1-1/2 POUNDS POTATOES, PEELED, CUT INTO 1/2-INCH CUBES

1/2 POUND DAIKON, PEELED, CUT INTO 1/2-INCH CUBES

1/4 CUP SAKE

3 CUPS CHICKEN STOCK

1 TABLESPOON KOSHER SALT, OR TO TASTE

1/2 TEASPOON FRESHLY GROUND WHITE PEPPER

1 CUP COCONUT MILK

1/4 CUP SLICED GREEN ONION TOPS

■ Melt the butter in a 3-quart saucepan over high heat. Add the gingerroot, garlic, leeks, and 1/3 cup sliced green onion whites. Cook until soft, about 3 minutes. Add the cubed potatoes and daikon and stir to coat. Add the sake and stock. Bring to a boil; then reduce the heat, cover, and simmer until the potatoes and daikon are quite soft, about 15 minutes. Stir in the salt and white pepper; the amount of salt you need will depend upon the saltiness of the stock.

Let the vegetables cool, then roughly chop them in a food processor or put them through the coarse blade of a food mill. If you are using a food processor, you will probably have to chop the vegetables in batches. Return the chopped vegetables to the cooking liquid and stir in the coconut milk. Refrigerate until thoroughly chilled.

Garnish each serving of soup with a sprinkling of green onion tops.

Makes about 8 cups (8 first-course or 4 main-dish servings).

Cream of Oriental Mushroom Soup

Many Oriental mushrooms are available to us, and they add flavor to all kinds of dishes. In this case, I've used three types—dried Chinese, straw, and enoki—to make what at first seems to be a traditional cream of mushroom soup thickened with egg yolks. To complement the mushrooms, I have used soy sauce, sake, and ginger rather than shallots and wine as seasonings. The soup makes a perfect beginning to an elegant dinner of poached or grilled salmon or Chicken Breast with Nori, page 62.

Chicken Breast with Nori, page 62.

1 OUNCE (ABOUT 16) DRIED CHINESE MUSHROOMS

1-1/2 CUPS BOILING WATER

2 TABLESPOONS UNSALTED BUTTER

1 TEASPOON MINCED FRESH GINGERROOT

1 TEASPOON MINCED GARLIC

3/4 CUP DIAGONALLY SLICED GREEN ONIONS

1 (15-OUNCE) CAN WHOLE PEELED STRAW MUSHROOMS, DRAINED, RINSED

2 CUPS CHICKEN STOCK

1 CUP WHIPPING CREAM

1 TABLESPOON SAKE

1 TABLESPOON LIGHT SOY SAUCE

HOT-PEPPER SAUCE TO TASTE

2 LARGE EGG YOLKS

18 ENOKI MUSHROOMS, ROOT ENDS TRIMMED

Place the dried Chinese mushrooms in a bowl and add the boiling water. Let soak for 20 minutes. Drain the mushrooms and squeeze them dry, reserving 1/2 cup liquid. Cut off and discard the stems; cut the caps into 1/8-inch-wide strips.

Melt the butter in a 2-quart saucepan over high heat. Add the gingerroot and garlic. Cook, stirring, for 30 seconds. Add the green onions and cook for 30 seconds longer. Add the Chinese and straw mushrooms; stir to mix well. Add the stock, cream, and reserved 1/2 cup mushroom liquid. Bring to a boil, then reduce the heat, cover, and simmer for 15 minutes. Stir in the sake, soy sauce, and hot-pepper sauce.

Place the egg yolks in a small bowl and whisk to blend. Slowly whisk in at least 1 cup of the hot soup to raise the temperature of the yolks; then pour the heated egg yolks back into the soup, whisking constantly. Cook, whisking, until the soup thickens slightly; do not let the soup boil or the egg yolks will curdle.

Spoon the hot soup into bowls and garnish each portion with 3 enoki mushrooms.

Makes 6 servings.

Thai Black Bean Soup

I love spicy foods and tend to add more garlic and chilies than recipes call for. I've learned through experience, however, that Thai dishes, more than those of other cuisines, tend to be extremely hot by Western standards. A soup may use eight hot chilies—but when I made this soup with only *two* bird's eye chilies, it was practically inedible. Just one makes it plenty hot. Remember, though, that heat varies with the type of chili and even among chilies of the same variety. To test a particular chili, I gently touch a cut piece against my lip. If it starts to burn, I know I had better be careful. If not, I may use more chilies.

When you prepare fresh chilies, always remove the seeds and ribs to cut down on the heat, and be sure to wash your hands, knife, and cutting board when you're done. And by all means, keep your hands away from your eyes when you have chili juice on your fingers. That really stings!

This is an excellent, surprisingly light, soup to start a meal. Follow it with something a bit milder in flavor, like Salmon in Papillote, page 110.

1 CUP (ABOUT 6-1/2 OUNCES) DRIED BLACK BEANS

1/4 CUP CHOPPED ONION

2 GARLIC CLOVES

5 CUPS WATER

8 UNCOOKED LARGE SHRIMP, SHELLED (LEAVE TAILS ON)

1 BIRD'S EYE CHILI, CORED, SEEDED, DERIBBED, CUT INTO THIN RINGS

1/2 RED BELL PEPPER, CORED, SEEDED, CUT INTO THIN SLICES

1/2 TEASPOON POWDERED LEMON GRASS (SEREH)

1/2 TEASPOON POWDERED GALANGAL (LAOS)

2 TABLESPOONS FISH SAUCE

3 TABLESPOONS LIME JUICE

1 STRIP LIME PEEL

Rinse and sort through the beans, removing any small stones that may be mixed in with them. Place the beans in a 3-quart pot and add the onion, garlic, and water. Bring to a boil; reduce the heat, cover, and simmer until the beans are soft, 2 to 2-1/2 hours. There should be enough liquid left so the beans are soupy; add more water if necessary. (This much can be done ahead.)

Bring a small pot of water to a boil. Butterfly the shrimp by cutting completely through their backs to the tail. Scrape away any dirty veins. Drop the shrimp into the boiling water, return to a boil, and cook just until the shrimp turn pink, about 30 seconds. Drain and set aside.

When you're ready to serve, heat the beans and their liquid. Add the chili, bell pepper, lemon grass, galangal, fish sauce, lime juice, and lime peel. Bring to a boil, then reduce the heat and simmer for 5 minutes.

Spoon the soup into individual bowls and garnish each serving with a shrimp.

Makes 8 servings.

Hot and Sour Chicken Noodle Soup

I love the sensation of hot and sour soup going down my throat. It's the perfect pick-me-up when I feel a cold coming on. Chicken noodle soup, chock-full of noodles and pieces of chicken, is another of my favorites. As this recipe shows, the two different soups go together beautifully.

1 (5-OUNCE) BONELESS, SKINLESS CHICKEN BREAST HALF, CUT INTO THIN STRIPS

2 TABLESPOONS PLUS 1/2 TEASPOON SOY SAUCE

1 TABLESPOON PLUS 1/2 TEASPOON CHINESE RICE WINE

1/4 TEASPOON SESAME OIL

4 CUPS CHICKEN STOCK

2 OUNCES (1 GENEROUS CUP) MEDIUM EGG NOODLES

1 LARGE EGG, WELL BEATEN

1/4 CUP CHINESE BLACK VINEGAR

1 TEASPOON FRESHLY GROUND BLACK PEPPER

1/4 CUP SLICED GREEN ONION TOPS

Toss the chicken with 1/2 teaspoon soy sauce, 1/2 teaspoon wine, and the sesame oil. Set aside.

In a large pot, bring the stock to a boil. Add the chicken and noodles. Reduce the heat and simmer, uncovered, until the noodles are tender, about 7 minutes.

Stirring the soup constantly, pour in the beaten egg so it forms lacy threads. Add the vinegar, pepper, remaining 2 tablespoons soy sauce, and remaining 1 tablespoon wine. Simmer for 1 minute. Taste and add more seasonings as needed. The soup should have a peppery, slightly sour flavor. Garnish with the green onions.

Makes 4 servings.

Chicken Minestrone

In the Philippines, tamarind is a common seasoning for chicken soup. Here, it imparts a pleasing light, tart flavor to minestrone. Serve this soup as a main course with a green salad and some crusty bread, or as a first course before a meat meal.

If you make the soup ahead, you will need to thin it a bit with water or stock upon reheating, since the macaroni continues to absorb liquid as the minestrone stands.

1/4 CUP TAMARIND PULP

1/2 CUP HOT WATER

1 OUNCE FRESH SPINACH, STEMS REMOVED, WASHED

2 TABLESPOONS OLIVE OIL

1 GARLIC CLOVE, MINCED

1 MEDIUM (5-OUNCE) ONION, CHOPPED

1/2 CUP DICED CARROT

1/2 CUP DICED POTATO

1/2 POUND TOMATOES, CORED, ROUGHLY CHOPPED

1 CUP CHICKEN STOCK

1 CUP WATER

2 TABLESPOONS FISH SAUCE

1/2 CUP ELBOW MACARONI

1/2 POUND BONELESS, SKINLESS CHICKEN, CUT INTO 1-INCH CUBES

FRESHLY GRATED PARMESAN CHEESE TO TASTE

Place the tamarind pulp in a bowl, add the hot water, and let soak for 20 minutes, stirring occasionally to help the pulp dissolve. Then press the mixture through a strainer to eliminate the seeds and undissolved pulp. You should have a scant 1/2 cup liquid. Set aside. Pile spinach leaves on top of each other, roll them up and cut them into thin strips. Set aside.

Heat the oil in a 3-quart pot over medium-high heat. Add the garlic and onion and sauté for 2 minutes. Add the carrot and potato and cook for 1 minute longer. Add the tomatoes and cook for about 1 minute longer. Pour in the stock, water, tamarind liquid, and fish sauce. Bring to a boil and add the macaroni. Reduce the heat and simmer for about 10 minutes; add the chicken and cook until both chicken and macaroni are tender, about 10 minutes longer. Stir in the spinach. At the table, offer cheese to sprinkle over the soup.

Makes 4 servings.

Hearty Vegetable Soup

In the winter, I make vegetable soups with whatever I have in the house. There are few rules—just about any combination guarantees good results. Use this recipe as a guide to giving the soup an Oriental feeling. I usually serve it for supper, accompanied with crusty French bread and cheese.

8 DRIED CHINESE MUSHROOMS (ABOUT 1/2 OUNCE *TOTAL*)

1 CUP BOILING WATER

2 TABLESPOONS OLIVE OIL

1 TABLESPOON MINCED FRESH GINGERROOT

1/2 CUP CHOPPED ONION

1 CUP 1/4-INCH POTATO CUBES

1/2 CUP 1/4-INCH CARROT CUBES

1 CUP 1/4-INCH DAIKON CUBES

4 CUPS CHICKEN STOCK

1 TABLESPOON SOY SAUCE

FRESHLY GROUND BLACK PEPPER TO TASTE

2 OUNCES CELLOPHANE NOODLES, BROKEN INTO 3-INCH PIECES

1 CUP 1/4-INCH FIRM TOFU CUBES

Place the mushrooms in a bowl and add the boiling water. Let soak for 20 minutes. Drain the mushrooms and squeeze them dry, reserving the liquid. Cut off and discard the stems; cut the caps into 1/4-inch squares.

Heat the oil in a 3-quart pot over high heat. Add the gingerroot and onion and cook for 1 minute. Add the potato, carrot, and daikon. Cook for 1 minute longer. Add the stock and reserved mushroom liquid. Bring to a boil. Add the mushrooms and cook for 10 minutes. Add the soy sauce and pepper.

Add the noodles and cook for 5 minutes longer. Stir in the tofu and cook for 1 minute longer. Taste and adjust the seasonings. Serve hot.

Makes 4 servings.

Curried Split Pea and Sausage Soup

Split pea soup, a beautiful bright green, is a wonderful winter meal, especially when chock-full of sliced knockwurst or other sausage. This time, the sausage is Chinese-style, adding a sweet counterpoint to the heat of the curry. I usually serve the soup as a main course with salad and bread; reheated leftover soup is good for lunch with grilled cheese or tuna sandwiches. Like most of my soups, this one is quite thick. You can thin it to taste with water.

2 TABLESPOONS OLIVE OIL

2 GARLIC CLOVES, MINCED

1 TABLESPOON MINCED FRESH GINGERROOT

1/2 CUP CHOPPED GREEN ONIONS

2 TEASPOONS RED CURRY PASTE, PAGE 189

1/4 POUND CARROTS, CUT INTO 1/4-INCH CUBES

1/2 POUND POTATOES, PEELED, CUT INTO 1/4-INCH CUBES

1/4 POUND DAIKON, PEELED, CUT INTO 1/4-INCH CUBES

1/2 POUND (ABOUT 1 CUP) DRIED GREEN SPLIT PEAS

3 CUPS CHICKEN STOCK

1/2 CUP SAKE

1/2 POUND CHINESE-STYLE PORK SAUSAGES, STEAMED FOR 15 MINUTES, CUT ON THE DIAGONAL INTO 1/4-INCH SLICES

1/4 CHOPPED FRESH CILANTRO LEAVES

▬ Heat the oil in a 2-quart saucepan over high heat. Add the garlic, gingerroot, and green onions. Cook for 1 minute, stirring often. Add the Red Curry Paste and stir until smooth. Add the carrots, potatoes, daikon, and split peas. Sauté for 1 minute. Stir in the stock and sake. Bring to a boil; then reduce the heat, cover, and simmer, stirring occasionally, until the peas are very soft, about 45 minutes. Add the sausage slices and cilantro and cook for 5 minutes longer.

Makes 4 servings.

Lentil Soup with Oriental Eggplant

Fermented black beans give this soup a wonderful flavor that's enhanced by slices of Oriental eggplant. It's an excellent way to start a dinner of Roast Chicken with Cilantro and Lime, page 72. It also makes a nice lunch or supper, either on its own or with grilled cheese sandwiches.

The soup is very thick, almost like a stew. If you prefer it thinner, add more water.

2 TABLESPOONS OLIVE OIL

1 TABLESPOON MINCED FRESH GINGERROOT

2 GARLIC CLOVES, MINCED

1 MEDIUM (5-OUNCE) ONION, CHOPPED

1/4 CUP FERMENTED BLACK BEANS, ROUGHLY CHOPPED

1 DRIED RED CHILI, HALVED

1 CUP (ABOUT 6-1/2 OUNCES) DRIED LENTILS, WASHED

2 CUPS CHICKEN STOCK

1 CUP WATER

1 (1/4-POUND) ORIENTAL EGGPLANT, CUT ON THE DIAGONAL INTO 1/4-INCH SLICES

Heat the oil in a 2-quart pot over high heat. Add the gingerroot and garlic and cook for 30 seconds to release the flavors. Add the onion and cook until softened, about 3 minutes. Add the black beans and chili; cook for 30 seconds. Add the lentils and stir to coat. Add the stock and water and bring to a boil. Reduce the heat, partially cover the pot, and simmer until the lentils are soft, about 30 minutes. Add the eggplant and simmer until tender, about 10 minutes longer.

Makes about 4 cups (4 first-course servings).

Fennel Fish Soup

With its mild licorice flavor, fennel is an ideal mate for plain white fish like cod. In a Mediterranean mood, I've enhanced the fennel flavor of this soup by adding Pernod, an aromatic liqueur. The stock, however, is dashi, an essential in any Japanese kitchen. Daikon and cellophane noodles add to the cross-cultural spirit.

This soup is light, but filling (and nourishing) enough to be a one-pot main dish. Serve it with French bread and a salad.

2 TABLESPOONS OLIVE OIL

1-1/2 CUPS SLICED LEEKS

1 CUP CHOPPED FENNEL

1 CUP THINLY SLICED DAIKON

1 CUP THINLY SLICED CARROTS

1/4 CUP PERNOD

6 CUPS DASHI, BELOW

1/4 CUP SOY SAUCE

FRESHLY GROUND WHITE PEPPER
TO TASTE

1 POUND BONELESS, SKINLESS
COD, CUT INTO 3/4-INCH CHUNKS

2 OUNCES CELLOPHANE NOODLES,
BROKEN INTO 2-INCH PIECES

Heat the oil in a large skillet or pot over high heat. Add the leeks and sauté for 2 minutes to soften. Add the fennel and sauté for 1 minute longer. Add the daikon and carrots and cook for 1 minute longer. Add the Pernod and cook for 30 seconds. Then add the Dashi, soy sauce, and white pepper. Bring to a boil and add the cod. Reduce the heat and simmer for 2 minutes. Add the noodles. Cook until the noodles are softened and the fish is opaque, about 2 minutes longer.

Makes 4 servings.

Dashi

The key ingredients in almost any Japanese dish are soy sauce, sake, and dashi, a delicate fish stock that no Japanese cook is ever without. Unlike Western stocks that simmer for hours, dashi is made in minutes. Some people grate their own dried fish for dashi; more are likely to use packaged dashi mixes. I opt for the middle road (and the most commonly used method today), starting with packaged bonito flakes and konbu. Since the ingredients are dried, I always keep them on hand and can have fish stock whenever the urge strikes. Using dashi is especially convenient if you don't have easy access to fish bones or if your family objects to the aroma of simmering fish stock.

Unlike heavier fish stocks, dashi does not stand up to freezing. Make it as you need it. It will keep in the refrigerator for several days.

1 (15-INCH) PIECE KONBU

6 CUPS WATER

2 (1.5-GRAM) PACKAGES BONITO
FLAKES

Place the konbu and water in a 2-quart pot. Bring the water to a boil and immediately remove the konbu. Remove the pot from the heat and sprinkle in the bonito flakes. Let the flakes settle to the bottom of the pot (it will take about a minute), then strain the stock through a damp kitchen towel, pressing down on the flakes.

Makes about 6 cups.

Clam Chowder

Most chowders seem to suffer from overcooking, but this chunky soup, cooked only a few minutes, tastes fresher. It's an excellent start to almost any meal; Twice-Cooked Pork, page 94, or Fried Chicken, page 67, would be great. The soup is also hearty enough to stand by itself for supper or lunch with a mixed green salad and crusty rolls.

Twice-Cooked Pork, page 94, or Fried Chicken, page 67

12 VERY LARGE CLAMS IN THE SHELL (ABOUT 2 QUARTS *TOTAL*), WELL SCRUBBED

1/2 CUP SAKE

1/2 POUND POTATOES, PEELED, CUT INTO 1/2-INCH CUBES

2 TABLESPOONS CLOUD EARS

2 TABLESPOONS VEGETABLE OIL

1 TEASPOON MINCED FRESH GINGERROOT

1 GARLIC CLOVE, MINCED

1/2 CUP CHOPPED GREEN ONIONS

1/2 POUND DAIKON, PEELED, CUT INTO 1/4-INCH CUBES

1 POUND TOMATOES, CORED, ROUGHLY CHOPPED

2 CUPS TOMATO JUICE

1/2 TEASPOON FRESHLY GROUND BLACK PEPPER

Place the clams in a large pot with 1/4 cup sake. Cover and cook over medium-high heat until all the clams are open, 15 to 20 minutes (start checking the clams after 15 minutes and remove those that are open to prevent them from overcooking). Let the clams cool. Remove the clams from their shells and chop them; you should have about 1-1/2 cups. Discard the shells, but reserve the cooking liquid. Measure the liquid; you should have about 1-1/2 cups. Add enough water to make 2 cups. Set aside.

Place the potatoes in a 3-quart pot and add cold water to cover. Bring to a boil and cook for 3 minutes. Drain and set aside. Place the cloud ears in a bowl and add boiling water to cover very generously. Let soak for 20 minutes. Drain, squeeze dry, and chop. Set aside.

Heat the oil in a 4-quart pot over high heat. Add the gingerroot and garlic and cook for 30 seconds. Add the green onions and cook for 30 seconds longer. Add the daikon and potatoes and cook briefly, stirring to coat. Add the tomatoes and cook for 30 seconds longer. Add the diluted clam cooking liquid, tomato juice, and the remaining 1/4 cup sake. Bring to a boil; then reduce the heat and simmer for 5 minutes. Add the clams, cloud ears, and pepper. Cook until heated through, about 1 minute longer.

Makes about 8 cups (8 first-course or 4 main-dish servings).

Agnolotti Soup

Won tons are a staple of Chinese restaurants, but they look an awful lot like Italian *tortellini* and Jewish *kreplach*. Similar in flavor, but very different in appearance, are small half-moon-shaped *agnolotti*. I like to cook them with broth and garnish them with Chinese mushrooms, ham, and spinach, in a dish much like traditional won ton soup. It makes a warming, light beginning to a meal. Follow with Charred Tile Fish with Pepper Sauce, page 113, or Aromatic Lamb with Melon, page 81. (If you can't find agnolotti, use tortellini.)

1/2 OUNCE (ABOUT 8) DRIED CHINESE MUSHROOMS

1 OUNCE BAKED HAM

1 OUNCE FRESH SPINACH LEAVES, WELL WASHED

6 CUPS CHICKEN STOCK

1/4 POUND CHEESE AGNOLOTTI

KOSHER SALT AND FRESHLY GROUND BLACK PEPPER TO TASTE

FRESHLY GRATED PARMESAN CHEESE TO TASTE

■ Place the mushrooms in a bowl and add boiling water to cover. Let soak for 20 minutes. Drain the mushrooms and squeeze them dry. Cut off and discard the stems; cut the caps into thin strips. Set aside.

Cut the ham into 1/4- by 1/4-inch sticks no more than 2 inches long. Pile the spinach leaves on top of each other, roll them up, and cut them into thin strips. Set the ham and spinach aside with the mushrooms.

Bring the stock to a boil in a large saucepan. Add the agnolotti and cook until tender but not soft, about 6 minutes. Add the mushrooms, ham, and spinach. Cook for 1 minute longer. Taste the stock and season the soup with salt and pepper. Ladle into bowls; sprinkle each serving with cheese.

Makes 8 servings.

Chicken is so generally available and affordable that we sometimes take it for granted. It is incredibly versatile and pairs well with all kinds of sauces. The recipes in this chapter range from whole roasted birds to vegetable-stuffed breasts. Aside from a few salads and one appetizer (Baked Chicken Wings), these are delicious main courses, offering excellent and inexpensive ways to bring new seasonings into your family's diet.

Along with the chicken, I have included a few recipes for game hens, duck, and turkey. These are a bit more unusual than the rest, but certain to delight.

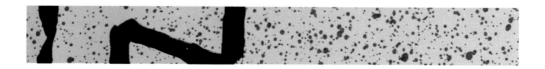

Lemon Chicken, page 61, is marinated in sake, soy sauce and sesame oil before cooking.

POULTRY

Stir-Fried Chicken Enchiladas

A European sauce and a Chinese filling give a new look to a familiar Mexican stand-by. In keeping with the Tex-Mex feeling, accompany the enchiladas with Black Beans, page 173, or Refried Adzuki Beans, page 172. Beyond that, you need add only a mixed green salad and frosty beer. For a simpler meal, serve the stir-fried chicken filling on its own with rice or tortillas on the side.

POULTRY

1 LARGE EGG

1/4 CUP PLUS 1 TABLESPOON CHINESE RICE WINE

1/4 CUP PLUS 2 TEASPOONS SOY SAUCE

1/4 CUP OLIVE OIL

2 TABLESPOONS CORNSTARCH

1 POUND BONELESS, SKINLESS CHICKEN, CUT INTO THIN STRIPS

1/2 TEASPOON SZECHUAN CHILI SAUCE

1/4 CUP WATER

PEEL OF 1 ORANGE, CUT INTO JULIENNE STRIPS

1 TABLESPOON MINCED FRESH GINGERROOT

2 GARLIC CLOVES, MINCED

1 RED BELL PEPPER, CORED, SEEDED, CUT INTO THIN STRIPS

1 TEASPOON CORNSTARCH DISSOLVED IN 2 TEASPOONS WATER

1 RECIPE RED PEPPER PUREE, PAGE 190

12 CORN TORTILLAS

In a bowl, lightly beat the egg. Mix in 1 tablespoon wine, 2 teaspoons soy sauce, 1 tablespoon oil, and 2 tablespoons cornstarch. Add the chicken and stir to coat thoroughly.

In a small bowl, mix the remaining 1/4 cup wine and the remaining 1/4 cup soy sauce with the chili sauce and water. Set aside.

Heat 2 tablespoons oil in a wok over high heat. Add the chicken mixture and cook, stirring often, until the chicken is cooked through, about 2 minutes. Remove the chicken from the wok and set aside. Heat the remaining 1 tablespoon oil in the wok and add the orange peel. Cook for about 30 seconds, then add the gingerroot and garlic. Cook for 30 seconds longer. Add the bell pepper and sauté for 1 minute. Add the wine-soy sauce mixture to the wok and bring to a boil. Return the chicken to the wok; stir. Stir the dissolved cornstarch; pour into the wok and cook, stirring, for 30 seconds longer. Remove the chicken mixture to a bowl.

Preheat the oven to 350F (175C). Heat the Red Pepper Puree in a skillet. Hold 1 tortilla with tongs and lay it lightly on top of the puree, pushing it lightly into the puree to soften. Then place the softened tortilla on your work surface, puree-coated side up. Place some of the chicken mixture on top of the tortilla and fold the sides over to cover. Place the filled tortilla, seam side down, in a 9- by 12-inch casserole. Repeat to fill the remaining tortillas. They should fit in a single layer in the casserole. Pour the remaining Red Pepper Puree on top and bake, uncovered, in the preheated oven until bubbly, about 20 minutes. Serve hot.

Makes 4 to 6 servings.

Lemon Chicken

For many years, Pearl's was one of New York's finest Chinese restaurants. Among the best dishes served there was lemon chicken, made with chicken breasts coated in water chestnut powder and topped with a sweet and sour lemon sauce. I have adapted the recipe, making it very lemony and leaving out the sugar. I've also changed the cooking technique: rather than deep-fry the chicken as the Chinese do, I brown it in olive oil.

With the chicken, you'll need a grain to soak up the sauce. I usually choose whole-grain kasha or brown rice. Before dinner, serve Fried Won Tons with Salsa, page 26, or Smoked Trout Mousse, page 40.

1/2 CUP PLUS 1 TABLESPOON SAKE

1 TABLESPOON SOY SAUCE

1/4 TEASPOON SESAME OIL

4 (5-OUNCE) BONELESS, SKINLESS CHICKEN BREAST HALVES

1 LARGE EGG WHITE

1/2 CUP WATER CHESTNUT POWDER

1 TABLESPOON CORNSTARCH

1/4 CUP LEMON JUICE

6 TABLESPOONS OLIVE OIL

1/2 CUP DIAGONALLY SLICED GREEN ONIONS, 1/8 INCH THICK

2 CUPS JULIENNED CARROTS

1 RED BELL PEPPER, CORED, SEEDED, CUT INTO JULIENNE STRIPS

1 GREEN BELL PEPPER, CORED, SEEDED, CUT INTO JULIENNE STRIPS

PEEL OF 1 LEMON, CUT INTO JULIENNE STRIPS

▬ Place 1 tablespoon sake, the soy sauce, and sesame oil in a bowl. Add the chicken and turn to coat. Let marinate for at least 1 hour.

Place the egg white in a shallow bowl and beat until frothy. Spread the water chestnut powder on a large plate. Lift the chicken pieces, 1 at a time, from the marinade. Shake off any excess liquid. Coat in the egg white, then in the water chestnut powder. Place on a clean plate.

In a small bowl, dissolve the cornstarch in 1 tablespoon lemon juice. Stir in the remaining 3 tablespoons lemon juice and the remaining 1/2 cup sake. Set aside.

Preheat the oven to 325F (165C). Heat the olive oil in a 10-inch skillet over high heat. Add the chicken in a single layer and cook until browned on the bottom, about 7 minutes. Then turn the pieces over; cook until well browned on the other side and almost cooked through, 6 to 7 minutes longer. Remove the chicken to a pan lined with paper towels and keep warm in the preheated oven.

Add the green onions to the same skillet. Cook for 15 seconds, then add the carrots, red and green bell peppers, and lemon peel. Cook for 2 minutes. Stir the lemon juice-sake mixture and pour it into the skillet. Bring to a boil; boil briefly to thicken. Spoon the vegetables and sauce onto a platter. Cover and keep warm.

Remove the chicken from the oven and cut it crosswise into 1/2-inch slices. Arrange the chicken over the vegetables.

Makes 4 servings.

Chicken Breast with Nori

Nori, the shiny dried sea vegetation familiar to most people as a wrapping for sushi rice, adds flavor and texture to an otherwise basic bread-crumb coating. I like this simple dish with a couple of side dishes, such as Braised Lentils, page 171, and Bean Sprout Salad, page 136.

3 TABLESPOONS DIJON MUSTARD

2 LARGE EGG YOLKS

1 TEASPOON CHOPPED FRESH TARRAGON

1 CUP FINE DRY BREAD CRUMBS

2 SHEETS NORI, TOASTED, CRUMBLED

4 (5-OUNCE) BONELESS, SKINLESS CHICKEN BREAST HALVES

ALL-PURPOSE FLOUR SEASONED WITH KOSHER SALT AND FRESHLY GROUND BLACK PEPPER

2 TABLESPOONS UNSALTED BUTTER

2 TABLESPOONS OLIVE OIL

In a small bowl, mix the mustard with the egg yolks and tarragon. In a separate bowl, mix the bread crumbs with the nori.

Dust each chicken breast half with some of the seasoned flour; shake off the excess. Coat each piece thoroughly with the mustard mixture; then coat with the bread-crumb mixture. Set aside. (You can prepare the chicken to this point in the morning and refrigerate it.)

To cook, heat the butter and oil in a 10-inch skillet over medium-high heat. Add the chicken in a single layer and cook until nicely browned on the bottom, about 7 minutes. Then turn the pieces over; cook until browned on the other side and cooked through, 7 to 8 minutes longer.

To serve, slice each chicken breast piece on the diagonal and fan the slices out on a dinner plate.

Makes 4 servings.

Soy-Roasted Chicken

Don't let all the peppercorns put you off—the flavor is surprisingly mild. Serve this chicken with Three-Bean Salad, page 174, and Baby Corn Salad, page 134.

1 TABLESPOON (ABOUT 3) CRUMBLED STAR ANISE

1 TABLESPOON MINCED FRESH GINGERROOT

1 TABLESPOON SZECHUAN PEPPERCORNS, TOASTED IN A DRY SKILLET, CRUSHED WITH YOUR FINGERS

1 (4-POUND) CHICKEN

1 TABLESPOON SOY SAUCE

1/4 CUP SAKE

1 TEASPOON SESAME OIL

▬ Mix together the star anise, gingerroot, and peppercorns. Sprinkle 1 tablespoon of the mixture inside the cavity of the chicken. Combine the remaining spice mixture with the soy sauce, sake, and sesame oil. Place the chicken in a bowl and pour the soy sauce mixture on top. Turn the chicken over and spoon the marinade all over the bird to coat it well. Let marinate for 2 hours, turning occasionally.

Preheat the oven to 400F (205C).

Remove the chicken from the marinade and place it, breast down, in a roasting pan (not on a rack). Roast in the preheated oven for 30 minutes. Then turn the bird breast up and roast for 1 hour longer, basting with the pan juices every 15 minutes. When the chicken is done, the juices should run clear when the thigh is pierced.

Remove the chicken to a carving board and let rest for about 5 minutes. Cut into serving-size pieces and serve hot or cold.

Makes 4 servings.

Thai Pie

I've always loved pot pies, especially relishing the crust—once crisp, now soggy with liquid absorbed from the filling. Chicken pot pies are usually filled with vegetables and meat in a velouté sauce. For this one, though, I have used a Thai curry sauce, based on coconut milk and flavored with hot chilies, lemon grass, galangal, shrimp paste, and fish sauce. In Thailand, the sauce would be served with chicken alone, but I added chunks of carrot, daikon, and potatoes and a handful of peas. All these mild ingredients are perfect foils for the spicy sauce.

You can make both the filling and the crust ahead and refrigerate them. Wait to assemble the pie until just before baking, or the crust will be overly soggy.

1 POUND BONELESS, SKINLESS CHICKEN, CUT INTO 1/2-INCH CUBES

1/4 POUND DAIKON, PEELED, CUT INTO 1/2-INCH CUBES

1/2 POUND POTATOES, PEELED, CUT INTO 1/2-INCH CUBES

1/2 CUP SLICED CARROT

2 CUPS COCONUT MILK

1 TABLESPOON SUGAR

2 TABLESPOONS FISH SAUCE

2 DRIED RED CHILIES

1 TEASPOON WHOLE BLACK PEPPERCORNS

1 TEASPOON DRIED SLICED LEMON GRASS

1/2 TEASPOON POWDERED GALANGAL (LAOS)

1 TEASPOON CORIANDER SEEDS

2 SHALLOTS

2 GARLIC CLOVES

1 TEASPOON SHRIMP PASTE

1 CUP FRESH PEAS; OR 1 CUP FROZEN PEAS, THAWED

2 TABLESPOONS CHOPPED FRESH CILANTRO LEAVES

PIE PASTRY, SEE PAGE 65

■■ Bring a 2-quart pot of water to a boil. Add the chicken and cook just until done through, about 3 minutes. Remove with a slotted spoon; place in a bowl. Add the daikon to the same boiling water and cook until barely tender, about 5 minutes. Lift out with a slotted spoon; add to the chicken. In the same way, cook the potatoes for about 3 minutes and the carrot for about 2 minutes. Set the bowl of chicken and vegetables aside.

Place the coconut milk, sugar, and fish sauce in a separate bowl.

Place the chilies, peppercorns, lemon grass, galangal, and coriander seeds in a spice grinder and grind to a powder. Stir the spice mixture into the coconut milk mixture.

Grind the shallots, garlic, and shrimp paste together in a spice grinder or chop very finely with a knife. Add to the coconut milk mixture. Stir to blend, then pour over the chicken and vegetables. Stir in the peas and cilantro. Cover and refrigerate until ready to assemble the pie. Prepare the Pie Pastry and refrigerate as directed.

To assemble the pie, preheat the oven to 450F (230C).

Divide the pastry into 2 pieces, one about twice as big as the other. On a floured board or between sheets of wax paper, roll the larger piece into a 12-inch circle. Fit the circle into a 2-quart casserole about 8 inches wide; where the pastry folds over on itself, press it to make neat pleats. Let the pastry extend beyond the edges of the casserole. Set aside. Roll the remaining piece of pastry into a 9-inch circle about 1/8 inch thick.

Spoon the chicken filling into the pastry-lined casserole. Place the circle of pastry on top. Fold the overhanging edges of the bottom crust up over the top piece of pastry; crimp to make a tight seal. With a small, sharp knife, make several slits in the top crust in an attractive pattern.

Bake in the preheated oven for 25 minutes. Reduce the oven temperature to 375F (190C) and bake until the crust is nicely browned, 20 to 25 minutes longer. Serve hot.

Makes 4 servings.

PIE PASTRY:

3 CUPS ALL-PURPOSE FLOUR

1 TEASPOON KOSHER SALT

3/4 CUP (12 TABLESPOONS) UNSALTED BUTTER, CUT INTO 1/4-INCH SLICES

1/4 TO 1/2 CUP ICE WATER

■ Place the flour and salt in a bowl. Add the butter and mix with your fingers until the butter is broken into pieces about the size of small peas. The mixture will be crumbly. Slowly add the ice water, using just enough to make the dough cling together. Dump the dough onto a sheet of wax paper and press off pieces with the palm of your hand to finish blending the ingredients. Shape into a ball, flatten into a disk, cover, and refrigerate for at least 1 hour.

Crunchy Chicken Salad

Oriental vegetables and crunchy peanuts make this chicken salad a bit different from the usual. The sambal in the dressing adds a subtle, intriguing flavor. The salad makes a wonderful lunch or summer dinner. Serve it over mixed greens or in warmed pita bread.

4 CUPS COOKED CHICKEN, IN 1/2-INCH CUBES

1/2 POUND SNOW PEAS, STRINGS REMOVED, HALVED DIAGONALLY, BLANCHED FOR 1 MINUTE

1 CUP SLICED WATER CHESTNUTS

1/2 CUP MAYONNAISE

2 TABLESPOONS LEMON JUICE

2 TEASPOONS SAMBAL OELEK

2/3 CUP ROUGHLY CHOPPED ROASTED UNSALTED PEANUTS

■ Place the chicken, snow peas, and water chestnuts in a bowl. In a separate bowl, mix together the mayonnaise, lemon juice, and sambal. Add the dressing to the chicken and stir to coat. Sprinkle the peanuts on top.

Makes 4 to 6 servings.

Chicken and Sun-Dried Tomato Salad with Ginger Vinaigrette

This is a very pretty salad. The pale chicken and white mozzarella stand out against the dark green background; the red tomato slivers and onion rings add to the visual appeal and make for a more interesting combination of tastes and textures. Serve for lunch or supper with pumpernickel rolls.

In keeping with the Eastern spirit, the chicken is seasoned and then steamed to give it a distinctive flavor even before the tangy vinaigrette is drizzled on top. If you can get fresh mozzarella, often available in Italian markets, use it here. The flavor is far superior to that of the plastic-wrapped supermarket varieties.

4 (5-OUNCE) BONELESS, SKINLESS CHICKEN BREAST HALVES

2 TEASPOONS SAKE

2 TEASPOONS SOY SAUCE

FRESHLY GROUND BLACK PEPPER TO TASTE

1/2 POUND FRESH SPINACH, STEMS REMOVED, WASHED WELL

1/4 POUND MOZZARELLA CHEESE, CUT INTO 1/4-INCH-THICK STRIPS

1/2 MEDIUM (5-OUNCE) RED ONION, CUT INTO THIN ROUNDS

1/2 CUP SUN-DRIED TOMATO PIECES PACKED IN OIL, DRAINED, CUT INTO JULIENNE STRIPS

1 RECIPE GINGER VINAIGRETTE, PAGE 183

Bring water to a boil in the bottom of a steamer or wok. Reduce the heat so the water simmers. In a bowl, toss the chicken with the sake, soy sauce, and pepper. Place the chicken on a steamer rack; set the rack in place over the simmering water. Cover and steam until the chicken is just cooked through, about 15 minutes. Let cool slightly, then cut into strips about 1/4 inch wide.

Arrange the salad on a large platter or on 4 dinner plates. Make a layer of the spinach on the platter or plate. Scatter the chicken and cheese neatly on top. Separate the onion slices into rings and scatter them on top with the tomatoes. Just before serving, drizzle the Ginger Vinaigrette over everything.

Makes 4 servings.

Fried Chicken

In the Orient, foods are usually sautéed or deep-fried, but this recipe follows a technique used in the American South: the chicken is cooked in about 1/4 inch of fat, enough to get it very crisp, but not enough to cover it. To suit Western tastes, the portions are good-sized; in an Eastern kitchen, the chicken would be cut into small pieces, allowing one bird to feed many. The seasonings here are definitely Asian, though. Serve with baked or fried yams, Daikon Chips, page 137, and some crunchy Coleslaw, page 139, or Kim Chee, page 134.

1 TEASPOON GRATED FRESH GINGERROOT

2 TABLESPOONS SOY SAUCE

2 TABLESPOONS SAKE

2 TABLESPOONS RICE WINE VINEGAR

1 (4-POUND) CHICKEN, CUT INTO 8 PIECES

1 CUP ALL-PURPOSE FLOUR

1 TEASPOON WASABI POWDER

1/2 TEASPOON KOSHER SALT

1/4 TEASPOON GROUND RED (CAYENNE) PEPPER

1 CUP VEGETABLE OIL

In a bowl, mix together the gingerroot, soy sauce, sake, and vinegar. Add the chicken pieces and turn to coat. Let marinate for at least 30 minutes.

Put the flour, wasabi powder, salt, and red pepper in a paper bag. Close the top of the bag and shake briefly to mix.

Pour the oil into a deep 12-inch skillet or chicken fryer. The oil should be about 1/4 inch deep. Heat until a haze forms above the oil.

Beginning with the dark meat, lift 1 chicken piece at a time from the marinade and drop it into the paper bag. Close the top and shake well to coat the chicken evenly with the flour mixture. Remove the chicken with tongs and shake off any excess flour mixture. Place the chicken, skin side down, in the hot oil. Continue in this way until all the chicken is in the skillet. It should fit in a tight but even layer. Cover the skillet and cook until the chicken is well browned on the bottom, about 15 minutes. Turn the chicken with tongs, cover again, and cook until browned on the other side, about 15 minutes longer.

Remove the chicken to a plate lined with paper towels and drain briefly before serving.

Makes 3 or 4 servings.

Steamed Chicken Rolls

Steaming is a wonderful fat-free way to cook. Unfortunately, when foods are steamed, some of their flavor usually leaches out into the liquid. Seppi Renggli, chef of The Four Seasons restaurant in New York, taught me to wrap chicken in plastic to seal in the flavor and moisture.

The chicken can be stuffed and wrapped early in the day, ready to go into the steamer just before cooking. Slicing the chicken on the diagonal makes for a pretty presentation. Fan the slices out to follow the curve of the plate, overlapping them slightly. Place a mound of brown rice—plain or cooked with coconut milk—in the center of the plate and spoon some sautéed spinach on the side. Follow with a mixed green salad dressed with a light vinaigrette.

POULTRY

4 (6-OUNCE) BONELESS, SKINLESS CHICKEN BREAST HALVES

1-1/2 TEASPOONS MINCED GARLIC

1-1/2 TEASPOONS MINCED FRESH GINGERROOT

2 TABLESPOONS SOY SAUCE

2 TABLESPOONS CHINESE RICE WINE

4 DRIED CHINESE MUSHROOMS (ABOUT 1/4 OUNCE *TOTAL*)

4 LARGE SAVOY CABBAGE LEAVES

1/4 POUND BAKED HAM, CUT INTO JULIENNE STRIPS

1 SMALL CARROT, CUT INTO JULIENNE STRIPS, BLANCHED FOR 2 MINUTES

1 SMALL ZUCCHINI, CUT INTO JULIENNE STRIPS

2 GREEN ONIONS, QUARTERED LENGTHWISE, CUT INTO 4-INCH PIECES

1/3 CUP JULIENNED DAIKON

FRESHLY GROUND BLACK PEPPER TO TASTE

Pound each chicken breast half until it is 1/4 inch thick. Place the pounded chicken pieces in a bowl with the garlic, gingerroot, soy sauce, and wine. Let marinate for at least 1 hour.

Place the mushrooms in a small bowl and add boiling water to cover. Let soak for 20 minutes. Drain the mushrooms and squeeze them dry. Cut off and discard the stems; cut the caps into thin strips. Set aside.

With a large paring knife, trim away the thick part of the rib on each cabbage leaf so the rib is no thicker than the rest of the leaf. Tear or cut a 16-inch-long piece of good-quality plastic wrap and place it on your work surface. Place 1 cabbage leaf, pared rib down, in the center of the plastic. Lift 1 chicken breast half from the marinade, leaving in place the bits of garlic and gingerroot that cling to it. Arrange the chicken, skinned side down, on top of the cabbage. Place 1/4 each of the ham, mushroom strips, carrot, zucchini, green onions, and daikon over the chicken so all the strips go the same way. Grind pepper on top.

Using the cabbage and plastic to help you, roll the chicken around the vegetables and the cabbage around the chicken to make a fairly tight roll. Wrap the plastic around the roll, tucking in the ends to make a tight seal. Place the wrapped chicken on a plate. Repeat with the remaining cabbage leaves, chicken, ham, and vegetables, making 3 more rolls.

When ready to serve, bring water to a boil in the bottom of a steamer. Reduce the heat so the water simmers. Place the chicken rolls on a steamer rack in a single layer. Set the rack in place over the simmering water, cover, and steam for 20 minutes.

Remove the chicken rolls to a work surface. Cut away the plastic wrap and slice each roll on the diagonal into about 8 pieces. Serve hot.

Makes 4 servings.

Coconut Milk Chicken

Coconut milk and lemon grass make a rich, fragrant sauce for this cut-up chicken. Serve it with rice or orzo to soak up the sauce. Some sautéed watercress or steamed asparagus adds color to the meal.

P
O
U
L
T
R
Y

2 TABLESPOONS VEGETABLE OIL

1 (4-POUND) CHICKEN, CUT INTO 8 PIECES

1 LARGE (1/2-POUND) ONION, THINLY SLICED

1/2 POUND CARROTS, CUT INTO THIN ROUNDS

1-1/2 CUPS COCONUT MILK

1/2 CUP WATER

2 TABLESPOONS FISH SAUCE

1 TEASPOON POWDERED LEMON GRASS (*SEREH*)

1/2 POUND FRESH MUSHROOMS, QUARTERED

▬ Heat the oil in a large skillet or chicken fryer over high heat. Add the chicken pieces, skin side down, and cook until lightly browned, about 10 minutes. Turn and cook until browned on the other side, about 10 minutes longer. Remove the chicken to a plate. Pour off and discard all but 1 tablespoon of the fat from the skillet. Then add the onion and cook until softened but not browned, about 2 minutes. Add the carrots and sauté for 2 minutes longer.

Pour in the coconut milk, water, fish sauce, and lemon grass. Return the chicken to the skillet in a single layer. Bring the liquid to a boil, reduce the heat, cover, and simmer for 15 minutes. Add the mushrooms. Continue to cook until the juices run clear when the chicken is pierced, about 15 minutes longer.

Remove the chicken to the center of a platter. With a slotted spoon, remove the vegetables and arrange them around the chicken. Keep warm. Bring the sauce to a boil, then cook and stir it briefly to blend. Serve the sauce on the side.

Makes 4 servings.

Baked Chicken Wings

For a snack or a nibble with drinks, chicken wings are perfect. They also make an ideal dinner for children, although adults usually have a hard time eating enough to satisfy. Rather than cook the wings whole, it is best to split them into three pieces—the bony wingtip (good to save for stocks), the single-bone piece that looks like a miniature leg, and the double-bone piece. Some poulterers package the wings already cut up, with the wingtips eliminated. That makes preparation very easy, especially if you want to make this recipe in quantity.

1 TABLESPOON MINCED FRESH
   GINGERROOT

1 TABLESPOON MINCED GARLIC

1 TABLESPOON CHOPPED FRESH
   CILANTRO LEAVES

1 JALAPEÑO CHILI, CORED, SEEDED,
   DERIBBED, MINCED

1 SHALLOT, MINCED

1/4 CUP SOY SAUCE

1/4 CUP RICE WINE VINEGAR

2 TABLESPOONS MIRIN

2 POUNDS (ABOUT 10) CHICKEN
   WINGS, CUT INTO PIECES AS
   DESCRIBED IN THE RECIPE
   INTRODUCTION ABOVE, WINGTIPS
   DISCARDED OR RESERVED FOR
   ANOTHER USE

Place the gingerroot, garlic, cilantro, chili, shallot, soy sauce, vinegar, and mirin in a glass dish. Add the chicken wings and let marinate for at least 3 hours, turning occasionally.

Preheat the oven to 400F (205C).

Remove the wings from the marinade and arrange in a single layer in a baking dish. Bake in the preheated oven until nicely browned and cooked through, about 10 minutes on each side.

Makes about 20 pieces.

NOTE: These are also excellent when grilled. Depending on the heat, cooking takes about 15 minutes.

Sautéed Chicken Livers

Because liver is such a rich meat, it pairs well with a tangy vinegar sauce. I've heightened the piquancy of the sauce by adding chopped pickled ginger—just enough to give the dish a mild bite. It is particularly good with brown or white rice and Broccoli and Mushrooms in Oyster Sauce, page 119.

8 DRIED CHINESE MUSHROOMS
   (ABOUT 1/2 OUNCE *TOTAL*)

2 TABLESPOONS OLIVE OIL

1 LARGE GREEN ONION, SLICED

1 POUND CHICKEN LIVERS, FAT
   REMOVED, QUARTERED

1/4 CUP CHOPPED PINK PICKLED
   GINGER

2 TABLESPOONS SOY SAUCE

1 TABLESPOON RICE WINE VINEGAR

1 TABLESPOON LIME JUICE

FRESHLY GROUND BLACK PEPPER
   TO TASTE

Place the mushrooms in a bowl and add boiling water to cover. Let soak for 20 minutes. Drain the mushrooms and squeeze them dry. Cut off and discard the stems; cut the caps into thin slices.

Heat the oil in an 8-inch skillet over medium-high heat. Add the green onion and cook for 1 minute. Add the livers and cook until browned on the outside but still pink in the center, about 3 minutes; turn the livers often to ensure even cooking. Add the mushrooms and ginger, then the soy sauce, vinegar, and lime juice. Stir to mix; cook for 2 minutes longer. Season with pepper.

Makes 3 or 4 servings.

Roast Chicken with Cilantro and Lime

Chicken pairs beautifully with all kinds of flavors. In this dish, the roasted bird is seasoned with ginger, garlic, and lots of lime and cilantro. Serve it with Spaghetti Squash with Oriental Vinaigrette, page 122, and Scallion Bread, page 176. Fennel Fish Soup, page 54, gets the meal off to an excellent start.

2 LIMES

1 TABLESPOON CHOPPED GARLIC

1 TABLESPOON CHOPPED FRESH GINGERROOT

2 TABLESPOONS CHOPPED FRESH CILANTRO LEAVES

1/4 TEASPOON CRUSHED RED PEPPER FLAKES

1 (4-POUND) CHICKEN

2 TEASPOONS KOSHER SALT

1/4 TEASPOON GROUND RED (CAYENNE) PEPPER

Preheat the oven to 400F (205C).

With a vegetable peeler, remove the peel from 1 of the limes. Mince the lime peel with the garlic, gingerroot, cilantro, and red pepper flakes.

With your fingers, carefully loosen the skin on the chicken over the breast and legs. Spread the seasoning mixture under the skin as evenly as you can.

Mix together the salt and ground red pepper. Sprinkle some of the mixture in the cavity of the chicken and rub the rest on the skin. Prick both the limes—both peeled and unpeeled—all over with a wooden pick or fork. Place the limes in the chicken cavity. Place the bird, breast down, in a roasting pan (not on a rack). Roast in the preheated oven for 30 minutes. Then turn the bird breast up and roast for 1 hour longer, basting with the pan juices every 15 minutes. When the chicken is done, the juices should run clear when the thigh is pierced.

Remove the chicken to a carving board and let rest for about 5 minutes. Remove and discard the limes; cut the chicken into serving-size pieces.

Makes 4 servings.

Cornish Game Hens with Tamarind Marinade

Tamarind is a nice change from vinegar in marinades. For company, I like to serve Cornish hens instead of chicken, since the smaller birds seem more festive. However, this marinade is fine on chicken, too. Vegetable Pancakes, page 175, are a good accompaniment for the hens.

1/2 CUP TAMARIND PULP

1 CUP HOT WATER

2 (1-1/2-POUND) CORNISH GAME HENS

2 TEASPOONS CHOPPED GARLIC

1 TABLESPOON SOY SAUCE

1 TABLESPOON SAKE

▬ Place the tamarind pulp in a bowl and add the hot water. Let soak for 20 minutes, stirring occasionally to help the pulp dissolve. Meanwhile, cut away the backbones from the hens. Press down firmly on the breastbones, breaking them so the birds will lie flat. Cut off the wing tips; save the wing tips and backbones for stock. Place the hens in a bowl or baking dish.

Press the tamarind mixture through a strainer to eliminate the seeds and undissolved pulp. Add all the strained liquid (1 scant cup) to the hens along with the garlic, soy sauce, and sake. Cover and let marinate in the refrigerator for several hours or overnight, turning occasionally.

When you are ready to cook, bring the hens to room temperature. Preheat a broiler or grill until hot. Remove the hens from the marinade; wipe off any excess marinade. Place the hens on a rack in a broiler pan or directly on the grill. Broil or grill until the juices run clear when the hens are pierced, about 15 minutes on each side. To serve, cut each cooked hen in half through the breastbone.

Makes 4 servings.

Duck Breasts with Black Bean Sauce

Duck breast makes an elegant main course, especially when the sliced meat is fanned out on a plate and accompanied by a colorful side dish like Curried Vegetables, page 126. The technique and presentation in this recipe are typically French; the sauce is Asian.

Duck is so rich that half a breast is an ample portion. Use the rest of the bird in Spicy Duck and Baby Corn with Cavatelli, page 163, or another pasta dish.

BONELESS BREAST HALVES WITH SKIN FROM 2 (5-POUND) DUCKS

1 TABLESPOON VEGETABLE OIL

1/2 CUP MINCED SHALLOTS

1 TABLESPOON MINCED FRESH GINGERROOT

1/4 CUP SAKE

1/2 CUP WHIPPING CREAM

1/4 CUP FERMENTED BLACK BEANS, RINSED, CHOPPED

■ Score the skin and fat of each duck breast half about 8 times. Heat the oil in a 10-inch skillet over medium-high heat. Add the shallots and gingerroot and cook for 1 minute. Add the duck pieces, skin side down, and cook for 5 minutes. Turn the pieces over and cook until done medium-rare, about 5 minutes longer. Remove the duck to a plate and keep warm.

Pour off and discard the fat from the skillet. Deglaze the still-hot skillet with the sake, scraping the bottom of the skillet with a wooden spoon to loosen any browned bits of meat and juices. Strain the liquid into a clean pot, pressing on the solids. Add the cream and bring to a boil. Add the black beans; also add any liquid that the duck has released. Boil for a few seconds longer.

Cut each piece of duck on the diagonal into 1/2-inch-thick slices. Arrange each portion of slices, slightly overlapping, in a curve around the edge of a dinner plate (the slices will go about halfway around the plate). Spoon some of the sauce over the duck. Serve a vegetable in the remaining space on the same plates.

Makes 4 servings.

Kung Pao Turkey with Pumpkin Seeds

Kung Pao chicken is a classic dish, said to have been invented in honor of a Hunanese general. The original recipe is made with deep-fried cubes of chicken tossed with a spicy sauce including fried peanuts and blackened chilies. I've substituted turkey and pumpkin seeds for the chicken and peanuts, giving the dish a Thanksgiving feeling, and omitted the deep-frying. The flavor is spicy, although not numbing. I always serve rice (usually brown) with this dish. For a more substantial meal, serve the turkey with a simple steamed vegetable like broccoli or green beans, and follow it with Carrot and Jicama Salad, page 138.

1 POUND BONELESS, SKINLESS TURKEY BREAST, CUT INTO 1/2-INCH CUBES

2 TEASPOONS GINGER WINE

2 TEASPOONS SOY SAUCE

1 TABLESPOON CORNSTARCH

1 TABLESPOON SZECHUAN CHILI SAUCE

1/4 CUP CHICKEN STOCK

1 TABLESPOON CHINESE RICE WINE

1 TEASPOON SUGAR

3 TABLESPOONS PEANUT OIL

1/2 CUP RAW SHELLED PUMPKIN SEEDS

6 DRIED RED CHILIES

1 TEASPOON MINCED FRESH GINGERROOT

1 TEASPOON MINCED GARLIC

1 CUP 2-INCH-LONG GREEN ONION PIECES

■ Place the turkey in a bowl. Add the ginger wine, soy sauce, and cornstarch. Mix to coat well and let marinate for 30 minutes.

In a separate bowl, mix together the chili sauce, stock, rice wine, and sugar; set aside.

Heat 2 tablespoons oil in a wok over medium heat. Add the pumpkin seeds and cook until lightly browned, about 2 minutes. The seeds will begin to pop if the oil is too hot, so watch out for flying seeds. Remove the seeds with a slotted spoon and set aside.

Add the remaining 1 tablespoon oil to the wok and increase the heat to high. Add the turkey and cook, stirring, until it is just cooked through, about 2 minutes. Remove with a slotted spoon and set aside with the pumpkin seeds.

Add the chilies to the still-hot oil and cook until they turn black, about 30 seconds. Add the gingerroot, garlic, and green onions; cook, stirring, for 30 seconds. Add the chili sauce mixture and bring to a boil.

Return the turkey and pumpkin seeds to the wok and cook to reheat and flavor, about 1 minute.

Makes 4 servings.

NOTE: Advise your guests not to eat the blackened chilies. They are very hot.

Although beef and other meats are not traditionally important in Asian cuisines, chefs in this century have had no trouble adapting and creating meat dishes quite unlike the typical Western fare of chops, steaks, and hamburgers. Perhaps because they have historically had less meat, Asian cooks have been more sensible in their approach, making a little go a long way. Combining the attitudes of both worlds, I serve less meat than I used to, but I'm not about to give it up entirely. The suggested portions in this chapter are quite large by Eastern standards, though real meat eaters will probably say that I'm being stingy.

More important than quantity, of course, is flavor—and I think you'll find all kinds of good ideas here for marinades with hoisin and miso, soy sauce and sake. In fact, I began experimenting with some of the more unusual ingredients in my cupboards by playing with marinades and simple meat sauces.

Aromatic Lamb with Melon, page 81, combines oriental spices and red wine.

MEAT

Lamb Kabobs with Hoisin

Meats grilled on skewers are popular throughout the world. Both Indonesian *satés* and Japanese *yakitoris* usually feature thin bamboo skewers threaded with bite-size pieces of meat that you eat right off the stick. In Japan, there are yakitori bars where diners can order an assortment of delicious skewers made with chicken, shrimp, or vegetables.

My Western-style kabobs, made with big chunks of lamb and vegetables, provide a more substantial meal. The marinade of hoisin, mirin, and rice wine vinegar comes from the East. You can prepare the skewers early in the day and cook them right before serving. To complete the meal, add plain rice or kasha and a chunky tomato and red onion salad with Soy Vinaigrette, page 183.

3 POUNDS BONELESS LEG OF LAMB, CUT INTO 1-INCH CUBES

1/2 CUP HOISIN SAUCE

1/4 CUP RICE WINE VINEGAR

2 TABLESPOONS MIRIN

2 TABLESPOONS SESAME OIL

1 POUND LARGE FRESH MUSHROOM, STEMS CUT OFF

2 MEDIUM (5-OUNCE) ONIONS, EACH CUT INTO 8 WEDGES, ROOT ENDS INTACT

2 RED BELL PEPPERS, CORED, SEEDED, CUT INTO 1-INCH SQUARES

2 GREEN BELL PEPPERS, CORED, SEEDED, CUT INTO 1-INCH SQUARES

HOT COOKED RICE OR WHOLE-GRAIN KASHA

Place the lamb in a bowl. Mix together the hoisin sauce, vinegar, and mirin; pour the mixture over the lamb, cover, and let marinate for at least 1 hour. Then drain the lamb, reserving the marinade.

Brush the sesame oil over the mushroom caps.

You will need twelve 10-inch metal skewers. On each skewer, thread lamb cubes, onion wedges, red and green bell pepper squares, and mushroom caps in a random pattern. Place the skewers in a dish and drizzle with the reserved marinade. Cover and let stand until ready to cook.

Preheat a grill or broiler until hot. Place the skewers on the grill or on a rack in a broiler pan; grill or broil, turning as needed, until done medium-rare, about 15 minutes.

Serve the skewers intact, or push the meat and vegetables off the skewers onto a pile of rice or kasha. Spoon any extra marinade on top.

Makes 6 to 8 servings.

Lamb Stew

This looks like a traditional Western stew, but the pleasantly hot kick of the chilies and the saltiness of the miso add subtle Eastern touches. The daikon cubes contribute an interesting flavor and texture surprise, since they look like chunks of potato.

There are far more vegetables than meat in this dish. While meat-and-potato lovers won't feel cheated, they will end up eating more vegetables than usual. If udon are unavailable, you can serve the stew over wide egg noodles.

2 TABLESPOONS SAKE

1 TABLESPOON MISO

1-1/2 POUNDS BONELESS LEG OF LAMB, CUT INTO 1-INCH CUBES

1/4 CUP OLIVE OIL

4 GARLIC CLOVES, MINCED

6 DRIED RED CHILIES

3/4 POUND ONIONS, CUT INTO 1/2-INCH WEDGES (ABOUT 2 CUPS)

1 POUND POTATOES, PEELED, CUT INTO 1-INCH CUBES

1/2 POUND DAIKON, PEELED, CUT INTO 1/2-INCH CUBES

1/2 POUND CARROTS, CUT INTO 1/2-INCH ROUNDS

1/2 POUND TURNIPS, PEELED, CUT INTO 1/2-INCH CUBES

1 (28-OUNCE) CAN WHOLE TOMATOES WITH PUREE

1 TABLESPOON SOY SAUCE

1/2 POUND SNOW PEAS, STRINGS REMOVED, HALVED ON THE DIAGONAL

1 POUND UDON

▬ In a bowl, mix together the sake and miso. Add the lamb and stir to coat. Let marinate for at least 1 hour.

Heat the oil in a very deep 10-inch skillet or a 5-quart heatproof casserole over medium-high heat. Remove the lamb from the marinade, reserving any remaining marinade. Add the lamb to the skillet in a single layer, leaving a little room between pieces. Brown each cube on all sides; as each piece is done, remove it to a plate and add another piece. When all the lamb has been browned, add the garlic to the skillet and cook for 30 seconds. Add the chilies and cook for 30 seconds longer. Add the onions and cook just to soften, about 2 minutes. Add the potatoes, daikon, carrots, and turnips. Sauté for 1 minute to mix. Crush the tomatoes with your hand or a spoon, then add them to the skillet along with their puree. Stir in all the browned lamb and any reserved marinade. Bring to a boil; then reduce the heat, cover, and simmer for 30 minutes. Add the soy sauce and simmer until the lamb and vegetables are tender, about 30 minutes longer.

Toward the end of the cooking time, bring a large pot of salted water to a boil. Add the snow peas and cook for 1 minute. Lift out with a strainer or slotted spoon and set aside. Add the udon to the same boiling water, return to a boil, and cook until tender but still chewy, about 8 minutes. Drain well.

Arrange the udon on a platter. Spoon the lamb stew over the udon and arrange the snow peas on top.

Makes 6 to 8 servings.

Marinated Leg of Lamb

Grilled boneless leg of lamb is one of my favorite company dishes. Lamb is popular with most people, and the leg is usually affordable. I marinate it early in the day and don't have to think about it again until I'm ready to cook. While the lamb is grilling, I finish the vegetable—another grilled dish like Grilled Vegetable Skewers on page 123, or something quick like Curried Vegetables, page 126. If I'm feeling energetic, I'll add some Scallion Bread, page 176. On the other hand, if I want a completely do-ahead meal, I'm opt for a room-temperature dish like Pickled Beets and Ginger, page 133. Seafood Salad with Miso Sauce, page 40, starts the meal off nicely, though I might make Shrimp Quenelles with Ginger-Wasabi Sauce, page 42, for special guests.

If you have leftover lamb, cut it into cubes and turn it into hash with cubed daikon and potato and some Chinese cabbage.

2 TABLESPOONS MINCED GARLIC

2 TABLESPOONS FRESH MINCED GINGERROOT

1/4 CUP SOY SAUCE

1/4 CUP WATER

1 TEASPOON SAMBAL OELEK

1/4 CUP CHINESE RICE WINE

1 (5-1/2-POUND) BONELESS LEG OF LAMB, BUTTERFLIED

Place the garlic, gingerroot, soy sauce, water, sambal, and wine in a large bowl or dish. Add the lamb and turn to coat. Cover and let marinate for several hours, turning occasionally.

Preheat a grill or broiler until very hot. Remove the meat from the marinade and place it on the grill or on a rack in a broiler pan. Grill or broil until done to your liking, about 15 minutes on each side for rare. Let rest for 5 minutes, then cut across the grain into thin slices.

Makes 10 servings.

Aromatic Lamb with Melon

Like many French game marinades, this one uses red wine. But the spices—star anise, Szechuan peppercorns, cinnamon, and cloves—are common to Asia. Rather than use an Oriental mushroom, I opted for woodsy-scented Italian porcini, assertive enough to hold their own with the spices. Warmed wedges of melon complement the lamb in color, texture, and flavor. On the side, you might serve rice flavored with a pinch of cardamom.

Use a soft Merlot or Burgundy in the marinade, and serve the rest with the meal. Clam Chowder, page 56, makes an excellent first course; after the lamb, a radicchio and Belgian endive salad with Soy Vinaigrette, page 183, would be good.

1-1/4 POUNDS BONELESS LEG OF LAMB, CUT INTO 1/4-INCH-THICK STRIPS NO MORE THAN 2 INCHES LONG

1 CUP DRY RED WINE

2 (1/2-INCH) PIECES CINNAMON STICK

4 WHOLE CLOVES

1 WHOLE STAR ANISE

1 TABLESPOON SZECHUAN PEPPERCORNS, TOASTED IN A DRY SKILLET

2 TABLESPOONS UNSALTED BUTTER

2 LARGE SLICES FRESH GINGERROOT

2 GARLIC CLOVES, SLICED

2 DRIED RED CHILIES

1 MEDIUM (5-OUNCE) ONION, THINLY SLICED

1/2 OUNCE PORCINI, SOAKED IN BOILING WATER FOR 15 MINUTES, DRAINED, SQUEEZED DRY, ROUGHLY CHOPPED

1/4 POUND FRESH MUSHROOMS, SLICED LENGTHWISE

1/3 CUP SLICED BAMBOO SHOOTS

2 TABLESPOONS SOY SAUCE

1/4 TEASPOON GROUND RED (CAYENNE) PEPPER

8 (1-INCH-WIDE) WEDGES RIPE MELON, SUCH AS CANTALOUPE, HONEYDEW, ETC., RIND TRIMMED OFF

■ Place the lamb in a bowl; set aside. Place the wine, cinnamon stick, cloves, star anise, and peppercorns in a pot. Bring to a boil, then reduce the heat and simmer for 5 minutes. Let cool completely, then pour over the lamb. Let marinate for at least 2 hours. Drain the lamb well; remove and discard all the spices. Set the lamb aside.

Melt 1 tablespoon butter in a large skillet over high heat. Add the gingerroot, garlic, and chilies. Cook for 30 seconds. Add the onion and cook until softened, about 1-1/2 minutes. Add the lamb and cook, stirring often, until it is done medium-rare, about 2 minutes. Add the porcini, fresh mushrooms, bamboo shoots, and soy sauce. Cook about 2 minutes longer to heat through. Spoon onto a platter and keep warm.

In a separate skillet, melt the remaining 1 tablespoon butter with the red pepper. Add the melon wedges and cook until heated through, about 30 seconds on each side. Arrange the melon around the lamb mixture on the platter.

Makes 4 servings.

Tortillas with Oriental Beef and Black Beans

Fajitas—seared slices of beef served in warm tortillas with salsa, guacamole, and sour cream—are fast becoming a restaurant staple. In this version, the beef is stir-fried with fermented black beans, giving it a flavor unknown in the Southwest. Serve it with Black Beans, Curried Guacamole, and your choice of Red Pepper Salsa or Tomato Salsa. I prefer to leave out the sour cream, but it is cooling and bright.

Although this is a filling meal, something light like Straw Mushrooms à la Grecque, page 135, would make a nice beginning. Serve with chilled Mexican beer.

1 POUND FLANK STEAK, THINLY SLICED ON THE DIAGONAL

1 TABLESPOON MINCED FERMENTED BLACK BEANS

1/4 CUP SAKE

1/2 TO 1 TEASPOON SAMBAL OELEK

1 TEASPOON MINCED FRESH GINGERROOT

1 TEASPOON MINCED GARLIC

1 TABLESPOON VEGETABLE OIL

FLOUR TORTILLAS, WARMED

1 RECIPE BLACK BEANS, PAGE 173

1 RECIPE CURRIED GUACAMOLE, PAGE 24

1 RECIPE RED PEPPER SALSA, PAGE 182, OR TOMATO SALSA, PAGE 182

SOUR CREAM, IF DESIRED

■ Place the steak in a bowl with the fermented black beans, sake, sambal, gingerroot, and garlic. Stir to coat. Let marinate for at least 1 hour.

Heat the oil in a wok over high heat. Add the meat mixture and cook until the meat is just done through, about 2 minutes.

To serve, have guests fill tortillas with meat, Black Beans, guacamole, salsa, and sour cream, if desired.

Makes 3 or 4 servings.

Negamaki with Cheese

Negamaki means "green onion" in Japanese, but the word also names a dish made by wrapping thin strips of beef around green onions, then braising the meat rolls in a salty-sweet liquid. In this version, I've added mozzarella cheese to the filling. As it melts during cooking, it adds both texture and flavor.

Negamaki is not very filling. Served on its own, it's a good first course before a hearty pasta dish. If you want to serve it as a main course, start the meal with a thick soup, accompany the negamaki with a vegetable like Carrots with Hijiki, page 120, or Ratatouille with Sambal, page 132, and follow with a salad.

1/2 POUND BEEF SIRLOIN

4 GREEN ONIONS, CUT INTO 2-INCH LENGTHS

2 OUNCES MOZZARELLA CHEESE, CUT INTO 8 (2-INCH-LONG) PIECES

1 TABLESPOON VEGETABLE OIL

2 TABLESPOONS SOY SAUCE

1 TABLESPOON SAKE

1 TABLESPOON WATER

1 TABLESPOON SESAME SEEDS, TOASTED IN A DRY SKILLET, GROUND TO A COARSE POWDER

Cut the beef into 8 equal pieces. Pound each piece between sheets of wax paper until it is about 1/8 inch thick. Each piece should be about 2 inches wide and 7 inches long.

Divide the green onion pieces into 8 bunches. Place 1 bunch on a slice of beef, close to a 2-inch end. Place a piece of cheese atop or next to the green onions; then roll the beef around the green onion and cheese. Tie the roll around the middle with string. Repeat with the remaining beef, green onions, and cheese, making 7 more rolls. Cover and refrigerate the rolls until ready to cook.

Heat the oil in an 8-inch skillet over medium-high heat. Add the beef rolls to the skillet in a single layer, placing them on their sides. Cook, turning often, until browned all over, about 5 minutes. Mix together the soy sauce, sake, and water; pour over the meat. Cook over medium heat, still turning the rolls to flavor them evenly, until the cheese is melted and oozing out, about 5 minutes longer.

Remove the beef rolls to a board and cut away the strings. Slice each roll in half crosswise, then arrange the rolls on a platter. Pour any sauce from the skillet on top; sprinkle with ground sesame seeds.

Makes 16 small rolls (2 to 4 servings).

Warm Beef Salad

This salad is great on hot nights when I want a light meal that includes meat. The greens and sliced tomatoes are Western, but the beef and dressing, flavored with fish sauce, lime juice, and red pepper flakes, are very much in the Thai style. I use only a little pepper; you can taste it, but the dressing won't raise your body temperature as many Thai sauces do. If you prefer more heat, use more pepper flakes.

Serve with French bread and a lightly chilled young red wine or Thai beer.

1 POUND BEEF CHUCK, ALL FAT REMOVED, THINLY SLICED ACROSS THE GRAIN

1/3 CUP PLUS 1 TABLESPOON LIME JUICE

1/4 CUP PLUS 1 TABLESPOON FISH SAUCE

1/4 TEASPOON CRUSHED RED PEPPER FLAKES

8 CUPS MIXED GREENS, SUCH AS BOSTON LETTUCE, RED LEAF LETTUCE, ROMAINE LETTUCE, RADICCHIO, BELGIAN ENDIVE, AND WATERCRESS, WASHED, TORN INTO BITE-SIZE PIECES

1/4 POUND BERMUDA ONION (ABOUT 1/4 ONION), CUT INTO 1/4-INCH SLICES, SEPARATED INTO RINGS

1 CUP SLICED CUCUMBERS (PREFERABLY UNWAXED, UNPEELED ONES)

1 TABLESPOON VEGETABLE OIL

2 LARGE SLICES FRESH GINGERROOT

2 PLUM TOMATOES, CORED, CUT INTO THIN SLICES

1/2 CUP FRESH CILANTRO LEAVES

▬ Place the beef in a bowl with 1 tablespoon lime juice and 1 tablespoon fish sauce. Toss well and let marinate for at least 1 hour.

To make the dressing, mix the remaining 1/3 cup lime juice and 1/4 cup fish sauce with the red pepper flakes. Set aside.

Toss together the greens, onion, and cucumbers. Arrange the mixture to cover a large platter.

Heat the oil in a wok over high heat. Add the gingerroot and cook for 30 seconds. Remove the meat from the marinade and add it to the wok; cook, stirring often, until the meat is just done through, about 2 minutes. Remove and discard the gingerroot.

Scatter the meat over the greens, onion, and cucumbers. Arrange the tomatoes and cilantro attractively on top. Pour the dressing over everything. Serve while the beef is still warm.

Makes 4 servings.

Meat Loaf

Meat loaf is a wonderful dish, easy to prepare and delicious hot or cold. Unfortunately for me, most recipes use ketchup, one of the few foods I've never developed a taste for. I much prefer this version, made with hoisin and other Oriental seasonings.

Serve meat loaf hot as a main course, with baked or steamed potatoes and a green vegetable like Stir-Fried Watercress with Garlic, page 129. Cold meat loaf makes wonderful sandwiches on rye or pumpernickel with mustard and tomato. It goes well with spicy Kim Chee, page 134, Tabbouleh, page 133, Coleslaw, page 139, or just about any cold salad.

2 POUNDS GROUND BEEF CHUCK

2 GARLIC CLOVES, MINCED

2 TEASPOONS MINCED FRESH GINGERROOT

2 TABLESPOONS SOY SAUCE

1/4 CUP HOISIN SAUCE

1/4 TEASPOON FRESHLY GROUND BLACK PEPPER

2 GREEN ONIONS, CHOPPED

3 TABLESPOONS FINE DRY BREAD CRUMBS

2 LARGE EGGS

1 CUP WATER

■ Preheat the oven to 350F (175C).

Place the beef in a bowl. Stir to loosen, then stir in the garlic, gingerroot, soy sauce, hoisin sauce, pepper, green onions, bread crumbs, eggs, and water. Pat the mixture into a 6-cup loaf pan, smooth the top, and bake in the preheated oven until firm to the touch, about 45 minutes.

Serve hot or cold, cut into slices.

Makes 6 to 8 servings.

Shiitake Hamburgers

Nothing could be more American than hamburgers—but these are rather unusual, mixed with braised shiitake mushrooms and green onion and served on English muffins with fruity tonkatsu sauce. French fries or Daikon Chips, page 137, are a good accompaniment.

The Japanese often braise mushrooms and vegetables in small amounts of liquid, as in this recipe. To keep the food from drying out, they use a dropped lid (otoshi-buta) that fits inside the pot and presses down on the food. If you don't have an otoshi-buta, keep the mushrooms moist by stirring them from time to time as they cook.

If you prepare more mushrooms than you need, cut the extras into strips and add them to salads, or use them as a vegetarian filling for sushi.

1/2 OUNCE (4 OR 5) DRIED SHIITAKE MUSHROOMS

2 TEASPOONS MIRIN

1 TEASPOON SOY SAUCE

1-1/4 POUNDS GROUND BEEF

4 TEASPOONS CHOPPED GREEN ONION

4 ENGLISH MUFFINS, SPLIT, TOASTED

TONKATSU SAUCE

TOMATO SLICES, IF DESIRED

■ Place the mushrooms in a bowl and add just enough boiling water to cover. Let soak for 20 minutes. Drain the mushrooms and squeeze them dry, reserving the liquid. Cut off and discard the stems and cut the caps into 1/4-inch squares.

In a small pot, combine 1/3 cup reserved mushroom liquid, the mirin, and soy sauce. Bring to a boil. Add the diced mushroom caps and simmer, covered as explained in the recipe introduction above, until the liquid is absorbed, about 15 minutes.

Place the cooked mushrooms in a bowl with the beef and green onion. Mix together quickly. Divide the meat into 4 portions and shape each into a 3/4-inch-thick patty.

Cook the meat patties in a hot skillet or on a hot grill until done to your liking, about 3 minutes on each side for rare.

Spread the toasted muffins with some tonkatsu sauce and place the meat patties on the muffins. Add tomato slices, if you like.

Makes 4 servings.

Potatoes with Spicy Beef Sauce

The Chinese often simmer cubes of tofu in spicy sauces like this one. In this case, cubed potatoes replace the tofu, yielding an equally tasty dish with a very different texture. It's a nice change of pace for meat-and-potato lovers. Serve with steamed carrots and sliced tomatoes.

2 POUNDS POTATOES, PEELED, CUT INTO 1/2-INCH CUBES

1 TABLESPOON VEGETABLE OIL

1 TEASPOON MINCED GARLIC

2 TEASPOONS MINCED FRESH GINGERROOT

2 TABLESPOONS MINCED SHALLOT

1/2 POUND GROUND BEEF

1 TABLESPOON SZECHUAN CHILI SAUCE

2 TABLESPOONS SOY SAUCE

2 TABLESPOONS CHINESE BLACK VINEGAR

2 TABLESPOONS WATER

1/2 CUP COOKED FRESH PEAS OR 1/2 CUP FROZEN PEAS, THAWED

▬ Place the potatoes in a 3-quart pot and add cold water to cover. Bring to a boil over high heat; then reduce the heat and simmer just until the potatoes are tender, about 10 minutes. Drain and set aside.

Heat the oil in a wok or large skillet over high heat. Add the garlic, gingerroot, and shallot; cook for 30 seconds. Add the beef, breaking it up with a spoon. Cook, stirring often, until the beef is browned, about 3 minutes. Add the chili sauce, soy sauce, vinegar, and water. Bring to a boil, then add the potatoes and peas. Reduce the heat and simmer for about 2 minutes to blend the flavors and heat throughout.

Makes 3 or 4 servings.

MEATS

Spicy Grilled Flank Steak

As this recipe shows, sometimes only a few ingredients are needed to make a delicious dish. With the meat, I like to serve Corn with Coconut Milk, page 121, Vegetable Pancakes, page 175, and Grilled Shiitake, page 140. Leftover steak is excellent in sandwiches with hot-sweet mustard and sliced tomatoes.

1 (2-POUND) FLANK STEAK

2 TABLESPOONS SZECHUAN CHILI SAUCE

2 TABLESPOONS CHINESE BLACK VINEGAR

▬ Place the steak in a dish and spread the chili sauce and vinegar on top. Turn the steak over a few times to coat both sides. Let marinate for several hours (or all day).

Preheat a grill or broiler until very hot. Place the meat on the grill or on a rack in a broiler pan; grill or broil until done to your liking, about 4 minutes on each side for rare. Let rest for 5 minutes, then cut diagonally across the grain into thin slices.

Makes 6 to 8 servings.

Veal with Ginger

The Italians cook veal scaloppine in dozens of ways, often losing the delicate meat in rich sauces. I prefer my veal with lighter sauces like this one, made with sake and lots of ginger. Serve this elegant dish with steamed asparagus and red-skinned potatoes. In keeping with the Italian spirit, start the meal with Italian-seasoned Pearl Balls, page 29.

1-1/2 POUNDS VEAL SCALOPPINE, SLICED NO MORE THAN 1/8 INCH THICK

ALL-PURPOSE FLOUR SEASONED WITH KOSHER SALT AND FRESHLY GROUND BLACK PEPPER

2 TABLESPOONS UNSALTED BUTTER

2 TABLESPOONS OLIVE OIL

6 TABLESPOONS SAKE

1 CUP PEELED, THINLY SLICED FRESH GINGERROOT

1/2 CUP SLICED GREEN ONIONS

1 TABLESPOON SOY SAUCE

FRESHLY GROUND BLACK PEPPER TO TASTE

Dip the veal slices in the seasoned flour to coat lightly. Shake off the excess.

If you have two 10-inch skillets, you can cook all the veal at once. If not, cook half the veal and set it aside, then wipe out the skillet and cook the remaining veal with fresh butter and oil. To cook the veal, heat 1 tablespoon butter and 1 tablespoon oil in each of two 10-inch skillets over medium-high heat. Add half the veal slices to each skillet in a single layer. Cook until the slices are lightly browned on the bottom, about 2 minutes. Turn the slices over and cook until browned on the other side, about 2 minutes longer. Remove the cooked veal to a platter and keep warm.

Pour the fat out of the skillet(s); deglaze the skillet(s) with the sake, adding 3 tablespoons to each skillet. Scrape the bottom of each skillet with a wooden spoon to loosen any browned bits of meat and cooking juices. Combine all the sake-cooking juice mixture in 1 skillet. Add the gingerroot and green onions and cook for 1 minute. Add the soy sauce and pepper and cook for 1 minute longer. Spoon the ginger sauce over the veal and serve hot.

Makes 4 to 6 servings.

Stuffed Breast of Veal

Veal breast, usually the least expensive cut of this delicate meat, needs long cooking. I like to stuff and braise it to serve hot or cold. Except for the strips of dark mushroom and bright carrot, this stuffing of rice and Chinese cabbage is as pale as the meat. For contrast on the plate, serve the veal with a dark green vegetable such as broccoli, broccoli de rabe, Swiss chard, or spinach.

1 (6-POUND) BREAST OF VEAL WITH BONES

1-1/2 CUPS COOKED RICE; OR 1/2 CUP UNCOOKED RICE, COOKED IN BOILING WATER FOR 10 MINUTES, DRAINED

8 DRIED CHINESE MUSHROOMS (ABOUT 1/2 OUNCE *TOTAL*)

2 TABLESPOONS OLIVE OIL

1 TABLESPOON MINCED FRESH GINGERROOT

1 TABLESPOON MINCED GARLIC

2 CUPS CHOPPED ONIONS

1/2 CUP JULIENNED CARROT, IN 1/4- BY 1/4- BY 2-INCH STICKS

1/2 CUP JULIENNED DAIKON, IN 1/4- BY 1/4- BY 2-INCH STICKS

1/2 POUND CHINESE CABBAGE, CUT INTO THIN SLICES

1/4 CUP FRESHLY GRATED PARMESAN CHEESE (ABOUT 3/4 OUNCE)

1/2 TEASPOON FRESHLY GROUND WHITE PEPPER

2 LARGE EGGS

KOSHER SALT AND FRESHLY GROUND WHITE PEPPER TO TASTE

2 CARROTS, ROUGHLY CHOPPED

1/2 CUP CHICKEN STOCK

1/4 CUP SAKE

■ Ask your butcher to cut a pocket in the breast of veal. You can also do it yourself: use a sharp knife, stay close to the bone, and work slowly so you don't cut holes in the pocket.

Place the rice in a large bowl. Place the mushrooms in a separate bowl and add boiling water to cover. Let soak for 20 minutes. Drain the mushrooms and squeeze them dry. Cut off and discard the stems; cut the caps into thin strips. Add the mushroom strips to the rice.

Heat the oil in a large skillet over high heat. Add the gingerroot and garlic and cook for 30 seconds. Add 1 cup onions and cook for 1 minute. Add the carrot sticks and daikon and cook for 1 minute longer. Add the cabbage and cook until well wilted, about 3 minutes. Add the vegetable mixture to the rice and mushrooms. Let the mixture cool, then stir in the cheese, 1/2 teaspoon white pepper, and eggs.

Preheat the broiler until hot.

Season the inside of the veal pocket with salt and white pepper. Spoon the stuffing inside; close up the opening with thin skewers or sew shut with kitchen twine. Season the outside of the veal with more salt and white pepper. Place the veal in a roasting pan and broil until lightly browned, about 5 minutes on each side.

Preheat the oven to 350F (175C). Pour most of the fat out of the roasting pan. Scatter the remaining 1 cup chopped onions and the chopped carrots in the pan, lifting the veal so the vegetables are underneath. Pour in the stock and sake and cover tightly with foil. Bake until the meat is tender and reaches an internal temperature of 170F (75C); be sure the tip of the meat thermometer is in the meat, not in the stuffing or touching bone. Baking will take about 2-1/2 hours.

Remove the meat to a cutting board and let rest while you strain the cooking liquid and skim off all the fat.

To serve the veal, carve it between the bones into thick slices and spoon some of the strained cooking liquid on top. If you prefer thinner slices, cut out the bones from the bottom (they should be very loose) and slice the now-boneless veal. Serve the bones on the side for those who like them. Spoon some of the cooking liquid over the meat.

Makes 6 to 8 servings.

Braised Brisket with Star Anise

Not only do I love eating brisket, I love the aroma that fills the kitchen as it slowly simmers. While Asians rarely braise big pieces of meat, star anise and other seasonings stand up beautifully to the long cooking. The chunks of daikon take on a rich mahogany color; your guests will probably assume they are potatoes with a slightly firmer texture.

Serve the sliced meat with Cranberry-Kumquat Relish, page 141, and Sesame Carrots, page 121. To start the meal, try Mackerel Seviche, page 36.

1/2 OUNCE (ABOUT 8) DRIED CHINESE MUSHROOMS, SOAKED IN BOILING WATER FOR 20 MINUTES

1 (2-1/2-POUND) THIN-CUT BEEF BRISKET, ALMOST ALL FAT REMOVED

2 GARLIC CLOVES, THINLY SLICED

2 TABLESPOONS MISO

1/4 CUP PLUS 1 TEASPOON SAKE

2 TABLESPOONS OLIVE OIL

1 POUND ONIONS, SLICED

1 TABLESPOON MINCED FRESH GINGERROOT

1/2 POUND DAIKON, PEELED, CUT INTO 1/2-INCH CUBES

2 TABLESPOONS SOY SAUCE

2 WHOLE STAR ANISE

■ Preheat the oven to 400F (205C).

Drain the mushrooms and squeeze them dry. Cut off and discard the stems; cut the caps into thin strips. Set aside.

With a thin knife, cut slits all over the brisket. Insert a garlic slice into each slit. Mix the miso with 1 teaspoon sake and rub the mixture all over the meat.

In an ovenproof skillet or casserole large enough to hold the meat flat, heat the oil over medium-high heat. Add the meat and cook until browned on the bottom, about 5 minutes. Turn and cook until browned on the other side, about 5 minutes longer. Remove the meat to a plate.

Add the onions and gingerroot to the skillet. Sauté for about 1 minute, then add the daikon and mushrooms. Sauté for 1 minute longer. Add the soy sauce and the remaining 1/4 cup sake. Bring to a boil. Return the meat to the skillet; add the star anise. Cover the skillet and bake in the preheated oven for 1 hour. Turn the meat over; continue to bake until the meat is fork-tender, about 45 minutes longer.

Remove the meat to a cutting board and thinly slice it across the grain. Remove and discard the star anise and serve the meat with the onions and daikon.

Makes 4 servings.

Braised Short Ribs with Rice Sticks

On a cold winter's night, a plate of tender short ribs is particularly satisfying. The meat does take a long time to simmer to tenderness, but the flavor makes it well worth the wait. All kinds of sauces, usually tomato-based, are delicious with ribs; in this case, I've added star anise, ginger, and fish sauce. Rice, couscous, and other grains pair well with the meat sauce, but boiled rice sticks are a nice change. To complete the meal, add zucchini, green beans, or another green vegetable.

3 TABLESPOONS OLIVE OIL

4 BEEF SHORT RIBS (ABOUT 3 POUNDS *TOTAL*)

1 LARGE (1/2-POUND) ONION, CHOPPED

1 (28-OUNCE) CAN WHOLE TOMATOES WITH PUREE

1 (3-INCH) CINNAMON STICK

1 WHOLE STAR ANISE

3 LARGE SLICES FRESH GINGERROOT

2 TABLESPOONS FISH SAUCE

2 TABLESPOONS RICE WINE VINEGAR

1/4 POUND RICE STICKS

MEATS

■ Heat 2 tablespoons oil in a deep 10-inch skillet over medium-high heat. Add the ribs and cook, turning as needed, until browned all over. Remove the ribs from the skillet and pour out the fat.

Add the remaining 1 tablespoon oil to the skillet along with the onion. Cook until the onion is softened, about 2 minutes. Add the tomatoes along with their puree to the skillet, crushing the tomatoes with a wooden spoon and scraping the bottom of the skillet to loosen any stuck bits of meat or onion. Add the cinnamon stick, star anise, gingerroot, fish sauce, and vinegar; bring to a boil. Return the ribs to the skillet, spooning some of the sauce over them. Reduce the heat, partially cover the skillet, and simmer until the meat is fork-tender, about 1-1/2 hours. Skim off and discard any fat that rises to the top. Taste the sauce and adjust the seasoning with fish sauce and vinegar as needed. Remove and discard the cinnamon stick, star anise, and gingerroot.

If cooking a day ahead, remove the ribs from the sauce; then cover and refrigerate the meat and sauce separately. This makes it easy to remove and discard any solidified fat from the sauce before reheating (reheat the ribs and sauce together).

Just before serving, bring a large pot of salted water to a boil. Add the rice sticks, return to a boil, and cook until soft, about 5 minutes. Serve the ribs and sauce with the rice sticks.

Makes 4 servings.

Pork-Filled Crêpes

Rather than serve this stir-fry dish with rice or another grain, I wrap it in Sesame Crêpes and bake it with a little Parmesan cheese. The pork is flavored with rosemary and hoisin, an unusual pairing that works well.

This dish makes a substantial meal that needs only a mixed green salad to complete it. If you'd like to serve a first course as well, try Hot and Sour Chicken Noodle Soup, page 50.

2 TABLESPOONS VEGETABLE OIL

1 JALAPEÑO CHILI, CORED, SEEDED, DERIBBED, CUT INTO VERY THIN STRIPS

3 LARGE SLICES FRESH GINGERROOT

1 POUND BONELESS LOIN OF PORK, CUT INTO THIN STRIPS

1/3 CUP SLICED GREEN ONIONS

1/4 POUND SNOW PEAS, STRINGS REMOVED, CUT ON THE DIAGONAL INTO 3/4- TO 1-INCH PIECES

1 RED BELL PEPPER, CORED, SEEDED, CUT INTO 1/4-INCH STRIPS

1 TABLESPOON FRESH ROSEMARY LEAVES OR 1 TEASPOON DRIED LEAF ROSEMARY

1/4 CUP HOISIN SAUCE (PLUS EXTRA HOISIN SAUCE FOR THE TABLE)

8 SESAME CRÊPES, PAGE 178

1 TABLESPOON UNSALTED BUTTER

1 TABLESPOON FRESHLY GRATED PARMESAN CHEESE

▬ Preheat the oven to 350F (175C).

Heat the oil in a large skillet or wok over high heat. Add the chili and gingerroot. Cook for 30 seconds. Add the pork and cook until the meat loses its raw look, about 2 minutes. Add the green onions, snow peas, bell pepper, and rosemary. Cook for 1 minute longer. Add 1/4 cup hoisin sauce and cook for about 1 minute longer, stirring to coat meat and vegetables.

Remove the skillet from the heat. Discard the gingerroot. Using a slotted spoon to leave extra liquid in the skillet, divide the mixture into 8 portions; roll each portion in a crêpe. Place the crêpes, seam side down, in a baking dish (about 12 by 8 inches). Dot the tops of the crêpes with butter, then sprinkle the crêpes with the cheese.

Bake, uncovered, in the preheated oven until heated through, about 15 minutes. Serve with extra hoisin sauce on the side.

Makes 4 servings.

Twice-Cooked Pork

Twice-cooked pork—first poached, then stir-fried—originated in Szechuan, but it is now popular all over China. Although the dish is usually made with bell peppers, I prefer to use the piquant, dark-skinned poblano chilies beloved of Mexicans and Southwestern Americans. The chilies add a flavor that's spicy but not numbing. For contrast in both taste and color, serve the meat with brown rice and a tomato salad.

1 POUND BONELESS LOIN OF PORK

2 LARGE SLICES FRESH GINGERROOT

1 TABLESPOON CHINESE BEAN PASTE

1 TEASPOON SZECHUAN CHILI SAUCE

2 TABLESPOONS SOY SAUCE

1 TABLESPOON CHINESE RICE WINE

1 TEASPOON SUGAR

1 TABLESPOON WATER

2 TABLESPOONS VEGETABLE OIL

3 GREEN ONIONS, CUT INTO 2-INCH PIECES

2 LARGE GARLIC CLOVES, MINCED

4 LARGE POBLANO CHILIES, CORED, SEEDED, DERIBBED, CUT INTO 1-INCH SQUARES

■ Place the pork and gingerroot in a 3-quart pot and add water to cover by at least 1 inch. Bring the water to a boil and skim the fat from the surface of the water. Reduce the heat, cover, and simmer until the meat is very tender, about 45 minutes. Remove and discard the gingerroot; remove the meat from the water and let cool completely. Cut the meat into thin slices about 2 inches square. Set aside.

In a small bowl, mix together the bean paste, chili sauce, soy sauce, wine, sugar, and water. Set aside.

Heat the oil in a wok or large skillet over high heat. Add the green onions and garlic and cook for 30 seconds. Add the chilies and cook, stirring often, for 2 minutes. Add the pork and the bean paste mixture, bring to a boil, and cook for 1 minute longer to blend and heat through.

Makes 3 or 4 servings.

Pork with Cilantro-Miso Sauce

The fresh tang of lime juice in both the marinade and the sauce makes this dish quite light. It's an easy way to add interest to a barbecue, since the sauce can be prepared ahead and the meat cooked quickly to order. If you have leftover meat and sauce, cube the pork and add it to a salad of cucumbers, tomatoes, and mixed greens; use the cilantro sauce as the dressing.

8 (ABOUT 3-OUNCE) BONELESS PORK CHOPS, EACH ABOUT 1/2 INCH THICK

JUICE OF 1 LIME

1 TABLESPOON SOY SAUCE

1/4 TEASPOON FRESHLY GROUND BLACK PEPPER

2 TABLESPOONS VEGETABLE OIL (IF SAUTÉING)

1 RECIPE CILANTRO-MISO SAUCE, PAGE 185

■ Place the pork in a shallow pan. Pour the lime juice and soy sauce on top; sprinkle with the pepper. Turn to coat completely. Cover and let marinate for several hours.

To cook, preheat a grill until hot. Remove the pork chops from the marinade and place them on the grill. Cook for about 2 minutes to sear; then lift each chop with tongs, rotate it a quarter turn, and return it to the grill, same side down. (Turning the chops in this way gives them an attractive diamond pattern of grill marks.) Cook for 2 minutes longer, then turn the chops over and continue to cook just until no longer pink in the center, 3 to 4 minutes longer. Although pork needs to be cooked through, it will get very dry if overcooked.

If you don't have a grill, heat the oil in a 10-inch skillet over medium-high heat. Add the pork chops in a single layer and cook until browned on the outside and no longer pink in the center, 4 to 5 minutes on each side.

Arrange the chops on a platter or individual plates and drizzle the Cilantro-Miso Sauce attractively across the tops of the chops.

Makes 4 servings.

Braised Pork Chops

Loin pork chops served on the bone are a common sight in America but unusual in Asia. The seasonings in this recipe, however, are more typical of Oriental cooking. The flavor is spicy but not hot, with a sweetness that comes from more than just the sugar. I like to spoon the sauce over rice instead of ladling it on the chops, since the meat picks up lots of spice as it cooks. To add some color to the plate, serve a mix of steamed carrots and snow peas on the side.

2 TABLESPOONS SOY SAUCE

1 TABLESPOON SUGAR

1/2 CUP CHICKEN STOCK

2 TABLESPOONS OYSTER SAUCE

2 TABLESPOONS FISH SAUCE

2 TABLESPOONS OLIVE OIL

4 (ABOUT 6-OUNCE) LOIN PORK CHOPS

1 LARGE (1/2-POUND) ONION, SLICED

1 TABLESPOON MINCED FRESH GINGERROOT

2 GARLIC CLOVES, MINCED

2 JALAPEÑO CHILIES, CORED, SEEDED, DERIBBED, CUT INTO THIN STRIPS

1 TEASPOON CORNSTARCH MIXED WITH 1 TEASPOON COLD WATER

HOT COOKED RICE

In a small bowl, mix together the soy sauce, sugar, stock, oyster sauce, and fish sauce. Set aside.

Heat 1 tablespoon oil in a large skillet over high heat. Add the pork chops in a single layer and cook until well browned on the bottom, about 5 minutes. Turn and cook until browned on the other side, about 5 minutes longer.

Remove the chops from the skillet; set aside. Pour the fat out of the skillet, then add the remaining 1 tablespoon oil. Add the onion, gingerroot, garlic, and chilies. Cook, scraping the bottom of the skillet, until the onion is softened, about 1 minute. Add the soy sauce mixture and bring it to a rapid boil. Scrape the bottom of the skillet to loosen any browned bits of meat and cooking juices.

Arrange the pork chops over the sauce in a single layer. Reduce the heat, cover the skillet, and simmer for 5 minutes; turn the chops and simmer until the meat is no longer pink in the center, about 5 minutes longer. Place the chops on a platter and keep warm.

Add a little of the sauce to the dissolved cornstarch to thin it further, then stir it into the sauce. Bring to a boil and cook until the sauce is slightly thickened, about 1 minute. Spoon the sauce over the pork chops or serve it on the side for the rice.

Makes 4 servings.

Braised Spareribs with Polenta

Polenta (cornmeal mush) is a wonderful change from rice and other starches. In Italy, it is used as a foil for rich, meaty dishes. It's terrific with pork ribs in a spicy Asian-style sauce.

Although the polenta must be made fresh, the ribs reheat beautifully. The meat goes well with steamed broccoli or sautéed spinach. For company, spoon the polenta in the center of a round platter and arrange the broccoli or spinach around the perimeter; then spoon the ribs over the polenta. Serve the sauce in a gravy boat on the side. For family, you might prefer to cook the broccoli along with the ribs, adding it to the pot toward the end of the cooking (or reheating) time. It will lose its bright green color, but you'll have one less pot to wash.

2 TABLESPOONS SOY SAUCE

1-1/4 CUPS WATER

1/4 CUP CHINESE RICE WINE

1/4 CUP FERMENTED BLACK BEANS, CHOPPED

1 TEASPOON SUGAR

2 TABLESPOONS VEGETABLE OIL

2 DRIED RED CHILIES, HALVED

1 CUP CHOPPED ONION

2 TABLESPOONS MINCED GARLIC

1 TABLESPOON MINCED FRESH GINGERROOT

1 (3-1/2-POUND) RACK PORK SPARERIBS, CUT INTO 2-INCH PIECES

1 RECIPE POLENTA, PAGE 174

In a bowl, mix together the soy sauce, water, wine, black beans, and sugar. Set aside.

Heat the oil in a large wok over high heat. Add the chilies and cook for 15 seconds. Add the onion, garlic, and gingerroot; cook for 1 minute. Add the ribs and cook, tossing often, until browned all over, about 10 minutes. Add the soy sauce mixture and stir to coat the meat. Bring the liquid to a boil; reduce the heat, cover the wok, and simmer until the ribs are very tender, about 30 minutes.

Remove the ribs from the wok and skim off as much fat from the sauce as possible (a fat separator comes in handy). If cooking the ribs a day ahead, remove the ribs from the sauce; then cover and refrigerate the meat and sauce separately. This makes it easy to remove and discard any solidified fat from the and sauce before reheating (reheat the ribs and sauce together).

Before serving, remove and discard the chilies. Serve the ribs and sauce with the Polenta, as explained in the recipe introduction above.

Makes 6 servings.

Barbecued Ribs

It's no surprise that barbecuing is popular all over the world: after all, open fires were our first ovens. Meats and methods vary, from whole pigs cooked over a slow flame in Texas to fresh-caught fish seared over a hibachi in Japan. Today, however, the term "barbecue" often refers to the sauce rather than the cooking technique, since many barbecue dishes — this one for example — are baked in the oven. The problem with actually grilling ribs is that they need long, slow cooking and more attention than most of us want to give. Without extra time and care, they'll end up charred and crusty on the outside, still rare inside—a fine condition for flank and other good steaks, but not acceptable for ribs.

To make sure the ribs have lots of flavor, I rub them with a spicy paste before cooking. The sauce goes on later, when the ribs are almost done. Because it's made with molasses, the sauce burns easily and can't take long cooking.

This is a messy, greasy meal. I like to serve the ribs with plain baked sweet potatoes, Sesame Potato Salad, page 136, Kim Chee, page 134, or Coleslaw, page 139, and plenty of icy beer.

1 TEASPOON GRATED FRESH GINGERROOT

4 GARLIC CLOVES, PUSHED THROUGH A GARLIC PRESS

2 TABLESPOONS PAPRIKA

2 TEASPOONS DRY MUSTARD

2 TEASPOONS GROUND RED (CAYENNE) PEPPER

2 TEASPOONS SOY SAUCE

2 TABLESPOONS CHINESE BLACK VINEGAR

2 TABLESPOONS HOISIN SAUCE

2 TEASPOONS WATER

2 (3-POUND) SLABS PORK SPARERIBS

2 LEMONS, SLICED

1 RECIPE ORANGE BARBECUE SAUCE, PAGE 191

■ Preheat the oven to 375F (190C).

In a bowl, mix together the gingerroot, garlic, paprika, mustard, red pepper, soy sauce, vinegar, hoisin sauce, and water to make a thick paste. Spread the paste over both sides of each slab of ribs. Place the slabs, top side up, in a shallow roasting pan. Arrange the lemon slices on top.

Bake in the preheated oven for 1-1/2 hours, turning the ribs every 30 minutes. After the ribs have baked for 1-1/2 hours, turn them again and brush with some of the Orange Barbecue Sauce. Bake for 15 minutes longer. Turn the ribs over again; brush the top with more sauce. Bake for 15 minutes longer. The meat should be tender enough to pull away from the bones with a fork. Serve with extra sauce on the side.

Makes 4 to 6 servings.

MEATS

Chinese Sausage and Peppers

The Italians sauté hot or sweet sausages with peppers or onions for a dinner dish or a sandwich filling. Chinese sausages, firmer and sweeter than the Italian type, give the dish a deliciously different flavor that somehow seems more festive.

1 POUND CHINESE-STYLE PORK
  SAUSAGES

3 TABLESPOONS OLIVE OIL

2 GARLIC CLOVES, MINCED

2 JALAPEÑO CHILIES, CORED,
  SEEDED, DERIBBED, CUT INTO
  THIN SLICES

2 LARGE (1/2-POUND) ONIONS,
  SLICED

2 RED BELL PEPPERS, CORED,
  SEEDED, SLICED

2 GREEN BELL PEPPERS, CORED,
  SEEDED, SLICED

1 TEASPOON KOSHER SALT, OR TO
  TASTE

FRENCH OR ITALIAN BREAD OR HOT
  COOKED RICE

■ Bring water to a boil in the bottom of a steamer or wok. Reduce the heat so the water simmers. Place the sausages on a steamer rack. Set the rack in place over the simmering water, cover, and steam until the sausages are softened and the fat becomes translucent, about 15 minutes. Remove to a cutting board and cut on the diagonal into 1/2-inch slices.

Heat the oil in a large skillet over high heat. Add the garlic and chilies; cook for 30 seconds. Add the onions and cook until slightly softened, about 2 minutes. Add the sausages, red and green bell peppers, and salt. Cook, stirring frequently, until the bell peppers are soft but not mushy, about 5 minutes. Serve with or in French or Italian bread, or with rice.

Makes 4 to 6 servings.

Americans who have been happily eating meat every night for years are now discovering the extraordinary bounty of oceans, seas, and lakes. There is something particularly elegant about pale seafood, pink and white on the plate. Its generally mild flavor makes it a perfect mate for a wide range of sauces and accompaniments, from thin slices of pickled ginger to piquant wasabi dressing. Seafood can be steamed, sautéed, grilled, or fried; almost anything works, as long as you avoid overcooking. Remove fish from the heat when it is barely done—still moist and flaky, never dry.

Since seafood is more readily available than meat in the East, Oriental chefs have been experimenting with it for years, finding just the right seasonings. One used just about everywhere in Southeast Asia is fish sauce, made of fermented fish. The aroma puts most Westerners off, at least at first—but the odor fades in the cooking, and the final flavor is surprisingly delicate. I've used it in many of these dishes to alter what would otherwise be more in the European tradition.

Cilantro and fish sauce add to new flavors to a classic—Salmon in Papillote, page 110.

SEAFOOD

Shrimp and Avocado Salad with Wasabi Dressing

Tossed with a zingy wasabi dressing, this salad blends different tastes, colors, and textures. The same dressing is excellent on tuna sandwiches or slices of leftover turkey.

1 POUND UNCOOKED MEDIUM-LARGE SHRIMP IN THE SHELL

2 TEASPOONS WASABI POWDER

2 TEASPOONS WATER

1/4 CUP MAYONNAISE

2 TEASPOONS RICE WINE VINEGAR

1/4 TEASPOON KOSHER SALT

2 CUPS MIXED GREENS, SUCH AS BIBB OR BOSTON LETTUCE, ROMAINE LETTUCE, RED LEAF LETTUCE, WATERCRESS, CHICORY, AND BELGIAN ENDIVE, TORN INTO BITE-SIZE PIECES

1/2 AVOCADO, PITTED, PEELED, CUT INTO 1-INCH CUBES

1 MEDIUM TOMATO, CORED, CUT INTO 1-INCH CUBES

1/4 CUP CHOPPED RED ONION

2 TABLESPOONS CHOPPED FRESH CILANTRO LEAVES

Bring a medium pot of salted water to a boil. Add the shrimp. Return to a boil and cook until the shrimp turn pink, about 30 seconds longer. Drain, shell, and devein the shrimp. Cut them into large chunks and set aside.

In a small bowl, mix together the wasabi powder and water. Cover and let stand for 5 minutes to develop the wasabi's flavor. Add the mayonnaise, vinegar, and salt. Stir until smooth. Set aside.

Toss the greens together and arrange them in a bed on a platter or in a shallow bowl. Scatter the shrimp, avocado, tomato, onion, and cilantro on top. Drizzle some of the wasabi dressing over everything. Serve the remaining dressing on the side.

Makes 4 servings.

Shrimp and Broccoli de Rabe on a Noodle Pillow

Barbara Tropp, owner of the extraordinary China Moon restaurant in San Francisco, christened Chinese shallow-fried noodle cakes "pillows." It's a wonderful name for a wonderful dish: pasta packages with a brown and crispy crust and a pale, soft interior. The Chinese make them with fresh egg noodles, but I find that packaged dried spaghetti works equally well. The pillows can take the place of rice with almost any stir-fried dish.

This spicy combination of shrimp and broccoli de rabe shows off the excellent, slightly bitter greens to advantage.

1 POUND UNCOOKED LARGE SHRIMP, SHELLED (LEAVE TAILS ON), DEVEINED, PREFERABLY BUTTERFLIED

1 TABLESPOON SOY SAUCE

2 TABLESPOONS SAKE

1 CUP CHICKEN STOCK

1 TABLESPOON CORNSTARCH

1 TABLESPOON SZECHUAN CHILI SAUCE

1 LARGE (ABOUT 1-POUND) BUNCH BROCCOLI DE RABE, CUT INTO 3-INCH PIECES

1/2 POUND SPAGHETTI

7 TABLESPOONS VEGETABLE OIL

4 LARGE GARLIC CLOVES, SLICED

■ Place the shrimp in a bowl, add the soy sauce and sake, and toss to coat. Set aside.

Mix 1 tablespoon stock with the cornstarch. Stir the chili sauce into the remaining stock. Set aside.

Bring 2 large pots of salted water to a boil. To 1 pot, add the broccoli de rabe and cook for 2 minutes. Drain well and set aside. To the second pot, add the spaghetti. Return to a boil and cook until barely tender, about 8 minutes. Drain well.

Heat 3 tablespoons oil in a well-seasoned 8-inch skillet over high heat. Add the drained spaghetti and press down to make a cake. Reduce heat to medium-high and cook until nicely browned on the bottom, about 5 minutes. Slide the cake onto a flat plate or pot lid. Add 1 more tablespoon oil to the skillet. Carefully turn the pasta cake over into the skillet, browned side up. Cook until browned on the bottom, about 3 minutes longer. Slide the cake out of the skillet and keep warm while you cook the topping.

Heat the remaining 3 tablespoons oil in a wok or large skillet over high heat. Add the garlic and cook for 30 seconds. Drain the shrimp and add to the wok. Toss and cook until the shrimp are almost cooked through, about 2 minutes. Add the broccoli de rabe and cook for 1 minute longer. Add the stock-chili sauce mixture, stir, and bring to a boil. Stir the cornstarch mixture, then add it to the wok. Cook until the sauce is thickened slightly, about 1 minute longer.

Place the noodle "pillow" on a platter and cut it into 4 or 6 wedges. Spoon the shrimp mixture on top.

Makes 4 or 6 servings.

Spicy Scallops

Scallops are one of the sweetest of the sea's treasures, perfect for all kinds of quick dishes. This one is made with a creamy sauce flavored with spices of the East. Serve it over plain rice, with quickly sautéed green beans, snow peas, or spinach on the side. To complete the meal, add a salad of mixed greens.

2 TABLESPOONS UNSALTED BUTTER

2 TABLESPOONS VEGETABLE OIL

1 TABLESPOON MINCED FRESH GINGERROOT

1 TABLESPOON MINCED GARLIC

1/2 CUP SLICED GREEN ONIONS

1-1/2 POUNDS BAY SCALLOPS

1/2 POUND CHERRY TOMATOES, HALVED

1/4 CUP SAKE

1/4 CUP WHIPPING CREAM

1 TEASPOON SAMBAL OELEK

2 TABLESPOONS CHOPPED FRESH CILANTRO LEAVES

1/2 TEASPOON KOSHER SALT

▬ Heat the butter and oil in a large skillet over high heat. Add the gingerroot and garlic and cook until fragrant, about 30 seconds. Add the green onions and cook for 30 seconds longer. Add the scallops and cook until barely opaque, about 1 minute longer. Add the tomatoes and cook until soft, about 2 minutes. Stir in the sake, cream, and sambal. Bring to a boil; stir in the cilantro and salt, then serve.

Makes 4 servings.

Shrimp and Chinese Cabbage Sauté

Pale green Chinese cabbage makes a perfect background for pink shrimp, especially when the dish is served on a black or jade green plate. To complete the meal, add brown rice to absorb the sauce and Sesame Carrots, page 121, or a tomato salad for color.

1 POUND UNCOOKED MEDIUM-LARGE SHRIMP, SHELLED, DEVEINED

2 TABLESPOONS SAKE

2 TABLESPOONS VEGETABLE OIL

2 GARLIC CLOVES, SLICED

1 LARGE (6-OUNCE) ONION, SLICED

1 POUND CHINESE CABBAGE, CUT CROSSWISE INTO 1/2-INCH PIECES

1 TEASPOON KOSHER SALT

2 TEASPOONS FISH SAUCE

FRESHLY GROUND BLACK PEPPER TO TASTE

■ Place the shrimp in a bowl, add the sake, and toss to coat. Set aside.

Heat the oil in a large skillet over high heat. Add the garlic and onion and sauté for 2 minutes. Add the cabbage and salt and cook until the cabbage softens a bit, about 3 minutes. Drain the shrimp and add them to the skillet with the fish sauce and pepper. Cook, stirring frequently, until the shrimp turn pink, about 3 minutes. Serve hot.

Makes 4 servings.

Soft-Shell Crabs with Black Bean Sauce

Soft-shell crabs are a sure sign of spring. These delicate sea creatures are molting blue crabs marketed when the hard shells have been shed, leaving the crabs unprotected and completely edible.

Seasoned with salty black beans, this dish is quick to make and certain to impress family and friends. Because the crabs are quite rich, keep the accompaniments simple—young spring asparagus, lightly steamed, and some fragrant rice.

8 (3-OUNCE) SOFT-SHELL CRABS

ALL-PURPOSE FLOUR

1/4 CUP (4 TABLESPOONS) UNSALTED BUTTER

1 CUP SAKE

4 GREEN ONIONS, SLICED

2 TEASPOONS MINCED GARLIC

2 TABLESPOONS FERMENTED BLACK BEANS, LIGHTLY RINSED, CHOPPED

■ Pat the crabs dry and coat them lightly with flour; shake off any excess.

If you have a skillet that is large enough to hold all the crabs in a single layer, melt all the butter in it over medium-high heat. Otherwise, divide the butter between 2 smaller skillets or cook the crabs in batches. Place the crabs in the skillet, shelled side down, and cook until lightly browned on the bottom, about 2 minutes. Turn the crabs over and cook until lightly browned on the other side, about 2 minutes longer. Remove the crabs to a platter and keep warm. Pour the sake into the skillet and deglaze over high heat, scraping the bottom of the skillet with a wooden spoon. (If using 2 skillets, divide the sake between the 2 and deglaze them; then combine all the liquid in 1 skillet.) Add the green onions and garlic and cook for 1 minute. Add the black beans and cook for 30 seconds longer. Spoon the sauce over the crabs and serve hot.

Makes 4 servings.

Clams with Black Beans on Polenta

In China, clams with black beans are traditionally served for good luck on New Year's Day. Such a felicitous combination certainly has a place in this country, although the dish presented here would be surprising to most Chinese. I've added chopped tomato to the classic sauce—for color, flavor, and a little more luck (red is a lucky color in China and Japan). The mild-flavored yellow polenta is the perfect foil for the salty sauce. I prefer serving this dish in small portions as a first course, followed by a mellow dish like Steamed Chicken Rolls, page 68.

2 TABLESPOONS VEGETABLE OIL

2 GARLIC CLOVES, MINCED

1 TABLESPOON MINCED FRESH GINGERROOT

1/4 CUP CHOPPED GREEN ONIONS

2 TABLESPOONS FERMENTED BLACK BEANS, RINSED WELL, ROUGHLY CHOPPED

1 DRIED RED CHILI

1 MEDIUM (1/4-POUND) TOMATO, CORED, CHOPPED

1/4 CUP CHICKEN STOCK

1 TABLESPOON OYSTER SAUCE

1/2 TEASPOON SUGAR

1 TEASPOON SOY SAUCE

24 LITTLE NECK CLAMS IN THE SHELL, WELL SCRUBBED

1/2 RECIPE POLENTA, PAGE 174

1 TABLESPOON CORNSTARCH DISSOLVED IN 1 TABLESPOON WATER

2 TABLESPOONS CHOPPED PARSLEY

Heat the oil in a large skillet or wok over medium-high heat. Add the garlic, gingerroot, green onions, and black beans. Cook, stirring often, for 1 minute. Add the chili, tomato, stock, oyster sauce, sugar, and soy sauce. Cook for about 30 seconds longer. Add the clams in a single layer, cover the skillet, and cook until the clams are open, about 10 minutes.

While the clams are cooking, divide the Polenta among 4 shallow soup bowls, arranging it in a neat pile in the center of each bowl.

Remove the cooked clams from the skillet and arrange them around the Polenta, 6 clams to a bowl. Bring the sauce in the skillet to a full boil. Stir the dissolved cornstarch, pour it into the skillet, and boil for 1 minute longer. Spoon the sauce over the Polenta and clams. Sprinkle some parsley on top of each serving.

Makes 4 servings.

Fish Cakes

Fish sauce enhances the flavor of these American fish cakes without making them "fishy" tasting. Serve them with Pickled Beets and Ginger, page 133, and a green vegetable such as Spinach with Black Sesame Seeds, page 120. A little spicy salsa is also an excellent accompaniment.

If you have a leftover fish cake, eat it for lunch on a roll with some Curried Mayonnaise, page 186, and sliced tomatoes.

1 POUND SCROD OR COD FILLET, CUT INTO CHUNKS

1/4 POUND DAIKON, PEELED, CUT INTO CHUNKS

1/4 POUND CARROTS, CUT INTO CHUNKS

1/4 POUND ONIONS, CUT INTO CHUNKS

2 TABLESPOONS FISH SAUCE

1 TEASPOON GRATED FRESH GINGERROOT

2 LARGE EGGS

1/8 TEASPOON GROUND RED (CAYENNE) PEPPER

1 CUP FINE DRY BREAD CRUMBS

2 TABLESPOONS VEGETABLE OIL

Put the fish, daikon, carrots, and onions through the small blade of a food grinder. If you don't have a grinder, process the fish and vegetables in a food processor in separate batches until minced. Place the mixture in a bowl and add the fish sauce, gingerroot, eggs, red pepper, and 1/2 cup bread crumbs. Mix well. If you have the time, cover the mixture and refrigerate it for 1 hour.

To cook, divide the fish mixture into 8 equal portions. Gently toss each portion back and forth between your wet hands to make a smooth, firm ball.

Spread the remaining 1/2 cup bread crumbs on a plate. Press 1 fish ball gently to flatten. Place it on the bread crumbs to coat the bottom; then turn to coat the top, patting the sides to make sure the cake is evenly breaded. Repeat to bread the remaining fish cakes.

Heat 1 tablespoon oil in each of two 8-inch skillets over medium-high heat. Put 4 fish cakes in each skillet and cook until well browned on both sides and cooked through, about 10 minutes on each side. Serve hot or cold.

Makes 4 servings.

Salmon Cooked with Coconut Milk

The flavoring comes from Thailand, but the portion sizes are definitely Western. This dish has only a hint of spiciness; if you prefer a hotter flavor, use an extra jalapeño. There is plenty of sauce, so serve plain rice, couscous, or kasha to soak it up. A steamed green vegetable balances the plate.

This recipe works equally well with any firm fish steak—salmon trout, cod, halibut.

1/2 TEASPOON POWDERED GALANGAL (LAOS)

1/2 TEASPOON CORIANDER SEEDS

1/2 TEASPOON WHOLE BLACK PEPPERCORNS

1/4 TEASPOON WHOLE CLOVES

1 TABLESPOON VEGETABLE OIL

1/2 TEASPOON GROUND NUTMEG

1/2 TEASPOON SHRIMP PASTE

1 TABLESPOON CHOPPED GARLIC

1 TABLESPOON CHOPPED SHALLOT

1 JALAPEÑO CHILI, CORED, SEEDED, DERIBBED, CUT INTO JULIENNE STRIPS

PEEL OF 1 LIME, CUT INTO JULIENNE STRIPS

1 TABLESPOON CHOPPED FRESH CILANTRO LEAVES

2 CUPS COCONUT MILK

2 TABLESPOONS FISH SAUCE

2 (1/2-POUND) SALMON STEAKS (SEE NOTE AT RIGHT)

HOT COOKED RICE OR OTHER GRAIN

— Place the galangal, coriander seeds, peppercorns, and cloves in a spice grinder and grind to a powder. Set aside.

Heat the oil in a 10-inch skillet over medium-high heat. Add the ground spices along with the nutmeg, shrimp paste, garlic, and shallot. Cook until the spices are fragrant, about 1 minute, pressing on the shrimp paste to break it up. Add the chili, lime peel, and cilantro; cook for 30 seconds longer to blend. Add the coconut milk and fish sauce and bring to a boil.

Add the salmon in a single layer. Reduce the heat, cover, and simmer until the fish is just opaque throughout, about 15 minutes. Remove the fish to a board. Divide each steak in half, place on a platter, and keep warm.

Bring the sauce to a full boil and cook for a few minutes to thicken slightly. Spoon some of the sauce over the fish and serve the rest on the side with rice or another grain.

Makes 4 servings.

NOTE: The steaks I use are about 1-1/2 inches thick. If those you buy are thicker or thinner, adjust the cooking time accordingly, allowing 10 minutes for each inch of thickness.

Salmon in Papillote

Fish sauce and cilantro lend a touch of the Orient to this elegant and very French dish. It's a great choice for company, since you can prepare the *papillotes* ahead and bake them just before serving. Each foil package contains both fish and vegetables, so you need only add rice or another grain to absorb the sauce. Begin the meal with a light vegetable soup.

2 LARGE LEEKS, (ABOUT 1 POUND *TOTAL*), WELL WASHED

3 TABLESPOONS UNSALTED BUTTER

1 SMALL ZUCCHINI, CUT ON THE DIAGONAL INTO 20 SLICES

1 POUND SALMON FILLET, CUT INTO 4 EQUAL PIECES (SEE NOTE BELOW)

1/2 POUND TOMATOES, CORED, SEEDED, DICED

1/4 CUP FRESH CILANTRO LEAVES

SZECHUAN PEPPERCORNS, TOASTED IN A DRY SKILLET

4 TEASPOONS FISH SAUCE

Preheat the oven to 400F (205C).

Cut the green tops off the leeks and discard them (or save them for soup). Cut the white parts into long, thin strips. Melt the butter in a small skillet over medium-high heat. Add the leeks and sauté until soft but not browned, about 2 minutes.

Place 4 sheets of foil, each about 18 inches long, on your work surface. Place 1/4 of the leeks on each sheet, arranging them about 5 inches up from the bottom of the shorter side. Overlap 5 zucchini slices on top of each pile of leeks. Place a piece of salmon over each portion of zucchini slices, then sprinkle the tomatoes and cilantro evenly over the salmon. Grind some peppercorns on top and sprinkle 1 teaspoon fish sauce over each portion. Fold the foil over to cover the fish, then seal the edges all around, making neat half-moons. Place the packages on a baking sheet and bake in the preheated oven for 10 minutes.

Serve each person an unopened package, or slit the packages open in the kitchen and slide the contents of each onto a dinner plate.

Makes 4 servings.

NOTE: You may cook the salmon with or without its skin. If you wish to remove the skin, scrape and pull it away with a paring knife and your fingers while the fish is cold. Most of the skin will come away easily.

Grilled Salmon with Miso

Miso imparts a special flavor to the fish in this very quick preparation, perfect for company (or family) when you are short on time or don't want to be stuck in the kitchen. Serve it with Baby Corn Salad, page 134, to add color to the plate. For a fairly quick start, begin with Udon with Cilantro Pesto, page 151.

2 TABLESPOONS MISO

1 TABLESPOON SAKE

4 (ABOUT 1/4-POUND) SALMON
    STEAKS, EACH ABOUT 1 INCH
    THICK

1 TABLESPOON SESAME OIL

4 WHOLE GREEN ONIONS, ROOTS
    TRIMMED

▬▬ Preheat a grill or broiler until hot. Mix the miso with the sake and set aside. Brush the salmon steaks on all sides with the sesame oil, then place them on the grill or on a rack in a broiler pan. Grill or broil for 3 minutes; then turn and cook for 3 minutes longer. Spread half the miso mixture on the fish. Turn the fish miso side down and cook for 2 minutes; brush with the remaining miso mixture, turn, and cook until opaque throughout, about 2 minutes longer.

While the fish is cooking, also grill or broil the green onions until soft, turning as necessary.

Serve the fish with the grilled or broiled green onions.

Makes 4 servings.

Sesame Red Snapper with Pickled Ginger

This is a very simple, elegant dish. The pickled ginger provides a tangy contrast to the milder fish—and it's pretty besides. I like to serve Mixed Vegetables with Cellophane Noodles, page 128, or a simply prepared green vegetable with this meal. Pearl Balls, page 29, or Crab Fritters, page 25, are excellent starters. You might end with Poached Pears and Kumquats, page 196.

4 (6-OUNCE) RED SNAPPER FILLETS

1/2 CUP SESAME SEEDS

1/4 CUP SESAME OIL

1/2 CUP THINLY SLICED PINK
    PICKLED GINGER

▬▬ Coat each snapper fillet with a layer of sesame seeds, pressing the seeds with your fingers so they stick onto both sides of the fish.

Heat 2 tablespoons sesame oil in each of 2 large skillets over medium-high heat (or use 1 skillet and cook half the fish at a time). Add the fish, skin side down. Cook until nicely browned on the bottom, about 5 minutes. Turn and cook until browned on the other side and opaque throughout, about 3 minutes longer. Remove to a platter or individual plates. Strew 1/4 of the ginger over each fillet.

Makes 4 servings.

Red Snapper with Ginger Beurre Blanc

Beurre blanc is a wonderful sauce that pairs beautifully with fish. The key is to make a reduction of wine, vinegar, and shallots, then beat in pieces of butter so they are absorbed by the reduction, becoming creamy but not melting. While this is not a sauce for beginners, I find it much easier to make than emulsion or egg-thickened sauces, which have a tendency to curdle. In keeping with the cross-cultural spirit, the reduction uses ginger, green onions, rice wine vinegar, and sake.

Because this dish is so rich, I usually use it as a first course before Marinated Leg of Lamb, page 80, or Spicy Grilled Flank Steak, page 88. If you make the portions larger, it can certainly serve as a main course as well. In that case, begin the meal with Thai Black Bean Soup, page 49, and accompany the fish with steamed asparagus or spinach.

1/4 CUP MINCED FRESH GINGERROOT

1/4 CUP MINCED GREEN ONIONS

1/2 CUP SAKE

1/4 CUP RICE WINE VINEGAR

1 POUND RED SNAPPER FILLETS, CUT INTO 6 EQUAL PIECES

12 (3-INCH) PIECES OF GREEN ONION TOP

1 CUP (1/2 POUND) UNSALTED BUTTER, CUT INTO ABOUT 30 PIECES

KOSHER SALT AND FRESHLY GROUND BLACK PEPPER TO TASTE

Place the gingerroot, green onions, sake, and vinegar in a heavy 1-quart saucepan. Bring to a boil and boil until reduced to a thick glaze, about 10 minutes. This can be done ahead.

Line 2 steamer racks with dampened cheesecloth. When ready to cook, arrange the fish, skin side down, in single layers on the racks. Bring water to a boil in the bottom of a steamer; reduce the heat so the water simmers. Set the racks in place over the simmering water, cover, and steam until the fish is opaque throughout, about 4 minutes. Toward the end of the cooking time, add the green onion tops to the steamer to soften.

While the fish is steaming, reheat the reduction over medium heat. Begin whisking in the butter, a few pieces at a time, allowing each portion to be completely absorbed before adding more. When all the butter has been added, press the sauce through a sieve into a clean bowl. Season with salt and pepper.

Spoon some beurre blanc onto each of 6 salad or 3 dinner plates. Arrange the fish, skin side up, over the sauce. Garnish each piece of fish with crossed pieces of green onion top.

Makes 6 first-course or 3 main-dish servings.

Charred Tile Fish with Pepper Sauce

Paul Prudhomme has made blackened fish a popular dish in restaurants all over the country. It is difficult to cook at home, however, because few of us have ranges that get hot enough or exhausts strong enough to keep the smoke detectors from going off. Unless your kitchen is suitably equipped or you want to place the skillet over a hot grill outdoors, you won't get blackened fish from this recipe—but the fillets will still be charred, moist, and delicious. To season the fish, I have used curry spices and paprika rather than all the chilies Prudhomme likes. Serve with brown rice and steamed broccoli. If tile fish isn't available, use any white-fleshed fish fillets.

3 DRIED RED CHILIES

1 TEASPOON DRIED SLICED LEMON GRASS

1 TEASPOON WHOLE BLACK PEPPERCORNS

1 TEASPOON CORIANDER SEEDS

1/2 TEASPOON CUMIN SEEDS

1/2 TEASPOON POWDERED GALANGAL (LAOS)

1 TEASPOON GROUND TURMERIC

1/2 TEASPOON KOSHER SALT

1 TABLESPOON PAPRIKA

1-1/2 POUNDS TILE FISH FILLETS, CUT INTO 4 (6-OUNCE) PIECES

1/4 CUP (4 TABLESPOONS) UNSALTED BUTTER, MELTED

2 TABLESPOONS UNSALTED BUTTER

1 MEDIUM (5-OUNCE) ONION, CHOPPED

2 JALAPEÑO CHILIES, CORED, SEEDED, DERIBBED, CUT INTO THIN STRIPS

1 TABLESPOON MINCED GARLIC

1 TABLESPOON MINCED FRESH GINGERROOT

■ Place the dried chilies, lemon grass, peppercorns, coriander seeds, and cumin seeds in a spice grinder and grind to a powder. Mix the ground spices with the galangal, turmeric, salt, and paprika.

Dip the fish fillets into the melted butter to coat. Sprinkle the spice mixture over the fillets, making sure to coat each completely.

The best pan for cooking the fish is a well-seasoned 12-inch cast-iron skillet. Place the skillet over high heat for at least 5 minutes. Turn your exhaust fan on high. Place the fish in the skillet in a single layer. Cook for about 3 minutes. Turn and cook just until opaque throughout, about 3 minutes longer. Remove the fish to a platter and keep warm.

Melt the 2 tablespoons butter in the skillet over medium-high heat. Add the onion, jalapeño chilies, garlic, and ginger-root. Cook until the onion is soft, about 3 minutes, scraping the skillet to mix in all the spices. Spoon the onion mixture over the fish.

Makes 4 servings.

Grilled Shark

This is a very fast main course, worthy of company. You can marinate the fish a full day ahead or about half an hour before cooking. Mixed Vegetables with Cellophane Noodles, page 128, are a perfect accompaniment. If shark isn't available, use cod or other white fish steaks.

1 TEASPOON RED CURRY PASTE,
   PAGE 189

1 TABLESPOON LIME JUICE

1 TABLESPOON FISH SAUCE

2 TABLESPOONS OLIVE OIL

1 POUND SHARK STEAKS

▄▄ In a bowl, mix together the Red Curry Paste, lime juice, fish sauce, and oil. Add the shark and turn to coat. Let marinate for at least 30 minutes.

Preheat a grill or broiler until hot. Measure the thickness of the fish; the cooking time will be about 10 minutes for each inch. For example, a 1-inch steak cooks in 10 minutes (5 minutes on each side); a 3/4-inch steak takes 7 to 8 minutes (3-1/2 to 4 minutes on each side).

Place the fish on the grill or on a rack in a broiler pan. Grill or broil until opaque throughout. Serve hot.

Makes 4 servings.

Steamed Catfish

Nothing could be more American than catfish, that Southern animal long popular for its low price. Like most other foods, it responds well to an Oriental treatment. Serve it with Grilled Eggplant with Miso, page 122, or Spaghetti Squash with Oriental Vinaigrette, page 122. Since the fish is so light, you could begin the meal with something rich, like Cream of Oriental Mushroom Soup, page 48.

2 (ABOUT 3/4-POUND) CATFISH
   FILLETS

1/4 CUP SOY SAUCE

2 GREEN ONIONS, CUT INTO 2-INCH
   PIECES

2 TABLESPOONS JULIENNED FRESH
   GINGERROOT

▄▄ Place the catfish in a shallow dish with the soy sauce. Turn the fillets to coat them with soy sauce. Let marinate for at least 1 hour.

Bring water to a boil in the bottom of a steamer or wok. Reduce the heat so the water simmers. Place the fish on 1 large or 2 small steamer racks. Arrange half the green onions and half the gingerroot on top of each fillet. Set the rack in place over the simmering water, cover, and steam just until the fish is opaque throughout, about 10 minutes.

Makes 4 servings.

Oriental Bouillabaisse

Bouillabaisse began as a simple fisherman's stew made with the catch of the day, but it has since evolved into a very elegant meal made with a variety of expensive fish and flavored with saffron. The recipe is easily adapted to other cuisines. The primary difference between my Oriental version and the soups served in the south of France is that this one replaces the traditional fish stock with dashi and a bit of fish sauce. It is also served with curry-seasoned mayonnaise rather than the usual garlicky aïoli.

Although bouillabaisse is a very impressive company dish, it is also very easy to make. I cook the base ahead, then return it to a boil and add the seafood just before serving. The soup is so filling that you need only a mixed green salad and some full-flavored goat cheese to round out the meal.

1 LOAF FIRM FRENCH BREAD

1 GARLIC CLOVE, HALVED

2 TABLESPOONS OLIVE OIL

2 TABLESPOONS MINCED FRESH GINGERROOT

2 TABLESPOONS MINCED GARLIC

1 CUP CHOPPED ONION

1/2 POUND DAIKON, PEELED, CUT INTO 1/8-INCH-THICK ROUNDS

1 POUND POTATOES, PEELED, CUT INTO 1/8-INCH-THICK ROUNDS

6 CUPS DASHI, PAGE 55

2 CUPS CHOPPED TOMATOES

1 TEASPOON CRUMBLED SAFFRON THREADS

1/4 CUP SAKE

1/4 CUP FISH SAUCE

1 (2-INCH) PIECE ORANGE PEEL

1 TEASPOON CRUSHED RED PEPPER FLAKES

1 POUND SCROD FILLET, CUT INTO 2-INCH SQUARES

1 POUND FLOUNDER FILLET, CUT INTO 2-INCH SQUARES

12 LITTLE NECK CLAMS IN THE SHELL, WELL SCRUBBED

1 (1-1/4-POUND) LOBSTER, CLAWS HALVED, BODY CUT INTO 6 PIECES WHILE STILL ALIVE

1 RECIPE CURRIED MAYONNAISE, PAGE 186

▬ Preheat the oven to 350F (175C).

Cut the bread on the diagonal into 1/4-inch slices. Rub both sides of each slice of bread with the cut sides of the halved clove of garlic. Then spread the slices in a single layer on a baking sheet. Bake in the preheated oven, turning as needed, until crisp and browned on both sides, 25 to 30 minutes. Set aside.

Heat the oil in a large pot over medium-high heat. Add the gingerroot and minced garlic and cook for 1 minute. Add the onion and cook until softened, about 2 minutes. Add the daikon and potatoes and stir to coat with the oil. Add the Dashi, tomatoes, saffron, sake, fish sauce, orange peel, and red pepper flakes. Bring to a boil and cook for 5 minutes.

Add the scrod, flounder, clams, and lobster, pushing the clams and lobster down into the pot so they are completely covered with liquid. Reduce the heat, cover, and simmer until all the seafood is done, about 15 minutes. The clams should pop open; the fish should be opaque throughout.

Spoon the soup into a tureen. Spread some of the croutons with Curried Mayonnaise; place them in shallow soup bowls. Ladle the soup on top. Serve additional croutons and Curried Mayonnaise on the side.

Makes 6 to 8 servings.

If you are hesitant about serving "foreign foods," this chapter is probably the place to start. The recipes that follow will seem new and unusual, yet familiar enough to accompany roast chicken and poached fish, meat loaf and pork chops. They might encourage you to sample more exotic ingredients and discover a wider world of vegetables and seasonings. Some of these dishes (Cheese Roulade, for example) make excellent vegetarian main courses although most meat-eaters will be happier seeing them at lunch or brunch than at dinner.

Here's a trio of vegetable dishes with oriental touches: Corn with Coconut Milk, page 121; Curried Vegetables, page 126; and Grilled Eggplant with Miso, page 122.

VEGETABLE DISHES

Broccoli with Fermented Black Beans

I hate to see recipes that use only the broccoli flowerets, ignoring the delicious stems. If you have the patience to peel the stems with your fingers rather simply cutting off the sides with a knife, you can preserve much of the irregular shape which makes for pretty slices.

This Chinese preparation is a nice change from plain steamed or boiled broccoli. Serve it with just about anything, from poached fish to roast beef. If you have any leftovers, heat them up with your breakfast omelet.

1 (ABOUT 1-1/4-POUND) BUNCH BROCCOLI

2 TABLESPOONS FERMENTED BLACK BEANS

1 TABLESPOON SAKE

1 TABLESPOON SOY SAUCE

2 TABLESPOONS WATER

1/8 TEASPOON GROUND RED (CAYENNE) PEPPER

2 TABLESPOONS VEGETABLE OIL

2 TEASPOONS MINCED GARLIC

2 TEASPOONS MINCED FRESH GINGERROOT

Remove the flowerets from the broccoli and cut them into pieces no more than 1/2 inch wide. Using a paring knife and your fingers, cut most of the thick peel away from the broccoli stems, leaving the pale, tender shoots underneath. Cut the stems on the diagonal into thin (about 1/8-inch) slices.

In a small bowl, mix together the black beans, sake, soy sauce, water, and red pepper. Set aside.

Heat the oil in a large wok or skillet over high heat. Add the garlic and gingerroot; cook for 30 seconds. Add the broccoli flowerets and stems and sauté for 2 minutes. Add the black bean mixture and cook, stirring, until the broccoli is cooked through but still firm, about 5 minutes longer.

Makes 4 servings.

Broccoli and Mushrooms in Oyster Sauce

Oyster sauce adds a wonderful flavor to broccoli. I like this dish with Meat Loaf, page 86, or Steamed Catfish, page 114, or with scrambled eggs for brunch or a late-night snack. It also makes a good filling for a roulade, as explained on page 126. If you want to turn the dish into a meal without the roulade, add some shrimp or flank steak.

1 (ABOUT 1-1/4-POUND) BUNCH BROCCOLI

2 TABLESPOONS OYSTER SAUCE

2 TABLESPOONS SOY SAUCE

2 TABLESPOONS CHINESE RICE WINE

1/4 CUP WATER

2 TABLESPOONS VEGETABLE OIL

1 TABLESPOON MINCED GARLIC

1 TABLESPOON MINCED FRESH GINGERROOT

1/4 CUP CHOPPED GREEN ONIONS

1/2 POUND FRESH MUSHROOMS, SLICED LENGTHWISE

2 TEASPOONS CORNSTARCH DISSOLVED IN 2 TEASPOONS WATER

Bring a large pot of salted water to a boil.

Cut the flowerets from the broccoli. If you are using this dish as filling for a roulade, cut the flowerets into fairly small pieces; otherwise, you can leave them quite large. Using a paring knife and your fingers, cut most of the thick peel away from the broccoli stems, leaving the pale, tender shoots underneath. Cut the stems on the diagonal into 1/2-inch slices. Drop the broccoli flowerets and stems into the boiling salted water and cook for 1 minute. Drain quickly and cool under cold running water. Drain again and set aside.

In a small bowl, mix together the oyster sauce, soy sauce, wine, and water. Set aside.

Heat the oil in a wok or large skillet over high heat. Add the garlic, gingerroot, and green onions. Cook for 30 seconds. Add the mushrooms and cook until softened, about 2 minutes. Add the broccoli and cook for 1 minute longer. Pour in the oyster sauce mixture and bring to a boil. Cook for about 30 seconds longer, then stir the dissolved cornstarch and pour it into the wok. Cook for 30 seconds longer. The broccoli should be cooked through but still firm, and the sauce should coat everything.

Makes 4 servings.

Spinach with Black Sesame Seeds

The Japanese often sprinkle black sesame seeds on white rice for both color contrast and flavor. The dark seeds are good on spinach, too, although they are hard to see against the deep green leaves.

1 POUND FRESH SPINACH, STEMS REMOVED, WELL WASHED

1 TABLESPOON BLACK SESAME SEEDS, TOASTED IN A DRY SKILLET TO RELEASE THEIR AROMA

1/4 TEASPOON KOSHER SALT

▬ Shake or pat off most but not all of the water clinging to the spinach leaves. Place the spinach in a large pot over medium-high heat. Cook, turning often, until the leaves are evenly wilted, 2 to 3 minutes. Remove to a bowl and toss with the sesame seeds and salt. Serve hot.

Makes 4 servings.

Carrots with Hijiki

Hijiki is sea vegetation with a licoricelike flavor. In dry form, it looks like black tea; when soaked, it turns to moist black shreds. It adds an interesting accent to ordinary steamed carrots—and as a bonus, it's a low-fat source of calcium.

2 TABLESPOONS HIJIKI

1 POUND CARROTS, CUT ON THE DIAGONAL INTO 1/4-INCH SLICES

1 GREEN ONION, SLICED

1/2 TEASPOON KOSHER SALT

PINCH OF GROUND RED (CAYENNE) PEPPER

▬ Place the hijiki in a bowl and add boiling water to cover generously. Let soak for 15 minutes; drain.

Bring water to a boil in the bottom of a steamer or wok. Reduce the heat so the water simmers. Scatter the carrots on a steamer rack lined with cheesecloth; scatter the hijiki over the carrots. Set the steamer rack in place over the simmering water, cover, and steam for 5 minutes. Add the green onion and steam until the carrots are cooked through but still firm, about 5 minutes longer.

Dump the carrots, hijiki, and green onion into a bowl. Season with the salt and red pepper. Serve hot or at room temperature.

Makes 4 servings.

Sesame Carrots

This simple dish gives steamed carrots a lift. It's a good choice whenever you want to add a color contrast to a dark meat like Duck Breasts with Black Bean Sauce, page 74, or Marinated Leg of Lamb, page 80. I particularly like serving the bright carrots in combination with pale potatoes or a leafy green.

1 POUND CARROTS, CUT ON THE DIAGONAL INTO 1/8-INCH SLICES

1 TABLESPOON SESAME SEEDS, TOASTED IN A DRY SKILLET

1 TABLESPOON SESAME OIL

1/4 TEASPOON KOSHER SALT

■ Bring water to a boil in the bottom of a steamer or wok. Reduce the heat so the water simmers. Place the carrots in an even layer on a steamer rack. Set the rack in place over the simmering water, cover, and steam until the carrots are cooked through but still firm, about 5 minutes.

Remove the carrots to a serving bowl and toss with the sesame seeds, sesame oil, and salt.

Makes 4 servings.

Corn with Coconut Milk

Living in the city, it's hard for me to get really fresh-picked corn. When I am lucky enough to find some, I tend to go overboard, buying and cooking so much that there are invariably a few ears left over. When that happens, I just cut the kernels off the cobs and use them in salads, chowders, and quick sautés like this one, great with Soy-Roasted Chicken, page 63. If fresh corn isn't available, substitute frozen kernels rather than the canned variety.

1 TABLESPOON UNSALTED BUTTER

1 TEASPOON MINCED FRESH GINGERROOT

2 TABLESPOONS CHOPPED GREEN ONION

2 CUPS COOKED CORN KERNELS (FROM ABOUT 4 EARS)

1/2 TEASPOON KOSHER SALT

FRESHLY GROUND BLACK PEPPER TO TASTE

1 CUP COCONUT MILK

2 TABLESPOONS ROUGHLY CHOPPED FRESH CILANTRO LEAVES

■ Melt the butter in an 8-inch skillet over medium-high heat. Add the gingerroot and cook for 30 seconds. Add the green onion, corn, salt, and pepper; cook for about 1 minute longer. Add the coconut milk and bring to a boil. Remove the skillet from the heat and stir in the cilantro.

Makes 4 to 6 servings.

Grilled Eggplant with Miso

This is an excellent vegetable dish to serve with other grilled foods—chicken, hamburgers, fish. The miso topping makes for a rich, flavorful sauce. The Oriental eggplants called for here are smaller and prettier than the Western variety. If you can't find them, substitute a regular eggplant, sliced about 1 inch thick.

V
E
G
E
T
A
B
L
E

D
I
S
H
E
S

1/4 CUP MISO
2 TABLESPOONS WATER
1 TABLESPOON SUGAR
1/2 TEASPOON GRATED FRESH
    GINGERROOT
4 (5-OUNCE) ORIENTAL EGGPLANTS
VEGETABLE OIL

■ Preheat a grill or broiler until hot.

In a small bowl, mix together the miso, water, sugar, and gingerroot. Set aside.

Cut each eggplant in half lengthwise. With a sharp knife, score the skin of each eggplant half several times. Brush the flesh with some oil. Place the eggplants on the grill or in a broiler pan—cut side down on the grill, cut side up in a broiler pan. Grill or broil until the cut side is soft and brown, about 2 minutes. Turn and continue to cook until soft throughout, about 3 minutes longer.

Place the eggplant halves, cut side up, on a platter. Spoon the miso sauce on top. Serve warm.

Makes 4 servings.

Spaghetti Squash with Oriental Vinaigrette

Spaghetti squash is fun to eat and easy to make for a small group. In this recipe, the baked squash is tossed with Chinese vinegar and soy sauce and served at room temperature. It's a low-calorie, healthful side dish for chicken, pork, or fish, and a great choice for picnics and buffet tables, too.

1 (4-1/2-POUND) SPAGHETTI
    SQUASH
1 POUND PLUM TOMATOES, CORED,
    SEEDED, CUT INTO THIN STRIPS
1/4 CUP CHOPPED FRESH CILANTRO
    LEAVES
2 TABLESPOONS CHINESE BLACK
    VINEGAR
2 TABLESPOONS SOY SAUCE
FRESHLY GROUND BLACK PEPPER
    TO TASTE

■ Preheat the oven to 350F (175C).

Cut the squash in half lengthwise; scoop out the seeds and stringy insides. Place the halves, cut side down, in a shallow baking dish. Add enough water to come about 1/2 inch up the sides of the squash. Bake, uncovered, in the preheated oven until tender, about 45 minutes.

Place the squash halves, cut side up, on your work surface. With a fork, pull out the pulp; it will separate into strands somewhat like spaghetti. Place the squash strands in a bowl and add the tomatoes, cilantro, vinegar, soy sauce, and pepper. Toss to mix thoroughly. Serve warm or at room temperature.

Makes 6 to 8 servings.

Grilled Vegetable Skewers

Once you have the grill lit to make Grilled Salmon with Miso, page 111, or Lamb Kabobs with Hoisin, page 78, it's easy to grill the vegetables, too. Threading them on skewers saves space on the grill and assures everyone of getting a colorful assortment.

1 MEDIUM RED BELL PEPPER, CORED, SEEDED, CUT INTO 1-1/2- TO 2-INCH PIECES

2 (ABOUT 6-OUNCE) ORIENTAL EGGPLANTS, CUT CROSSWISE INTO 1-INCH SLICES

1 LARGE (1/2-POUND) RED ONION, CUT INTO 1-INCH WEDGES, ROOT END INTACT

12 LARGE FRESH MUSHROOM CAPS

2 TABLESPOONS RICE WINE VINEGAR

2 TABLESPOONS SOY SAUCE

1 TABLESPOON MIRIN

2 TABLESPOONS SESAME OIL

2 TABLESPOONS PEANUT OIL

1/4 TEASPOON CRUSHED RED PEPPER FLAKES

1 TEASPOON MINCED FRESH GINGERROOT

1 TABLESPOON SESAME SEEDS, TOASTED IN A DRY SKILLET, GROUND TO A COARSE POWDER

On four 10-inch metal skewers, alternate bell pepper pieces, eggplant slices, onion wedges, and mushroom caps; begin and end each skewer with mushroom caps, rounded sides facing in.

To make the sauce, in a bowl, whisk together the vinegar, soy sauce, mirin, sesame oil, peanut oil, red pepper flakes, and gingerroot.

To cook, preheat a grill until hot. Brush each skewer with some of the sauce. Place the skewers on the grill and cook until all the vegetables are tender, about 15 minutes, turning the skewers as needed and brushing the vegetables with with the sauce occasionally. Serve with extra sauce and a sprinkling of ground sesame seeds.

Makes 4 servings.

Mo-shu Vegetables

The bits of egg in any mo-shu mixture must have reminded someone of delicate cassia blossoms, hence the dish's name—*mo-shu* is Chinese for "cassia blossoms." This is a fairly traditional vegetarian version of mo-shu. However, I serve it with warm flour tortillas rather than mo-shu pancakes, which are difficult to find and time-consuming to make. The pancakes and tortillas taste much the same, and tortillas are now a supermarket staple.

VEGETABLE DISHES

1/2 CUP DRIED TIGER LILY BUDS

2 TABLESPOONS CLOUD EARS

3/4 CUP SOYBEAN SPROUTS

6 LARGE EGGS

2 TABLESPOONS PLUS 1-1/2 TEASPOONS LIGHT SOY SAUCE

1-1/2 TEASPOONS SUGAR

5 TABLESPOONS VEGETABLE OIL

4 GREEN ONIONS, SLICED ON THE DIAGONAL

4 LARGE SLICES FRESH GINGERROOT

3/4 CUP JULIENNED CARROTS

3/4 CUP JULIENNED GREEN BEANS

3 TABLESPOONS CHINESE RICE WINE

8 FLOUR TORTILLAS, WARMED

HOISIN SAUCE

Place the tiger lily buds and cloud ears in separate large bowls; add boiling water to the bowls to cover the lily buds and cloud ears. Let soak for 20 minutes (the cloud ears will expand considerably).

Drain the lily buds and squeeze them dry. Cut off and discard any tough ends; then shred the buds lengthwise with your fingers. Place the shredded buds in a bowl. Squeeze the cloud ears dry and roughly chop them. Add to the lily buds. Set aside.

Bring a small pot of water to a boil. Add the bean sprouts and cook for 1 minute. Drain well and pat dry. Set aside.

In a bowl, whisk together the eggs, 1-1/2 teaspoons soy sauce, and the sugar. Heat 2 tablespoons oil in a wok over medium heat. Add the egg mixture and cook, turning often, until the eggs are set but still moist. Break them into small pieces with a spatula or wooden spoon and turn into a clean bowl.

Wipe the wok clean with a paper towel; then heat the remaining 3 tablespoons oil over high heat. Add the green onions and gingerroot. Cook, stirring, for 1 minute. Add the carrots and beans; cook, stirring, for 2 minutes longer. Add the bean sprouts, lily buds, and cloud ears; then stir in the remaining 2 tablespoons soy sauce and the wine. Toss and bring to a boil. Add the eggs and cook for 1 minute longer.

Arrange the vegetable mixture on a platter with the tortillas. Set a bowl of hoisin sauce alongside. To eat, spread some hoisin on a tortilla and top with some of the vegetable mixture; roll up and eat with your hands.

Makes 4 servings.

Curried Vegetables

I make this dish for company because the actual cooking is so brief that I can do it while I'm finishing the main course or assembling the plates. The curry flavor is mild, but still noticeable enough to give the sauce an intriguing character. Serve with Soy-Roasted Chicken, page 63, Steamed Catfish, page 114, or Veal with Ginger, page 89.

2 TABLESPOONS UNSALTED BUTTER

1/2 POUND GREEN BEANS, ENDS BROKEN OFF, HALVED LENGTHWISE

1/2 POUND CARROTS, CUT INTO 4-INCH-LONG MATCHSTICKS

1/2 TEASPOON KOSHER SALT

1 TEASPOON RED CURRY PASTE, PAGE 189

1 TABLESPOON SAKE

1/2 POUND ZUCCHINI, CUT INTO 4-INCH-LONG MATCHSTICKS

■ Melt the butter in a large skillet over medium-high heat. Add the beans, carrots, and salt. Cook for 2 minutes.

Stir the Red Curry Paste and sake together to dissolve the curry paste. Stir the curry mixture and the zucchini into the skillet. Cook until the vegetables are cooked through but still firm, about 1 minute longer.

Makes 6 servings.

VEGETABLE DISHES

Cheese Roulade with Broccoli Filling

A roulade is a soufflé baked in a jelly-roll pan, so it doesn't rise to spectacular heights—and when it cools, what did rise deflates. Nonetheless, the result is a delicious, tender sheet that can be rolled around a range of fillings to make a perfect brunch or supper dish. Many stir-fries, such as Shrimp and Broccoli de Rabe, page 103, and Mo-Shu Vegetables, page 124, are excellent in roulades. In this case, I used Broccoli and Mushrooms in Oyster Sauce with a bit of Tomato Salsa on the side.

Although the process sounds complicated, a roulade can be finished off fairly quickly if you prepare the soufflé base and cut up all the vegetables in advance. About half an hour before serving, beat the egg whites and fold them into the base. You'll have time to stir-fry the broccoli while the roulade is cooling.

To complete the meal, you need only a beautiful salad of radicchio, endive, and Bibb lettuce with slices of Parmesan cheese.

3 TABLESPOONS FRESHLY GRATED
  PARMESAN CHEESE

3 TABLESPOONS UNSALTED BUTTER

3 TABLESPOONS ALL-PURPOSE
  FLOUR

1-1/4 CUPS MILK

1 TEASPOON DIJON MUSTARD

3 OUNCES SWISS CHEESE, GRATED
  (ABOUT 3/4 CUP)

1/4 TEASPOON GROUND RED
  (CAYENNE) PEPPER

1/2 TEASPOON KOSHER SALT

5 LARGE EGGS, SEPARATED

1 RECIPE BROCCOLI AND
  MUSHROOMS IN OYSTER SAUCE,
  PAGE 119

1 RECIPE TOMATO SALSA, PAGE 182

Preheat the oven to 400F (205C).

Lightly butter an 11- by 17-1/2-inch jelly-roll pan. Line it with wax paper, letting the paper hang over the pan by about 1 inch at either end. Butter the paper and sprinkle on 1 tablespoon Parmesan cheese. Set aside.

To prepare the roulade base, melt 3 tablespoons butter in a 1-quart saucepan over medium heat. Add the flour and stir to blend, then cook for 1 minute. Slowly add the milk, stirring vigorously to make a smooth sauce. Increase the heat, bring the sauce to a boil, and cook for 30 seconds. Remove the pan from the heat and scrape the sauce into a clean bowl. Stir in the mustard, Swiss cheese, red pepper, and salt. Let the sauce cool a bit, then stir in the egg yolks. If not finishing the roulade at this time, cover the base and refrigerate.

In a clean bowl, beat the egg whites until stiff but not dry. Carefully fold the egg whites into the base. Spread the mixture gently in the prepared pan, smoothing the top with a spatula. Bake in the preheated oven until lightly browned and set, 12 to 14 minutes.

Place the pan on a rack and let cool for 10 minutes. Meanwhile, prepare Broccoli and Mushrooms in Oyster Sauce. Keep warm.

Butter a sheet of foil large enough to cover the jelly-roll pan. If necessary, use 2 overlapping pieces of foil. Sprinkle the remaining 2 tablespoons Parmesan cheese on top of the roulade. Cover the pan with the buttered foil, then turn the pan over. Carefully lift the pan from the roulade. With your fingers and a small knife, peel away the wax paper.

Drain the broccoli mixture and spread it across the roulade in an even line from end to end, about 1 inch above a 17-1/2 inch side. Using the foil to help you, carefully roll the roulade around the broccoli mixture. Still using the foil, turn the roulade onto a long platter. Discard the foil. Cut the roulade into slices about 1 inch thick. Serve with salsa on the side.

Makes 4 to 6 servings.

Mixed Vegetables with Cellophane Noodles

This is the kind of vegetable dish that keeps meat eaters happily coming back for more. It's a variation on the Korean *jap chae.* Serve it with Meat Loaf, page 86, Spicy Scallops, page 105, or an omelet.

2 OUNCES CELLOPHANE NOODLES

8 DRIED CHINESE MUSHROOMS (ABOUT 1/2 OZ. *TOTAL*)

2 TABLESPOONS SESAME OIL

3 TABLESPOONS SOY SAUCE

1 TABLESPOON SAKE

2 TABLESPOONS SUGAR

2 TABLESPOONS VEGETABLE OIL

1 TABLESPOON MINCED FRESH GINGERROOT

2 CELERY STALKS, THINLY SLICED ON THE DIAGONAL

2 CARROTS (1/4 POUND *TOTAL*), CUT INTO JULIENNE STRIPS

1 LARGE (6-OUNCE) ONION, SLICED

1/2 POUND CHINESE CABBAGE, SHREDDED

1/2 POUND ZUCCHINI, THINLY SLICED ON THE DIAGONAL

2 CUPS SPINACH LEAVES, STEMS REMOVED, WELL WASHED, DRIED, CUT INTO THIN STRIPS

1 TABLESPOON SESAME SEEDS, TOASTED IN A DRY SKILLET

Place the noodles and mushrooms in separate bowls. Add boiling water to the bowls to cover the noodles and mushrooms. Let the noodles soak for 10 minutes, then drain well. Let the mushrooms soak for 20 minutes, then drain and squeeze dry. Cut off and discard the stems; cut the caps into thin strips. Set the noodles and mushrooms aside.

In a separate bowl, mix together the sesame oil, soy sauce, sake, and sugar. Set aside.

Heat the vegetable oil in a wok or large skillet over high heat. Add the gingerroot and cook for 30 seconds. Add the celery and carrots and cook for 30 seconds longer. Add the onion and cook for 2 minutes, then add the cabbage and cook for 2 minutes longer. Add the zucchini and toss to mix. Stir in the mushrooms and spinach and cook for 1 minute. Stir in the soy sauce mixture, then the noodles. Cook for about 30 seconds longer. Pour into a bowl or deep platter and scatter the sesame seeds on top.

Makes 4 to 6 servings.

Stir-Fried Watercress with Garlic

Once known only as an essential ingredient in fancy sandwiches at British teas, watercress is increasingly available in American markets. The peppery-tasting leaves are wonderful raw in salads and cooked in soups and sauces, but watercress really gets to star when served by itself with a liberal lacing of garlic. Try this dish the next time your kids don't want spinach.

2 TABLESPOONS OLIVE OIL

1/4 CUP MINCED GARLIC

2 BUNCHES WATERCRESS, RINSED BUT NOT DRIED, LARGE STEMS REMOVED

1/4 CUP CHICKEN STOCK

1/2 TEASPOON KOSHER SALT

▬ Heat the oil in a wok over medium-high heat. Add the garlic and cook for 30 seconds. Add the watercress and cook until it begins to wilt, 1 to 2 minutes. Add the stock and salt; cook until the watercress is tender, about 2 minutes longer.

Makes 4 to 6 servings.

Snow Pea Quiche

This unusual quiche is flavored with hoisin, giving it a most exotic taste. Serve it as a first course before a grilled or roasted bird, or as a supper or lunch with a salad of watercress and endive.

1 TEASPOON UNSALTED BUTTER

1 TEASPOON MINCED FRESH GINGERROOT

1/4 CUP CHOPPED GREEN ONIONS

1 (10-INCH) PARTIALLY BAKED PASTRY SHELL, PAGE 202

1/4 POUND GRUYÈRE CHEESE, GRATED (ABOUT 1 CUP)

1/4 POUND SNOW PEAS, STRINGS REMOVED, CUT INTO 1/2-INCH PIECES, BLANCHED FOR 1 MINUTE

1 CUP WHIPPING CREAM

1/4 CUP HOISIN SAUCE

3 LARGE EGGS

1/8 TEASPOON GROUND RED (CAYENNE) PEPPER

▬ Preheat the oven to 400F (205C).

Melt the butter in a small skillet over medium heat. Add the gingerroot and green onions and sauté for 1 minute, then scrape into the prepared Pastry Shell. Sprinkle the cheese on top. Scatter the snow peas over the cheese.

In a bowl, whisk together the cream, hoisin sauce, eggs, and red pepper. Pour the cream mixture over the ingredients in the Pastry Shell.

Bake in the preheated oven until set, about 30 minutes. Let cool slightly, then cut into wedges and serve.

Makes 6 to 8 servings.

I made so many vegetable dishes in working on this book that I divided them somewhat arbitrarily into smaller groups. In this chapter are all kinds of room-temperature salads to serve as first courses or with meat or fish main dishes. I often make more than one at a time, offering my family and guests a choice of tastes and textures as well as adding color to the plate. Many of these salads can be made ahead and left to marinate in the refrigerator, ready to pull out for picnics, parties, and unexpected company. You'll also find a few dishes meant to be served hot or warm, from simple Grilled Shiitake to a spicy Cornbread Stuffing.

Like the recipes in the last chapter, most of these dishes will seem familiar at first. However, the flavors are generally more Asian than appearances might indicate.

Baby Corn Salad, page 134, is garnished with Sweet & Sour Lotus Root, page 140.

SALADS

Ratatouille with Sambal

In the Mediterranean, beautiful ripe tomatoes are often cooked with zucchini and eggplant to make a vegetarian stew called *ratatouille*. I've adapted the recipe to the East, livening up the mixture with a bit of sambal and using the skinny Oriental eggplants that never seem to be bitter. Like the original version, this ratatouille makes a wonderful filling for omelets and tastes great on ham and cheese sandwiches or over hamburgers. Serve it hot or cold.

SALADS

2 TABLESPOONS OLIVE OIL

1 TABLESPOON MINCED FRESH GINGERROOT

3 GARLIC CLOVES, MINCED

4 GREEN ONIONS, CHOPPED

2 (ABOUT 6-OUNCE) ORIENTAL EGGPLANTS, CUT INTO 1/8-INCH-THICK ROUNDS

2 MEDIUM (1/4-POUND) ZUCCHINI, CUT INTO 1/4-INCH-THICK ROUNDS

1 RED BELL PEPPER, CORED, SEEDED, CUT INTO 1/2-INCH SQUARES

1 GREEN BELL PEPPER, CORED, SEEDED, CUT INTO 1/2-INCH SQUARES

1 (14-OUNCE) CAN PLUM TOMATOES, DRAINED

1-1/2 TABLESPOONS RICE WINE VINEGAR

2 TABLESPOONS SAKE

1 TABLESPOON SAMBAL OELEK

1/4 CUP CHOPPED FRESH CILANTRO LEAVES

Heat the oil in a large skillet over high heat. Add the gingerroot and garlic and cook for 1 minute. Add the green onions and cook for 1 minute longer. Add the eggplants, zucchini, and red and green bell peppers; cook for about 1 minute longer to soften slightly. Crush the drained tomatoes with your hand or a spoon and add them to the skillet; then add the vinegar, sake, and sambal. Stir to mix well. Reduce the heat, cover the skillet, and simmer until the vegetables are soft but still retain their shape, about 15 minutes. Taste and adjust the seasonings. Stir in the cilantro. Serve hot, warm, or at room temperature.

Makes 4 servings.

Tabbouleh

Tabbouleh is a Middle Eastern salad of cracked wheat, also called bulgur. It's an excellent choice for summer meals, especially good as an accompaniment to cold roast chicken or ham. Instead of the usual mint, I've seasoned the salad with cilantro and sushi su, sweetened Japanese rice vinegar.

When you buy the bulgur, make sure it's the unflavored variety. If your supermarket doesn't have it, look in health food stores.

1 CUP BULGUR WHEAT

4 CUPS BOILING WATER

1/4 CUP SUSHI SU

2 TEASPOONS SOY SAUCE

1/2 CUP 1/4-INCH RADISH CUBES

1/2 CUP CHOPPED GREEN ONIONS

1/4 CUP CHOPPED PINK PICKLED GINGER

1/4 CUP CHOPPED FRESH CILANTRO LEAVES

■ Place the bulgur in a large bowl. Add the boiling water and let soak until the bulgur is soft, 1 to 2 hours. Drain well.

Toss the bulgur with the sushi su and soy sauce. Stir in the radish cubes, green onions, ginger, and cilantro. Serve at room temperature.

Makes about 4 cups.

Pickled Beets and Ginger

Paper-thin slices of pale pink pickled ginger, traditionally served with sushi and sashimi, are a delicate palate refresher. Although they lose their pretty color when mixed with beets, the sacrifice is worth it because they add such a wonderful tanginess to the sweet vegetable. I serve this pickled salad in the summer with Soy-Roasted Chicken, page 63, or Marinated Leg of Lamb, page 80, and corn on the cob.

Since the salad lasts for a week or more, I often double the recipe and keep it in the refrigerator to serve with sandwiches or spoon over hamburgers.

2 POUNDS BEETS, ALL BUT 1 INCH OF ROOTS CUT OFF, WELL WASHED

1/2 CUP THINLY SLICED PINK PICKLED GINGER

1/4 CUP RICE WINE VINEGAR

4 TEASPOONS MIRIN

2 TEASPOONS KOSHER SALT

■ Place the beets in a 3-quart pot and add water to cover generously. Bring to a boil; then reduce the heat, cover, and simmer until the beets are soft enough to pierce through easily with a skewer, 30 to 45 minutes. (The cooking time varies with the age of the beets.)

Drain the beets and let them cool. The skins should be soft enough to come off when you rub them with your fingers. Rub off the skins; cut any hard bits of skin away with a small knife.

Cut the beets into thin rounds. Place them in a bowl with the ginger, vinegar, mirin, and salt. Stir to mix well. Let stand at room temperature for at least an hour to let the flavors develop.

Makes about 3 cups.

Kim Chee

All kinds of foods can be pickled, but probably no pickled dish is as interesting as *kim chee,* spicy sour cabbage that is as essential to most Korean homes as salt and pepper are to American kitchens. It is a wonderful addition to many meals, especially when used in unusual ways. Try some on your next hamburger or roast beef sandwich; serve it as a change from coleslaw. The stuff is really addictive.

1 (2-POUND) HEAD CHINESE CABBAGE, HALVED LENGTHWISE, CUT CROSSWISE INTO 1-INCH PIECES

1/4 CUP KOSHER SALT

1 TABLESPOON MINCED GARLIC

1 TABLESPOON MINCED FRESH GINGERROOT

4 GREEN ONIONS, CHOPPED

2 TEASPOONS CHILI POWDER

1 TABLESPOON SUGAR

Place a layer of cabbage in a large bowl. Sprinkle with some of the salt. Continue layering cabbage and salt until both are used up. Place a plate over the cabbage, set some cans or other weights on it, and let stand at room temperature for 1 day to wilt the cabbage.

Pour off the liquid that has accumulated in the bowl; then add the garlic, gingerroot, green onions, chili powder, and sugar. Stir to mix well. Place in a clean bowl, cover, and let stand at room temperature until the cabbage is sour enough for your taste—about 3 days in winter, less time in summer. Then put the kim chee in a jar, cover, and refrigerate. It will keep for months.

Makes about 4 cups.

Baby Corn Salad

Tiny ears of yellow corn add a splash of color to this Mediterranean salad, flavored with an Eastern vinaigrette. It's a perfect accompaniment to any grilled dish. For a first course, spoon it into cupped leaves of Boston lettuce. Be sure to let the salad marinate for at least an hour so the cheese and corn can absorb the flavors of the dressing.

2 (15-OUNCE) CANS BABY CORN,
    DRAINED, SOAKED IN ICE WATER
    FOR 30 MINUTES
1/2 CUP CHOPPED RED ONION
1/4 POUND MOZZARELLA CHEESE,
    CUT INTO 1/4-INCH CUBES
1/2 CUP CHOPPED PITTED KALAMATA
    OLIVES
1 CUP FRESH TOMATO STRIPS
2 TABLESPOONS CHINESE BLACK
    VINEGAR
4 TEASPOONS SOY SAUCE
2 TEASPOONS DIJON MUSTARD
1/4 TEASPOON FRESHLY GROUND
    BLACK PEPPER
1/4 CUP OLIVE OIL
2 TEASPOONS SESAME OIL

▬ Drain the corn and pat dry. Place it in a bowl with the onion, cheese, olives, and tomato strips. In a separate bowl, whisk together the vinegar, soy sauce, mustard, and pepper. Whisk in the olive oil and sesame oil. Pour the dressing over the salad and mix well.

Let marinate at room temperature for at least 1 hour before serving.

Makes 6 to 8 servings.

Straw Mushrooms à la Grecque

As a rule, I find that canning destroys most of the charm and flavor of mushrooms. However, straw mushrooms have such a wonderful texture that they hold up to the process. They still need a little help with seasoning, though, and this variation on a typical Greek marinade works very well. Serve the mushrooms with salami and cheese as part of an antipasto assortment, add them to green salads, or drain them and serve as is with drinks. They will keep in the refrigerator for at least a week.

1 (15-OUNCE) CAN WHOLE PEELED
    STRAW MUSHROOMS, DRAINED,
    RINSED
1/4 CUP OLIVE OIL
2 TABLESPOONS LEMON JUICE
1/2 CUP WATER
1 LARGE GARLIC CLOVE
1 DRIED RED CHILI, HALVED
1 TEASPOON KOSHER SALT
1/2 BAY LEAF
2 LARGE SLICES FRESH
    GINGERROOT

▬ Bring a small pot of water to a boil. Add the mushrooms and cook for 1 minute. Drain well and place in a bowl.

Place the oil, lemon juice, water, garlic, chili, salt, bay leaf, and gingerroot in a separate small pot. Bring to a boil; then reduce heat and simmer for 5 minutes. Pour the lemon juice mixture over the mushrooms, cover, and let marinate for at least several hours.

Makes 2 cups.

Bean Sprout Salad

This makes a nice change from coleslaw at a picnic or barbecue. The flavor of the bean sprouts improves with blanching.

8 CUPS SOYBEAN SPROUTS

1 CUP JULIENNED CARROTS

1/4 CUP SLICED GREEN ONIONS

1/2 CUP SUSHI SU

1/4 TEASPOON FRESHLY GROUND
   WHITE PEPPER

▬ Bring a large pot of water to a boil. Add the bean sprouts and carrots and cook for 1 minute. Drain well. Place the warm vegetables in a bowl with the green onions, sushi su, and white pepper. Toss well and refrigerate until thoroughly chilled.
   Makes 8 cups.

SALADS

Sesame Potato Salad

This version of the old American standby has water chestnuts for crunch and an Asian-inspired dressing. Nonetheless, it fits in perfectly at any picnic or barbecue with ham sandwiches or hamburgers. Season the potatoes while they are still warm, so they'll absorb more of the vinaigrette.

2 TABLESPOONS RICE WINE
   VINEGAR

1/4 CUP SESAME OIL

1 TABLESPOON SOY SAUCE

FRESHLY GROUND WHITE PEPPER
   TO TASTE

2 POUNDS POTATOES, BOILED,
   PEELED, CUT INTO 1-INCH
   CHUNKS

1/3 CUP SLICED WATER CHESTNUTS

1/4 CUP SLICED GREEN ONIONS

1/2 CUP 1/2-INCH RED BELL PEPPER
   SQUARES

▬ In a bowl, whisk together the vinegar, sesame oil, soy sauce, and white pepper. Add the potatoes, water chestnuts, green onions, and bell pepper. Toss to mix well.
   Makes 4 to 6 servings.

Baked Eggplant Salad

Long popular in Eastern and Middle Eastern countries, eggplant has now become common in the West. It can be grilled, sautéed, or baked; for this salad, it's baked with bell peppers. The fish sauce adds a subtle flavor that few will identify but most will enjoy. Because of that bit of fish, this salad is excellent with steamed or grilled seafood. The red strips of peppers and tomatoes are a pretty contrast to pale fish.

When buying eggplant, choose one that feels very light. That means it has few seeds.

1 (1-POUND) EGGPLANT

2 GARLIC CLOVES, THINLY SLICED

2 RED BELL PEPPERS

1 MEDIUM (1/4-POUND) TOMATO, CORED, THINLY SLICED

1 TABLESPOON FISH SAUCE

2 TABLESPOONS RICE WINE VINEGAR

1 TABLESPOON OLIVE OIL

— Preheat the oven to 400F (205C).

With a small, sharp knife, cut slits all over the eggplant. Push a slice of garlic into each slit. Place the eggplant and the bell peppers in a baking dish. Bake in the preheated oven until very soft, about 45 minutes, turning the eggplant and peppers as needed to brown evenly. Let cool.

Cut the stem off the eggplant. With your fingers or a paring knife, peel off all the skin. Cut or tear the flesh into long, thin strips. Discard any big lumps of seeds but leave the rest. Place the eggplant in a bowl with the garlic slices that cling to the pulp.

The skin on the bell peppers should be soft enough to peel off easily. Remove as much skin as possible, then discard the stems, cores, and seeds. Cut the flesh into long, thin strips and add to the eggplant. Then add the tomato, fish sauce, vinegar, and oil. Toss to mix well. Taste and adjust the seasonings.

Makes 3 cups.

Daikon Chips

Deep-fried rounds of daikon are slightly sweet, excellent served in place of French fries with Meat Loaf, page 86, Shiitake Hamburgers, page 87, or Grilled Shark, page 114. Although they brown like potato chips, they do not get as crisp.

VEGETABLE OIL FOR DEEP-FRYING

1 POUND DAIKON, PEELED, CUT INTO VERY THIN ROUNDS

KOSHER SALT

— In a deep pot, heat 4 inches of oil to 400F (205C) or until a 1-inch bread cube turns golden brown in 20 seconds.

Drop a few daikon slices into the oil; cook until browned, about 1 minute on each side. Drain on paper towels and sprinkle with salt. Repeat to cook the remaining daikon. Adjust the heat as needed to keep the temperature of the oil constant.

Makes 4 to 6 servings.

Three-Radish Salad

Combining the tastes and textures of red, black, and white (daikon), radishes makes for an interesting salad, excellent with grilled foods.

2 BUNCHES RED RADISHES, COARSELY GRATED

2 MEDIUM (ABOUT 6-OUNCE) BLACK RADISHES, PEELED, COARSELY GRATED (SEE NOTE BELOW)

3/4 POUND DAIKON, PEELED, COARSELY GRATED

1/2 CUP LIME JUICE

3 TABLESPOONS SOY SAUCE

1/4 CUP OLIVE OIL

1/2 TEASPOON HOT SESAME (CHILI) OIL

2 TABLESPOONS FRESH THYME OR 2 TEASPOONS DRIED LEAF THYME

■■ Place the red and black radishes and the daikon in a large bowl. In a separate bowl, whisk together the lime juice, soy sauce, olive oil, hot sesame oil, and thyme. Pour the dressing over the radishes and stir to mix well. Let stand at room temperature for at least 30 minutes before serving.

Makes 8 to 10 servings.

NOTE: Black radishes are much larger than red ones—more the size of a turnip—and not as sharp in flavor. Look for them in produce stores.

Carrot and Jicama Salad

Jicama, native to Mexico, is a crunchy tuber that looks something like a large, brown, thick-skinned turnip. It is delicious both cooked and raw. In this dish, grated raw jicama is mixed with carrots and tossed with a Thai vinaigrette for a pretty orange and white salad, good with all kinds of roasted or grilled meats or fish. In the summer, I like to serve a trio of salads, combining Carrot and Jicama Salad, Pickled Beets and Ginger, page 133, and Cucumber Salad, page 139, for a rainbow of colors on the plate.

1 POUND JICAMA, PEELED, GRATED

1 POUND CARROTS, PEELED, GRATED

1/4 CUP FISH SAUCE

2 TABLESPOONS SUGAR

2 LARGE GARLIC CLOVES, MINCED

1/3 CUP LIME JUICE

FRESHLY GROUND BLACK PEPPER TO TASTE

2/3 CUP CHOPPED ROASTED UNSALTED PEANUTS

■■ Place the jicama and carrots in a bowl with the fish sauce, sugar, garlic, lime juice, and pepper. Toss to mix well. Sprinkle the peanuts on top.

Makes about 4 cups.

Cucumber Salad

Wakame—dried green sea vegetation that turns soft and slippery when soaked—adds color and flavor contrast to this Japanese salad. It's excellent with cold cuts as well as hot meats. Like most cucumber salads, this one will last for several days in the refrigerator, although the cucumbers will get softer as they sit.

1/8 OUNCE WAKAME

1 POUND (ABOUT 5) KIRBY (PICKLING) CUCUMBERS

1 TEASPOON MINCED FRESH GINGERROOT

1/4 CUP RICE WINE VINEGAR

1 TABLESPOON SOY SAUCE

1 TEASPOON SUGAR

Place the wakame in a bowl and cover with warm water. Let soak for 25 minutes. Drain well and cut away the hard edge. Cut the wakame into 1-inch pieces. Place in a clean bowl.

Cut the cucumbers into thin slices; place in the bowl with the wakame. Add the gingerroot. In a separate bowl, mix together the vinegar, soy sauce, and sugar. Pour over the cucumber mixture and toss to mix.

Makes about 3 cups.

Coleslaw

The word "coleslaw" comes from *koolsla*, Dutch for "cabbage salad." This one uses Chinese cabbage, daikon, and rice wine vinegar, but it's as good as any creamy version alongside grilled chicken or on a roast beef sandwich.

4 CUPS SHREDDED CHINESE CABBAGE

1 TABLESPOON PLUS 1 TEASPOON KOSHER SALT

2 TABLESPOONS WATER

1 LARGE CARROT, SHREDDED

1/4 POUND DAIKON, PEELED, SHREDDED

2 TEASPOONS MINCED FRESH GINGERROOT

1/4 CUP RICE WINE VINEGAR

1 TABLESPOON VEGETABLE OIL

FRESHLY GROUND BLACK PEPPER TO TASTE

Place the cabbage in a large bowl with 1 tablespoon salt and 2 tablespoons water. Place a plate, dropped lid (otoshi-buta), or other weight on the cabbage. Let stand for 30 minutes. Rinse the cabbage under cold running water, drain, and squeeze dry.

Place the cabbage in a bowl with the carrot, daikon, gingerroot, vinegar, oil, remaining 1 teaspoon salt, and pepper. Toss to mix well. Let stand at room temperature for at least 1 hour before serving.

Makes about 2 cups.

Sweet and Sour Lotus Root

Whenever my niece is over, she always checks to see if I have a jar of Sweet and Sour Lotus Root on hand. It's a delicious snack and an interesting addition to green salads. Much as I like to use the slices whole to show off their wonderful shape, I often cut them up and add them to tuna or egg salad, sushi rice, and other dishes. They keep for months.

2 TABLESPOONS RICE WINE
  VINEGAR
1/2 POUND LOTUS ROOT
3/4 CUP SUSHI SU

Add the rice wine vinegar to a large bowl of cold water. Peel the lotus root and cut it into thin rounds. As you cut the slices, drop them into the acidulated water to preserve their white color. Let soak for 5 minutes.

Meanwhile, bring a 2-quart pot of fresh water to a boil. Drain the lotus root and add to the boiling water. Cook just until the lotus root is tender but still crisp, about 2 minutes. Drain well and toss with the sushi su.

Spoon into a jar, cover, and refrigerate until chilled.

Makes about 3 cups.

SALADS

Grilled Shiitake

Fabulously meaty shiitake mushrooms were long known in this country only in their dried form. Today, however, several companies cultivate the mushrooms and sell them fresh in gourmet produce markets. Since shiitake are expensive, I like to cook them quite simply on the grill, as a special accompaniment to any plain grilled meat, fish, or poultry. I often cook red onion wedges and poblano chili strips alongside for an unusual array of vegetables my guests always love.

1 TABLESPOON OLIVE OIL
1 TABLESPOON SOY SAUCE
8 FRESH SHIITAKE MUSHROOMS
  (ABOUT 1/4 POUND TOTAL)

Preheat a grill until hot.

In a bowl, mix together the oil and soy sauce. Cut off the mushroom stems (they are too tough to eat, but you can add them to soup for extra flavor). Brush the mushroom caps on both sides with the oil mixture. Place on the grill and cook until soft, about 2 minutes on each side.

Makes 4 servings.

Cranberry-Kumquat Relish

Tart kumquats taste wonderful with cranberries. This easy-to-make relish is a good side dish with braised brisket or Thanksgiving turkey; you can serve any leftovers on turkey sandwiches. Make the relish a day ahead to let the flavors develop. If you like a sweeter flavor, use more sugar.

3/4 POUND (3-1/3 CUPS) CRANBERRIES, WASHED, DRAINED

1 CUP THINLY SLICED KUMQUATS, SEEDS REMOVED

2 (1/2-INCH) CUBES FRESH GINGERROOT

2 CUPS SUGAR

1/2 CUP ORANGE JUICE

1/2 CUP CHOPPED WALNUTS

■ Place the cranberries, kumquats, gingerroot, sugar, and orange juice in a 2-quart saucepan. Bring to a boil over medium heat, stirring to dissolve the sugar. Boil until all the cranberries pop, about 10 minutes. Remove to a bowl and stir in the walnuts. Refrigerate until ready to serve. Just before serving, remove the gingerroot.

Makes 3 cups.

Lotus Root Remoulade

The French often serve hors d'oeuvre assortments that include celery root in a remoulade sauce. Crunchy lotus root works just as well, and it's slightly more exotic. The only drawback to the substitution is that the beautiful, lacy pattern of the lotus root is somewhat masked by the thick sauce.

2 TABLESPOONS RICE WINE VINEGAR

10 OUNCES LOTUS ROOT

1/2 CUP MAYONNAISE

1 TEASPOON MINCED SHALLOT

1 TEASPOON DIJON MUSTARD

1 TEASPOON MINCED CAPERS

1 TEASPOON LEMON JUICE

■ Add the vinegar to a large bowl of cold water. Peel the lotus root and cut it into thin rounds. As you cut the slices, drop them into the acidulated water to preserve their white color. Let soak for 5 minutes.

Meanwhile, bring a 2-quart pot of fresh water to a boil. Drain the lotus root and add it to the boiling water. Cook just until the lotus root is tender but still crisp, about 2 minutes. Drain well and let cool to room temperature.

In a bowl, mix together the mayonnaise, shallot, mustard, capers, and lemon juice; toss with the lotus root. Serve cold.

Makes about 4 cups.

In most Asian homes, rice or pasta is served all day long—at breakfast, for lunch and snacks, and always at dinner. I've adopted the custom, using rice or noodles as a first course, main dish, or accompaniment at almost every meal. Pasta and rice just seem to complete a menu as few other foods can.

In Asia, rice is usually served plain to soak up sauces and gravies, just as Americans use bread. The recipes in this section present it in more interesting ways: as a stuffing for cabbage leaves and chilies, for example, and in wonderful side dishes and salads. For a fabulous first course, try the creamy Oriental Risotto. Paella makes a filling main course, perfect for a crowd. I often serve it at Super Bowl parties.

Because pasta of some sort is popular in almost every country, it offers an ideal base for cross-cultural dishes. The noodles themselves are made from many different flours—buckwheat, rice, mung bean, semolina—and formed into an endless variety of shapes, from long, flat strands to curly ribbons to wagon wheels. The dishes may be as simple as pasta with butter and cheese or as complex as a baked lasagne.

I always have pasta on hand in the cupboard or the freezer, and can whip up a meal without fail just by combining it with leftover meat, a few vegetables, and some canned or dried seasonings. Of course, a little planning and shopping ahead can often turn the merely good into the sublime.

With the exception of Oriental Lasagne, the pasta dishes in this section can be assembled quickly if you've done all the chopping early in the day or the night before. I usually finish the sauce after I put the pasta on to boil. Most leftovers can be reheated, but they're rarely as good as they were when fresh. I like to eat leftover pasta for breakfast—unconventional, but usually healthful.

The American Southwest and the Orient are combined in Poblano Chiles Stuffed with Glutinous Rice, page 146.

RICE AND
PASTA

Sushi Salad

The first time I had a large party, I served scattered sushi—a room-temperature Japanese dish—alongside the tortellini salad. The rice, flavored with pickled ginger and topped with braised vegetables and shreds of egg, was a big hit. This version is similar in flavor but quicker to make, since not all the parts need to be cooked ahead. It also has more seasoning than the Japanese dish and more vegetables and salmon than rice. It's substantial enough to make a summer dinner or luncheon, served as is or with mixed greens.

You can season the rice ahead, but don't add the snow peas too early. The vinegar in the rice will cause them to discolor.

R I C E   A N D   P A S T A

1 RECIPE SUSHI RICE, BELOW

1 CUP COOKED BONELESS, SKINLESS SALMON OR 1 (ABOUT 7-3/4-OUNCE) CAN SALMON, DRAINED, BONES AND SKIN REMOVED

1 MEDIUM (1/4-POUND) TOMATO, CORED, SEEDED, CHOPPED

1 LARGE GREEN ONION, CHOPPED

2 TABLESPOONS CHOPPED PINK PICKLED GINGER

MIXED GREENS SUCH AS BOSTON LETTUCE, ARUGULA, BELGIAN ENDIVE, CHICORY, AND WATERCRESS

2 OUNCES SNOW PEAS, STRINGS REMOVED, CUT ON THE DIAGONAL INTO THIRDS, BLANCHED FOR 1 MINUTE

1/4 CUP SLICED RADISHES (ROUND SLICES)

■■■ Place the Sushi Rice in a bowl and add the salmon, tomato, green onion, and ginger. With a rice paddle or wooden spoon, toss the ingredients together until well mixed.

Line a platter with the greens. Neatly mound the rice on top. Shortly before serving, arrange the snow peas and radishes attractively over the rice.

Makes 3 or 4 servings.

Sushi Rice

The word *sushi* means vinegared rice, not raw fish. In fact, many sushi dishes are made without any fish at all, and I only make vegetarian or cooked fish sushi. The rice itself is so flavorful, it combines beautifully with all kinds of other ingredients.

This recipe makes 2 cups rice. You can increase or decrease it depending on your needs. The key is to flavor the rice while it is still warm. After that, it can sit at room temperature for hours. Experts say you should never refrigerate sushi, but I do refrigerate leftovers and they never go to waste.

2 CUPS WARM BASIC RICE, BELOW
2 TABLESPOONS SUSHI SU

■ With a rice paddle or a wooden spoon, fold the rice over itself to fluff. Sprinkle the sushi su on top; mix and fold to blend the vinegar with the rice. To be authentic, you should work in a wooden bowl and fan the rice as you mix to keep it from becoming too wet from condensing steam.

Makes 2 cups.

Basic Rice

Although Oriental kitchens have few electric gadgets, the first one most cooks will buy is a rice maker. It makes perfect rice without any attention from the cook, and the fancier machines keep the rice nicely hot for hours—a real pleasure for hosts. If you, like most Americans, don't have a rice maker, just cook your rice according to the directions below. Oriental rice differs from Western rice in that it is cooked with less water and no fat or salt, and it's intentionally sticky, making it easier to eat with chopsticks.

1 CUP UNCOOKED SHORT-GRAIN
  RICE
1 CUP PLUS 2 TABLESPOONS WATER

■ Place the rice in a bowl and add cold water to cover. Stir the mixture around; then pour out the now-cloudy water. If using the rice for sushi, keep rinsing it until the water runs clear. For ordinary use, a single rinsing is enough.

Place the rice and 1 cup plus 2 tablespoons fresh water in a heavy medium pot with a lid. Place the pot over high heat and cook, covered, for about 5 minutes. The water should be actively boiling; if the pot lid is not very heavy, it will move. (To be sure, I always peek.) Reduce the heat so the water simmers and cook until all the water has been absorbed, 8 to 10 minutes. Increase the heat to high and cook for about 20 seconds longer to let the rice dry a bit. Let the rice stand, covered, another 10 minutes or so. To serve, fluff the rice up a bit with a wooden spoon or a Japanese rice paddle.

Makes about 2 cups.

Wild Rice Salad

Actually a water grass, not a rice, wild rice is a distinctly North American product. It was long grown and harvested exclusively by Indians, but today others have entered the market, making the product more generally available and affordable. Since wild rice takes a while to cook, I like to use it cold in salads and stuffings. That way, I don't have any long cooking to do just before dinner. The sesame oil in this salad enhances the rice's robust flavor, and the assorted vegetables brighten up its dark color.

1/4 CUP SESAME OIL

1 TABLESPOON MINCED FRESH GINGERROOT

1 TABLESPOON MINCED GARLIC

1/2 CUP CHOPPED ONION

2 CUPS UNCOOKED WILD RICE

5 CUPS WATER

1 TABLESPOON KOSHER SALT

1 (15-OUNCE) CAN BABY CORN, DRAINED, RINSED

1/2 CUP 1/4-INCH DAIKON CUBES

1/2 CUP WATER CHESTNUTS, CUT INTO 1/8- BY 1/8-INCH STICKS

1 RED BELL PEPPER, CORED, SEEDED, CUT INTO 1/2-INCH SQUARES

2 TABLESPOONS CHINESE BLACK VINEGAR

Heat 2 tablespoons sesame oil in a large pot over medium-high heat. Add the gingerroot and garlic and cook until fragrant, about 30 seconds. Add the onion and cook just to soften, about 1 minute. Add the rice and stir to coat well with the oil. Add the water and bring to a boil; then reduce the heat, cover, and simmer for 30 minutes. Add the salt and continue to cook until the rice is tender and almost all the water has been absorbed, about 30 minutes longer. Uncover and cook over high heat for about 1 minute to dry out the rice a bit.

While the rice is cooking, cut the corn into 1/2-inch rounds. Place in a bowl of ice water and let stand for 30 minutes to firm up. Drain well and set aside.

Place the rice in a bowl and stir it often to help it cool. When the rice is tepid, add the corn, daikon, water chestnuts, bell pepper, vinegar, and the remaining 2 tablespoons sesame oil. Serve cold or at room temperature.

Makes about 10 cups (8 to 10 servings).

Poblano Chilies Stuffed with Glutinous Rice

Whenever I am in California or the Southwest, I marvel at the fabulous produce, including piles of poblano chilies and tomatillos, two Mexican/Southwestern ingredients that I have to search for in New York. When I do find them, I feel obliged to purchase some so the produce buyers will know to buy more.

I was never a fan of stuffed peppers until I tasted *chiles rellenos* made with fresh poblano chilies. Both sweet and peppery, these big chilies add a wonderful flavor to the finished dish. For this recipe, I stuff my chilies with shrimp and glutinous rice instead of the usual cheese or ground meat. The results are delightful: the combination of tastes and textures is quite special, and the filling is solid enough not to ooze or fall out when the chilies are coated in batter and fried.

If you can't find fresh poblano chilies, you can use bell peppers and add a bit of hot-pepper sauce or red pepper flakes to the sauce.

4 (1/4-POUND) POBLANO CHILIES

1 CUP UNCOOKED GLUTINOUS RICE

2 CUPS WATER

1/2 POUND UNCOOKED SHRIMP IN
    THE SHELL

2 TEASPOONS OYSTER SAUCE

1 TABLESPOON SOY SAUCE

1 TABLESPOON RICE WINE VINEGAR

1/2 CUP ALL-PURPOSE FLOUR

6 TABLESPOONS YELLOW CORNMEAL

1/2 TEASPOON BAKING POWDER

1/4 TEASPOON KOSHER SALT

1/2 CUP MILK

1 LARGE EGG, LIGHTLY BEATEN

VEGETABLE OIL FOR FRYING

1 RECIPE TOMATO SAUCE, PAGE
    190

■■■ Preheat the grill or broiler until hot. Roast the chilies over the grill or under the broiler until the skin is blackened all over, turning as needed. Do not let the flesh under the skin burn or the chilies will get too soft and fall apart. Set the charred chilies aside to cool, then peel them and cut out the cores. With a knife, cut a slit down the length of each chili and remove the seeds, trying to keep the chiles as whole as possible. Set aside.

Bring water to a boil in the bottom of a steamer or wok, then reduce the heat so the water simmers. Meanwhile, rinse the rice in several changes of cold water until the water runs clear. Then place the rice in a wide pan and add 2 cups water. Place the pan on a steamer rack; set the rack in place over the simmering water, cover, and steam until the rice is tender and all the water has been absorbed, about 35 minutes.

Bring a 1-quart pot of water to a boil. Add the shrimp, return to a boil, and cook until the shrimp turn pink, about 30 seconds. Drain and let cool; then shell, devein, and cut into 1/4-inch pieces. Place the rice and shrimp in a bowl and add the oyster sauce, soy sauce, and vinegar. Stir to mix well. Stuff each chili with 1/4 of the rice mixture. Reshape the stuffed chilies and set aside until ready to cook.

In a separate bowl, blend the flour, cornmeal, baking powder, and salt. Stir in the milk and egg and whisk until smooth.

In a 10-inch skillet, heat 1/2 inch of oil until a haze forms above the oil. Dip a chili into the batter, turn to coat, and drop into the hot oil. Cook until browned on the bottom, about 3 minutes; turn and cook until browned on the other side, about 3 minutes longer. You will be able to cook 2 chilies at a time. Keep the cooked chilies warm in a low oven while you cook the remaining chilies. Serve with Tomato Sauce.

Makes 4 servings.

Stuffed Cabbage Rolls

One of my favorite things to order for dim sum is sticky rice wrapped in a lotus leaf. Lotus leaves aren't readily available outside of Chinatown, though, so I wrapped the rice for this dish in cabbage leaves—which have the additional advantage of being edible. In deference to typical Western tastes, the filling contains more meat than rice. If you like very spicy foods, use the full amount of chili sauce; otherwise, use less.

R I C E   A N D   P A S T A

1 CUP UNCOOKED GLUTINOUS RICE

5 OUNCES SKINLESS, BONELESS CHICKEN, CUT INTO 1/4-INCH CUBES

1/2 TEASPOON SZECHUAN PEPPERCORNS, TOASTED IN A DRY SKILLET, CRUSHED BETWEEN YOUR FINGERS

1 TEASPOON SOY SAUCE

2 TABLESPOONS VEGETABLE OIL

1 TABLESPOON MINCED FRESH GINGERROOT

1 TABLESPOON MINCED GARLIC

1/2 POUND GROUND PORK

1 TO 3 TEASPOONS SZECHUAN CHILI SAUCE

1/4 CUP HOISIN SAUCE

1 HEAD SAVOY CABBAGE

1 RECIPE TOMATO SAUCE, PAGE 190

Rinse the rice in several changes of cold water until the water runs clear. Place the rice in a bowl, cover generously with cold water, and let soak for 1 hour.

Place the chicken in a bowl with the peppercorns and soy sauce. Toss to blend. Heat the oil in a medium skillet over high heat. Add the gingerroot and garlic and cook for 1 minute. Add the pork and cook, stirring to break up lumps, until no longer pink. Then add the chicken and stir occasionally until the chicken is cooked through, about 3 minutes. Stir in the chili sauce and hoisin sauce. Remove the mixture to a bowl. Drain the rice, add to the meat mixture, and stir to blend.

Separate the cabbage into leaves. With a large paring knife, trim away the thick part of each rib so it is no thicker than the rest of the leaf. To fill each leaf, place it on your work surface, pared rib down. Place about 1/3 cup of the filling in the bottom curve of the leaf. Fold the bottom of the leaf up over the filling; fold in the sides to cover the filling, then roll up. Continue to fill leaves until all the filling has been used.

Place the filled rolls in a single layer, seam side down, on a steamer rack lined with cheesecloth. (The leaves may be filled ahead and cooked just before serving.)

When ready to cook, bring water to a boil in the bottom of a steamer or wok. Reduce the heat so the water simmers. Set the steamer rack in place over the simmering water, cover, and steam the cabbage rolls for 20 minutes. Meanwhile, heat the Tomato Sauce.

To serve, spoon some of the sauce onto individual plates and arrange the cabbage rolls on top; or put the cabbage rolls on a platter and serve the sauce on the side.

Makes 4 servings.

Oriental Risotto

Risotto is one of the few Western rice dishes in which the rice is intentionally sticky and creamy. Slow cooking and lots of stirring make it that way. The Italians prepare risotto in dozens of variations, adding everything from assorted cheeses to fresh and dried mushrooms, seasonal vegetables, and seafood. The dish is usually served by itself as a first course in place of pasta, but I like it as a side dish with roasted chicken. This risotto is flavored with ginger, dry shiitake, Chinese rice wine, and soy sauce, ingredients found in few, if any, traditional Italian kitchens.

If you want to cut down on the last-minute cooking, begin the dish earlier in the day and stop when you have added most of the stock. Cover, then reheat and finish cooking just before serving.

4 OR 5 DRIED SHIITAKE MUSHROOMS (1/2 OUNCE *TOTAL*)

1 CUP BOILING WATER

1/4 POUND SNOW PEAS, STRINGS REMOVED, CUT ON THE DIAGONAL INTO 1/2-INCH PIECES

2 CUPS CHICKEN STOCK MIXED WITH 1 CUP WATER

2 TABLESPOONS UNSALTED BUTTER

1 TABLESPOON MINCED FRESH GINGERROOT

1/4 CUP MINCED GREEN ONIONS

1-1/2 CUPS UNCOOKED SHORT-GRAIN RICE

1/4 CUP CHINESE RICE WINE MIXED WITH 1/4 CUP WATER

2 TEASPOONS SOY SAUCE

FRESHLY GROUND BLACK PEPPER TO TASTE

▬ Place the mushrooms in a bowl and add the boiling water. Let soak for 20 minutes. Drain the mushrooms and squeeze them dry, reserving the liquid. Cut off and discard the stems. Cut the caps into 1/4-inch squares. Set aside.

Bring a small pot of salted water to a boil. Add the snow peas and cook for 1 minute. Drain and set aside.

Place the diluted stock in a medium pot and bring to a simmer. Melt the butter in a 2-quart pot over medium-high heat. Add the gingerroot and green onions and cook for 30 seconds. Add the rice and stir to coat with the butter. Ladle in 1/2 cup simmering stock. Cook, stirring often, until the rice has absorbed all the liquid. Add another 1/2 cup stock; stir until absorbed. Add the remaining stock in the same way, 1/2 cup at a time. When all the stock has been added, stir in the reserved mushroom liquid, 1/2 cup at a time, then the diluted wine. The whole process will take about 30 minutes. The rice should be very creamy and cooked through but not mushy. If necessary, add simmering water and continue to cook. When the rice is done, stir in the mushrooms, snow peas, soy sauce, and pepper. Serve hot.

Makes 4 servings.

Paella

Paella, practically the national dish of Spain, points up the differences between Eastern and Western attitudes toward meat and fish. If it were made in the Orient, the dish would be largely rice, with scattered small pieces of chicken, shrimp, and sausage. But Westerners prefer generous amounts of meat and ample portion sizes—and this paella, though it features Eastern seasonings and Chinese sausage, is definitely Western in spirit.

Paella is a meal in itself, great for a crowd. It can star on a buffet, along with a baked ham and a few cold salads. When I make it for dinner, I usually follow it with a salad of mixed greens.

The traditional paella pan looks something like a flat, shallow wok. If you don't have a paella pan, do the preliminary cooking in a large skillet, then transfer the seasoned rice to a large ovenproof casserole and add the chicken, shrimp, snow peas, and shellfish.

1 (4-POUND) CHICKEN, CUT INTO SERVING-SIZE PIECES (SEE NOTE BELOW)

1 TABLESPOON SZECHUAN CHILI SAUCE

1/4 CUP PLUS 3 TABLESPOONS SAKE

1 POUND UNCOOKED SHRIMP, SHELLED, DEVEINED, BUTTERFLIED

2 TABLESPOONS SOY SAUCE

1/2 TEASPOON CRUMBLED SAFFRON THREADS

5-3/4 CUPS CHICKEN STOCK

24 MUSSELS IN THE SHELL (ABOUT 1-1/2 POUNDS *TOTAL*), WELL SCRUBBED

16 LITTLE NECK CLAMS IN THE SHELL, WELL SCRUBBED

1/4 CUP PLUS 2 TABLESPOONS OLIVE OIL

1 TABLESPOON MINCED FRESH GINGERROOT

1-1/2 TABLESPOONS MINCED GARLIC

1 CUP CHOPPED GREEN ONIONS

1/4 POUND CHINESE-STYLE PORK SAUSAGES, STEAMED 15 MINUTES, CUT ON THE DIAGONAL INTO THIN SLICES

3 CUPS UNCOOKED SHORT-GRAIN RICE

1 CUP JULIENNED SNOW PEAS

1/4 CUP CHOPPED FRESH CILANTRO LEAVES

■ Preheat the oven to 350F (175C). Place the chicken in a bowl with the chili sauce and 2 tablespoons sake; place the shrimp in a separate bowl with 1 tablespoon soy sauce and 1 tablespoon sake. Dissolve the saffron in some of the stock. Set aside. Soak the mussels and clams in several changes of cold water while preparing the paella.

Heat 1/4 cup oil in a paella pan or wok over medium-high heat. Add the chicken pieces, a portion at a time, and cook until nicely browned, about 5 minutes on each side. Set the browned chicken aside.

Pour off the fat from the pan, then add the remaining 2 tablespoons oil. Add the gingerroot and garlic. Cook for 1 minute. Add the green onions and cook for 30 seconds longer. Add the sausage slices and cook for 1 minute longer. Add the rice and stir until coated. Pour in the stock, dissolved saffron, remaining 1/4 cup sake and remaining 1 tablespoon soy sauce. Bring to a boil. Cook over medium-high heat for 10 minutes.

Bury the snow peas, shrimp, and chicken pieces in the rice. Arrange the clams and mussels on top of the rice, sticking up so they can open. Bake, uncovered, in the preheated oven until the clams and mussels are open, 30 to 40 minutes. Sprinkle the cilantro on top and serve from the pan.

Makes 8 or more servings.

NOTE: Cut the chicken to eliminate the backbone and wingtips (save them for stock). Then cut the thighs and wings in half; cut each breast half in thirds.

Brown Rice Steeped in Coconut Milk

An excellent accompaniment to sauceless dishes like roast chicken or steamed fish, this creamy rice is flavored with warm Eastern spices and a bit of lemon peel instead of the more exotic lemon grass. In dishes like this, I prefer fuller-flavored brown rice to white rice.

1 CUP COCONUT MILK
1-1/2 CUPS WATER
1 CUP UNCOOKED BROWN RICE
1 TEASPOON KOSHER SALT
1/2 TEASPOON GROUND CINNAMON
1/8 TEASPOON GROUND CLOVES
1 (2-INCH) PIECE LEMON PEEL

In a 2-quart pot, bring the coconut milk and water to a boil. Add the rice, salt, cinnamon, cloves, and lemon peel. Reduce the heat, cover, and simmer until the rice is tender and all the liquid has been absorbed, about 45 minutes. Uncover the pot and cook over high heat for 1 minute to dry out the rice a bit.

Makes 4 servings.

Udon with Cilantro Pesto

The essence of spring, pesto is a fresh Italian pasta sauce of pureed basil, pine nuts, Parmesan cheese, and oil. To adapt the recipe to the East, I use cilantro and peanuts in place of basil and pine nuts, and toss the sauce with udon. It makes a light first course or snack and a good side dish with Spicy Grilled Flank Steak, page 88, or roast chicken. The sauce also works well over rotelle and other pastas. If you have any leftover, use it instead of mustard on a ham sandwich on a crusty roll.

1 LARGE GARLIC CLOVE
2 TABLESPOONS ROASTED
   UNSALTED PEANUTS
2 TABLESPOONS FRESHLY GRATED
   PARMESAN CHEESE
1/3 CUP FRESH PARSLEY LEAVES
1/3 CUP FRESH CILANTRO LEAVES
1/4 CUP OLIVE OIL
1 TEASPOON RICE WINE VINEGAR
1/2 TEASPOON KOSHER SALT
1/2 POUND UDON
2 MEDIUM TOMATOES, CORED,
   SEEDED, CUT INTO STRIPS

With the food processor running, drop the garlic through the feed tube and process to mince. Add the peanuts and roughly chop. Add the cheese and process until everything is well mixed and very finely chopped. Add the parsley and cilantro and process with on-and-off pulses to chop well. Scrape down the sides of the work bowl as needed. With the machine running, pour the oil through the feed tube; then pour in the vinegar and salt. Taste and adjust the seasonings.

Bring a large pot of salted water to a boil. Add the udon, return to a boil, and cook until tender but still chewy, about 8 minutes. Drain well and toss with the cilantro pesto. Add the tomato strips and serve hot or at room temperature.

Makes 4 first-course or side-dish servings.

Penne à la Sake

A popular light pasta dish in recent years has been *penne à la vodka*, made with vodka, hot chilies, tomatoes, and cream. Sake makes an excellent alternative to the vodka: although lower in alcohol than vodka, it too is a clear, fresh liquor. I've also left out the cream and enhanced the Oriental flavor of the dish by using sambal and ginger. Cubes of green avocado, barely warmed by the sauce, add color and another texture.

RICE AND PASTA

1/2 POUND PENNE (SEE NOTE BELOW)

1 TABLESPOON OLIVE OIL

2 LARGE SLICES FRESH GINGERROOT

1 TEASPOON MINCED GARLIC

1/4 CUP SAKE

1/2 CUP CHOPPED TOMATO

1/2 TEASPOON SAMBAL OELEK

1/2 TEASPOON KOSHER SALT

1/2 RIPE AVOCADO, PEELED, CUT INTO 1/2-INCH CUBES

■ Bring a large pot of salted water to a boil. Add the penne, return to a boil, and cook until barely tender, about 10 minutes.

While the pasta is cooking, heat the oil in a large skillet over high heat. Add the gingerroot and garlic and cook for 30 seconds. Add the sake and bring to a boil. Add the tomato, sambal, and salt. Cook until the tomato begins to wilt, about 1 minute. Remove the gingerroot, if desired.

Drain the pasta well and toss with the tomato mixture. Divide among 4 salad plates; pile some avocado in the center of each plate.

Makes 4 first-course servings.

NOTE: Penne is a medium-sized tubular pasta; the ends of each tube are cut on the diagonal. If you cannot find penne, ziti is a fine substitute.

Rotelle with Sesame Sauce

The Chinese may have invented pasta, but the Italians certainly get the credit for creating imaginative shapes. One I particularly like is corkscrewlike rotelle, ideally shaped for holding sauce in all its nooks and crannies. Serve this for a snack or as a first course before Meat Loaf, page 86.

1 POUND ROTELLE

3 TABLESPOONS SMOOTH PEANUT BUTTER

1 TABLESPOON SESAME OIL

2 TABLESPOONS SOY SAUCE

1 TABLESPOON CHINESE BLACK VINEGAR

1 TABLESPOON SZECHUAN CHILI SAUCE

1/4 CUP WATER

2 TABLESPOONS SESAME SEEDS, TOASTED IN A DRY SKILLET

■ Bring a large pot of salted water to a boil. Add the rotelle, return to a boil, and cook until barely tender, about 10 minutes.

While the pasta is cooking, whisk together the peanut butter, sesame oil, soy sauce, vinegar, chili sauce, and water. Drain the pasta well and toss it immediately with the sauce. Sprinkle the sesame seeds on top.

Makes 8 first-course servings.

Radiatore with Spicy Vinaigrette

Even more fun than rotelle is radiatore, shaped like wide ribbon curls and excellent with this spicy vinaigrette. It makes a delicious accompaniment to steamed fish, chicken, or beef. If you prefer a more substantial dish to serve as a light main course, add a cup of cooked chicken, crab, salmon, or tuna.

1/2 POUND RADIATORE

1 TABLESPOON CHINESE BLACK VINEGAR

1 TABLESPOON SESAME OIL

1/2 TO 1 TEASPOON HOT SESAME (CHILI) OIL

1 TABLESPOON SOY SAUCE

1/2 CUP CHOPPED GREEN ONIONS

2 TABLESPOONS CHOPPED FRESH CILANTRO LEAVES

■■■ Bring a large pot of salted water to a boil. Add the radiatore, return to a boil, and cook until barely tender, about 10 minutes. Drain well.

In a large bowl, whisk together the vinegar, sesame oil, hot sesame oil, and soy sauce. Add the drained pasta, green onions, and cilantro; toss well. Serve warm, at room temperature, or chilled.

Makes 4 side-dish servings or 2 main-dish servings (if made with chicken or seafood).

Soba with Tomato and Basil

Tomato and basil are perfect summer partners, often served with cheese—admittedly an element foreign to the Oriental kitchen, yet the combination of fresh tomatoes, feta, and slivered basil works well with Japanese soba. Try this dish as a first course before grilled fish or chicken, or as a main course at supper with hot biscuits or crusty bread. Because the olives and cheese are salty, you won't need to add any salt to the sauce.

1/2 POUND SOBA

1 TABLESPOON OLIVE OIL

1 CUP SLICED GREEN ONIONS

1 TEASPOON MINCED FRESH GINGERROOT

1 POUND TOMATOES, CORED, CUT INTO 1/2-INCH CUBES

2 TABLESPOONS SAKE

1/2 TO 1 TEASPOON SAMBAL OELEK

1 CUP CRUMBLED FETA CHEESE (ABOUT 1/4 POUND)

1/4 CUP CHOPPED PITTED KALAMATA OLIVES

1/4 CUP JULIENNED FRESH BASIL LEAVES

■■■ Bring a large pot of salted water to a boil. Add the soba, return to a boil, and cook until barely tender, about 7 minutes.

While the pasta is cooking, heat the oil in an 8-inch skillet over high heat. Add the green onions and gingerroot and cook for 1 minute. Add the tomatoes and cook for 2 minutes longer to let the tomatoes begin releasing their juice. Add the sake, sambal, cheese, and olives. Cook for about 2 minutes longer; some of the cheese will dissolve into the sauce, but many bits will remain solid.

Drain the pasta well and toss it with the sauce. Sprinkle the basil on top.

Makes 6 first-course or 3 main-dish servings.

Chinese Egg Noodles with Zucchini and Peanuts

Laced with lime juice and peel, this is a very light, refreshing dish. I serve it for a late-night supper or as a starter for a summer dinner of grilled salmon with Fermented Black Bean and Tomato Sauce, page 184. Aside from the occasional dark strip of sun-dried tomato, the colors are pale. The final cooking time is brief.

If you don't have Chinese noodles, use any long pasta, from spaghetti to fettuccine.

RICE AND PASTA

1/2 POUND FRESH THICK CHINESE EGG NOODLES

2 TABLESPOONS OLIVE OIL

2 LARGE SLICES FRESH GINGERROOT

1/2 POUND ZUCCHINI, CUT INTO 1/4- BY 1/4- BY 3-INCH STICKS

1/2 POUND YELLOW SUMMER SQUASH, CUT INTO 1/4- BY 1/4- BY 3-INCH STICKS

1/4 CUP CHOPPED UNROASTED UNSALTED PEANUTS

1/2 CUP SLICED GREEN ONIONS

1/2 CUP CHOPPED FRESH CILANTRO LEAVES

PEEL OF 1 LIME, CUT INTO JULIENNE STRIPS

JUICE OF 1 LIME

2 TABLESPOONS FISH SAUCE

2 TABLESPOONS SAKE

1/4 CUP SUN-DRIED TOMATOES PACKED IN OIL, CUT INTO JULIENNE STRIPS, PATTED DRY

FRESHLY GRATED PARMESAN CHEESE TO TASTE

Bring a large pot of salted water to a boil. Add the noodles, return to a boil, and cook until barely tender, about 4 minutes. Drain well.

Heat the oil in a large skillet over medium-high heat. Add the gingerroot, zucchini, and yellow squash. Cook until slightly soft, about 2 minutes. Add the peanuts, green onions, cilantro, and lime peel. Cook for 1 minute longer. Add the lime juice, fish sauce, and sake. Bring to a boil. Remove the gingerroot, if desired.

Drain the liquid off the vegetable mixture; toss the liquid with the pasta. Arrange the pasta on a platter. Add the sun-dried tomatoes to the vegetable mixture, toss to mix, and spoon over the pasta. Serve with cheese on the side.

Makes 4 first-course or 2 main-dish servings.

Fettuccine with Spicy Peanut Sauce

If you have homemade peanut sauce on hand, you can make this unusual pasta dish quickly. Serve it before Fish Cakes, page 108, and Stir-Fried Watercress with Garlic, page 129.

1 (ABOUT 1-1/4-POUND) BUNCH BROCCOLI

1/2 POUND CARROTS, THINLY SLICED ON THE DIAGONAL

1/2 POUND FETTUCCINE

1/2 CUP WATER

1/2 CUP INDONESIAN-STYLE PEANUT SAUCE, PAGE 191

Cut the flowerets from the broccoli stems. Cut the flowerets into bite-size pieces. Using a paring knife and your fingers, cut most of the thick peel away from the broccoli stems, leaving the pale, tender shoots underneath. Cut the stems on the diagonal into thin slices. Scatter the carrots and all the broccoli on a steamer rack. Set aside.

Bring a large pot of salted water to a boil. Add the fettuccine, return to a boil, and cook until barely tender, about 10 minutes. Also bring water to a boil in the bottom of a steamer or wok. Reduce the heat so the water simmers. Set the rack of vegetables in place, cover, and steam over the simmering water until the vegetables are just cooked through but still firm, about 5 minutes.

While the pasta and vegetables are cooking, slowly whisk 1/2 cup water into the peanut sauce to thin it.

Drain the pasta well and toss with the peanut sauce, then with the hot vegetables. Serve hot.

Makes 4 first-course servings.

Fettuccine with Oriental Mushrooms

Fettuccine lends itself to all sorts of sauces, from heavy, rich concoctions to simple butter and pepper. This particular sauce is made with an assortment of dried mushrooms, some meatier than others, tossed with cream and topped with Parmesan cheese. This is an excellent first course before any roasted, grilled, or braised main dish. (To avoid monotony, don't serve a main dish that features a cream sauce or mushrooms.)

1/4 CUP DRIED TIGER LILY BUDS

2 TABLESPOONS CLOUD EARS

1 OUNCE (ABOUT 16) DRIED CHINESE MUSHROOMS

1/2 POUND FETTUCCINE

1 TABLESPOON OLIVE OIL

2 GARLIC CLOVES, SLICED

1/4 CUP SLICED SHALLOTS

1 JALAPEÑO CHILI, CORED, SEEDED, DERIBBED, MINCED

1 CUP WHIPPING CREAM

2 TABLESPOONS SOY SAUCE

FRESHLY GRATED PARMESAN CHEESE TO TASTE

■ Place the tiger lily buds in a bowl and add boiling water to cover. Let soak for 20 minutes. Place the cloud ears and Chinese mushrooms in a separate bowl and add boiling water to cover. Let soak for 20 minutes.

Drain the tiger lily buds and squeeze them dry. Cut off and discard any tough ends, then shred the buds lengthwise with your fingers. Place in a bowl.

Drain the cloud ears and Chinese mushrooms and squeeze them dry. Roughly chop the cloud ears and add to the tiger lily buds. Cut off and discard the mushroom stems; cut the caps into strips. Add to the cloud ears and lily buds.

Bring a large pot of salted water to a boil. Add the fettuccine, return to a boil, and cook until barely tender, about 10 minutes. Drain well and set aside.

Heat the oil in a large skillet over high heat. Add the garlic, shallots, and chili. Cook until lightly browned and fragrant, about 2 minutes. Add the lily buds, cloud ears, and Chinese mushrooms and sauté briefly. Add the cream and soy sauce; bring to a boil. Reduce the heat and simmer for about 1 minute. Add the pasta to the skillet and stir briefly to reheat and coat. Serve with cheese on top.

Makes 4 first-course servings.

Tortellini with Snow Peas and Straw Mushrooms

On Sundays we usually have salad and pasta for dinner—often tortellini, since they make such a satisfying meal. There are dozens of good sauces, but this one is a favorite. The bright snow peas and dark mushrooms contrast well with the pale tortellini in appearance, texture, and taste.

Because the sauce is so quick to make, this dish is great for company. If you serve it as a first course, follow with a lighter main course such as Steamed Catfish, page 114, or Marinated Leg of Lamb, page 80.

RICE AND PASTA

1/4 POUND SNOW PEAS, STRINGS REMOVED, HALVED DIAGONALLY

1/2 POUND CHEESE TORTELLINI

2 TABLESPOONS UNSALTED BUTTER

1 TEASPOON MINCED FRESH GINGERROOT

1 LARGE GARLIC CLOVE, MINCED

2 TABLESPOONS MINCED SHALLOT

1 (15-OUNCE) CAN WHOLE PEELED STRAW MUSHROOMS, DRAINED, RINSED

1 TEASPOON SOY SAUCE

PINCH OF GROUND RED (CAYENNE) PEPPER

FRESHLY GRATED PARMESAN CHEESE TO TASTE

ENOKI MUSHROOMS, ROOT ENDS TRIMMED

Bring a large pot of salted water to a boil. Add the snow peas and cook for 1 minute. Lift out with a strainer or slotted spoon, rinse under cold water, drain, and set aside.

Add the tortellini to the same water and return to a boil; then cook until barely tender, 8 to 10 minutes. While the pasta is cooking, melt 1 tablespoon butter in a skillet over high heat. Add the gingerroot and garlic and cook for 30 seconds. Add the shallot and cook for 30 seconds longer. Add the straw mushrooms and snow peas to the skillet along with the remaining 1 tablespoon butter, soy sauce, and red pepper. Stir to mix well; cook for 2 minutes.

Drain the tortellini well. Toss the vegetables with the tortellini. Sprinkle with cheese, garnish with enoki mushrooms, and serve hot.

Makes 4 first-course or 2 main-dish servings.

Somen with Shrimp and Vegetables

I first had somen one summer in Japan, where the noodles were served in bowls of ice water, with each bite to be lifted out and dipped into a light sauce. It was a perfect refresher on a steamy day. The Japanese, who take seasonality very seriously, serve the white somen in clear glass bowls to enhance the feeling of iciness that is so appealing in hot weather. It is not unusual for families to use those glass bowls for only the summer season.

In keeping with the Japanese spirit, I have created a very light but more substantial salad with this delicate pasta. There's no dipping sauce on the side; instead, the white noodles are tossed with a fragrant raspberry vinaigrette, then topped with bright green and red vegetables and a scattering of pink shrimp. The dish makes a lovely summer lunch or late-night snack, ideally served on glass plates.

Since the Japanese pack somen in neat bundles of five (a lucky number), I use two bundles for this dish rather than a half-pound.

1/2 POUND UNCOOKED SHRIMP, SHELLED, DEVEINED, HALVED LENGTHWISE

1 TABLESPOON DRY VERMOUTH

2 (ABOUT 3-1/4-OUNCE) BUNDLES SOMEN

1/4 CUP PLUS 1 TABLESPOON RASPBERRY VINEGAR

1/2 TEASPOON GRATED FRESH GINGERROOT

1 TABLESPOON MIRIN

1 (1/4-POUND) ZUCCHINI, SLICED ON THE DIAGONAL INTO 1/8-INCH-THICK SLICES, EACH SLICE CUT INTO 1/8-INCH-WIDE STICKS

2 LARGE RADISHES, CUT INTO 1/8- BY 1/8-INCH STICKS

1 PLUM TOMATO, CORED, CUT INTO 1/4- BY 1/4-INCH STRIPS

1/2 CUP WATERCRESS LEAVES

1 TABLESPOON WALNUT OIL

1/2 TEASPOON KOSHER SALT

▬ Toss the shrimp with the vermouth and let marinate for 30 minutes.

Bring 1 large and 1 small pot of salted water to a boil. Drop the shrimp into the small pot. Return to a boil; cook until the shrimp turn pink, about 30 seconds. Drain and set aside. Add the somen to the large pot of boiling water, return to a boil, and cook until barely tender, about 3 minutes. Drain well and place in a bowl of cold water and ice cubes. Let stand until well chilled.

Mix 1/4 cup vinegar with the gingerroot and mirin. Drain the chilled noodles and toss with the vinegar mixture, then place on a large, round glass platter or on individual plates. Neatly arrange piles of the zucchini, radishes, and tomato over the noodles. If you are using a platter, divide each vegetable into 3 portions and alternate the 3 types around the edge of noodles. If using individual plates, just use 1 pile of each vegetable. Place the watercress in a bunch in the center of the noodles; scatter the shrimp on top.

Mix the remaining 1 tablespoon vinegar with the walnut oil and salt. Drizzle the mixture over the salads.

Makes 4 main-dish (lunch or supper) servings.

Somen Salad with Pork

Lime and fish sauce give this salad a Vietnamese flavor, although Vietnamese cooks would use more sugar and leave out the oil. The presentation, with the dish seasoned in the kitchen, bows to the West. In Vietnam, such a salad would be presented with dipping sauces and seasonings, and each diner would make his own sauce.

Because it's served cold, the salad is excellent on a hot night or as part of a buffet. The parts can be made a day ahead, but it's best to assemble them a few hours before serving.

1/2 POUND BONELESS LOIN OF PORK, CUT INTO THIN SLICES

2 TABLESPOONS MINCED SHALLOT

1 TABLESPOON PLUS 1 TEASPOON MINCED GARLIC

1/4 CUP PLUS 1 TABLESPOON FISH SAUCE

GRATED PEEL OF 1 LIME

JUICE OF 2 LIMES

1 TABLESPOON VEGETABLE OIL

2 OR 3 (3-1/4-OUNCE) BUNDLES SOMEN

2 CARROTS, GRATED

1/2 CUP GRATED DAIKON

1 SMALL RED BELL PEPPER, CORED, SEEDED, CHOPPED

1/4 CUP WATER

1/2 TEASPOON CRUSHED RED PEPPER FLAKES

1 TABLESPOON SUGAR

2 TABLESPOONS OLIVE OIL

1/4 CUP CHOPPED ROASTED UNSALTED PEANUTS

2 TABLESPOONS CHOPPED FRESH CILANTRO LEAVES

Place the pork in a bowl with the shallot, 1 teaspoon garlic, 1 tablespoon fish sauce, lime peel, and juice of 1 lime. Let marinate for at least 1 hour.

Heat the vegetable oil in a wok or large skillet over high heat. Drain the pork, reserving the marinade. Add the pork to the hot oil; cook, stirring often, until the pork loses its raw look, about 2 minutes. Add the marinade and cook for 1 minute longer. Remove from the heat and let cool.

Bring a large pot of salted water to a boil. Add the somen, return to a boil, and cook until barely tender, about 3 minutes. Drain well and place in a bowl with the carrots, daikon, and bell pepper.

In a separate bowl, whisk together the remaining 1 tablespoon garlic, remaining 1/4 cup fish sauce, juice of 1 lime, 1/4 cup water, red pepper flakes, sugar, and olive oil. Pour over the pasta and vegetables and toss to mix well. Arrange the mixture on a platter; top with the pork and its juices. Sprinkle the peanuts and cilantro on top.

Makes 4 main-dish servings.

Soba Primavera

Pasta *primavera*—pasta and cream with fresh spring vegetables—takes on a whole new complexity when made with soba and seasoned with a hint of fish sauce. This colorful dish makes an excellent first course before Lamb Stew, page 79, served with Ratatouille with Sambal, page 132. I like a fruity red wine with the meal.

1/2 POUND SOBA

2 TABLESPOONS UNSALTED BUTTER

2 GREEN ONIONS, SLICED ON THE DIAGONAL

1/2 POUND ASPARAGUS, WOODY ENDS BROKEN OFF, STALKS CUT INTO 2-INCH PIECES

1/4 POUND CARROTS, THINLY SLICED ON THE DIAGONAL

3/4 CUP WHIPPING CREAM

2 TABLESPOONS FISH SAUCE

1 CUP BARELY COOKED FRESH PEAS OR 1 CUP FROZEN PEAS, THAWED

1/4 POUND SNOW PEAS, STRINGS REMOVED, CUT ON THE DIAGONAL INTO THIRDS

1 RED BELL PEPPER, CORED, SEEDED, CUT INTO THIN STRIPS

1/4 CUP CHOPPED FRESH CILANTRO LEAVES

Bring a large pot of salted water to a boil. Add the soba, return to a boil, and cook until barely tender, about 7 minutes.

While the pasta is cooking, melt the butter in a large skillet over medium-high heat. Add the green onions and cook for 1 minute. Add the asparagus and carrots; cook for 2 minutes longer. Add the cream and bring to a boil. Stir in the fish sauce, peas, snow peas, and bell pepper. Cook until the vegetables are all just cooked through but still firm, about 2 minutes longer. Stir in the cilantro.

Drain the pasta well. Toss the hot vegetable mixture with the pasta and spoon onto individual plates.

Makes 6 first-course servings.

Orzo with Shrimp and Pork

Orzo is one of my favorite pastas. Since it looks like plump grains of rice, I've seasoned it like fried rice for a fun variation on a traditional Chinese stir-fried dish. You might include it in an assortment of salads at a buffet or picnic. It's good served hot or at room temperature. The recipe calls for raw pork and shrimp, but you can substitute leftover cooked ham or chicken.

1/2 POUND BONELESS LOIN OF PORK, CUT INTO THIN SLICES

1/4 TEASPOON HOT SESAME (CHILI) OIL

2 TEASPOONS SAKE

1/2 POUND UNCOOKED SHRIMP, SHELLED, DEVEINED, COARSELY CHOPPED

1/4 CUP SOY SAUCE

2 TEASPOONS UNSALTED BUTTER

2 LARGE EGGS, LIGHTLY BEATEN

1 OUNCE (ABOUT 16) DRIED CHINESE MUSHROOMS

1 CUP ORZO

2 TABLESPOONS VEGETABLE OIL

1 LARGE GARLIC CLOVE, MINCED

1/4 CUP CHOPPED GREEN ONIONS

1/3 CUP CHOPPED WATER CHESTNUTS

1/2 CUP WATERCRESS LEAVES

1 TABLESPOON DRY SHERRY

1/4 CUP CHICKEN STOCK

■ Place the pork in a bowl with the hot sesame oil and sake. Stir to mix, then set aside. In a separate bowl, toss the shrimp with 1 tablespoon soy sauce; set aside.

Melt the butter in a 6-inch skillet over medium heat. Add the eggs and stir gently until set but still moist. Cut into 1-inch pieces and set aside.

Place the mushrooms in a bowl and add boiling water to cover. Let soak for 20 minutes. Drain, then squeeze dry. Cut off and discard the stems; cut the caps into thin strips. Set aside with the eggs.

Bring a pot of salted water to a boil. Add the orzo, return to a boil, and cook until barely tender, about 8 minutes. Drain well.

Place a wok over high heat. Add the vegetable oil, then the garlic. Cook, stirring, for 30 seconds. Add the pork and shrimp and cook just until done, about 4 minutes. Add the green onions, water chestnuts, eggs, mushrooms, and watercress. Cook, stirring, for 1 minute longer. Add the orzo and mix well. Add the remaining 3 tablespoons soy sauce along with the sherry and stock. Stir to mix. Cook until well blended and hot, about 2 minutes longer.

Makes 4 main-dish servings.

Spicy Duck and Baby Corn with Cavatelli

I usually cut my ducks up, using the breasts for one meal, the rest of the meat for something else. This slightly spicy pasta dish makes wonderful use of the legs. It's a meal in itself, perfect for supper with a green salad; it's also a satisfying first course before a light main dish like Grilled Shark, page 114. The sauce has an Asian flavor that's highlighted by the baby corn, but the olives and pasta speak of the Mediterranean.

1 POUND CAVATELLI OR ROTELLE

3 TABLESPOONS VEGETABLE OIL

1/2 CUP CHOPPED GREEN ONIONS

2 TABLESPOONS MINCED FRESH
  GINGERROOT

2 JALAPEÑO CHILIES, CORED,
  SEEDED, DERIBBED, CUT INTO
  THIN STRIPS

MEAT FROM THIGHS AND LEGS OF 2
  (5-POUND) DUCKS, SKINNED, CUT
  INTO THIN STRIPS

2 (15-OUNCE) CANS BABY CORN,
  DRAINED, RINSED, HALVED
  LENGTHWISE

1/2 CUP CHOPPED PITTED KALAMATA
  OLIVES

1/4 CUP CHICKEN STOCK

1/4 CUP SOY SAUCE

2 TABLESPOONS SAKE

1/2 TEASPOON DRIED LEAF THYME

2 TEASPOONS SESAME OIL

▬ Bring a large pot of salted water to a boil. Add the pasta, return to a boil, and cook until barely tender, about 10 minutes.

While the pasta is cooking, heat the vegetable oil in a wok or large skillet over high heat. Add the green onions, gingerroot, and chilies; cook for 1 minute. Add the duck and cook, stirring, until it loses its raw look, about 2 minutes longer. Add the corn and olives; cook, stirring, for 1 minute longer. Add the stock, soy sauce, sake, and thyme. Bring to a boil and cook for 2 minutes longer.

Drain the cooked pasta well. Toss the sauce with the hot pasta and the sesame oil.

Makes 8 first-course or 4 main-dish servings.

Oriental Lasagne

Although Asians eat pasta from dawn to dusk, baked dishes like lasagne are virtually unknown in Asian countries. This lasagne is assembled in the classic style, but the flavor offers a few surprises. The sauce gets a rich sweetness from Chinese sausages, and the traditional mozzarella is mixed with cubes of tofu. Serve with a mixed green salad with a soy dressing and hot bread with garlic-ginger butter.

1/2 POUND LASAGNE NOODLES

1/2 POUND CHINESE-STYLE PORK SAUSAGES, STEAMED FOR 15 MINUTES, CUT ON THE DIAGONAL INTO 1/4-INCH SLICES

1 RECIPE TOMATO SAUCE, PAGE 190

2 LARGE EGGS

1 POUND FRESH RICOTTA CHEESE OR 1 (15- TO 16-OUNCE) CONTAINER RICOTTA CHEESE

1/4 CUP CHOPPED FRESH CILANTRO LEAVES

1 TABLESPOON CHOPPED FRESH GINGERROOT

1/2 POUND MOZZARELLA CHEESE, CUT INTO 1/4-INCH CUBES

2 CAKES FIRM TOFU (ABOUT 1/2 POUND *TOTAL*), DRAINED, CUT INTO 1/3-INCH CUBES

1/3 CUP FRESHLY GRATED PARMESAN CHEESE (ABOUT 1 OUNCE)

■ Bring a large pot of salted water to a boil. Add the lasagne noodles, return to a boil, and cook until barely tender, about 10 minutes. Drain well and set aside, making sure the strips don't stick to each other.

Stir together the sausages and Tomato Sauce; set aside. In a small bowl, beat the eggs just to mix. Beat in the ricotta cheese, cilantro, and gingerroot. Set aside 1/3 cup of the mozzarella cheese; mix the remaining mozzarella with the tofu.

Preheat oven to 350F (175C). Spoon a little of the Tomato Sauce (without any sausage pieces) into the bottom of a 9- by 13-inch baking pan. Top with a single layer of pasta. Spoon half the remaining sauce over the pasta. Top with dollops of half the ricotta mixture; sprinkle on half the mozzarella-tofu mixture. Top with another layer of pasta; then add the remaining sauce, ricotta mixture, and mozzarella-tofu mixture. Top with a third pasta layer. Sprinkle the reserved 1/3 cup mozzarella cheese and the Parmesan cheese on top.

Bake in the preheated oven until bubbly and heated through, about 30 minutes.

Makes 6 to 8 main-dish servings.

Baked Soba

Baked macaroni with a Cheddar béchamel sauce is an American classic. To make this variation, I used soba and dried mushrooms, left out the Cheddar, and added a dash of fish sauce. The result may not be as popular with the kids as the standard dish, but adults will probably love it. It can be an interesting first course before a roast chicken or a pleasant supper with salad and cheese.

1/2 OUNCE (ABOUT 8) DRIED CHINESE MUSHROOMS

1/2 OUNCE DRIED PORCINI

1/2 POUND SOBA

2-1/2 TABLESPOONS UNSALTED BUTTER

1/4 CUP CHOPPED GREEN ONIONS

1-1/2 TEASPOONS MINCED FRESH GINGERROOT

1 GARLIC CLOVE, MINCED

1 TABLESPOON ALL-PURPOSE FLOUR

3/4 CUP MILK

1/2 CUP CHICKEN STOCK

1 DRIED RED CHILI

1 TEASPOON FISH SAUCE

1/8 TEASPOON FRESHLY GROUND BLACK PEPPER

2 TABLESPOONS MINCED FRESH CILANTRO LEAVES

1/4 CUP FRESHLY GRATED PARMESAN CHEESE (ABOUT 3/4 OUNCE)

Place the Chinese mushrooms and porcini in a bowl and add boiling water to cover. Let soak for 20 minutes. Meanwhile, preheat the oven to 425F (220C). Butter a 6-cup baking dish (a ceramic quiche pan works well) and set aside.

Drain the mushrooms and squeeze them dry, reserving 1/2 cup liquid. Cut off and discard the stems from the Chinese mushrooms; cut the caps into thin strips. Also cut the porcini into thin strips. Set the mushrooms aside.

Bring a large pot of salted water to a boil. Add the soba, return to a boil, and cook until barely tender, about 7 minutes. Drain well and set aside in a bowl.

Melt 1-1/2 tablespoons butter in a small skillet over high heat. Add the green onions, gingerroot, and garlic. Sauté for 1 minute. Add the mushrooms and cook for about 2 minutes longer. Add the mushroom mixture to the soba.

Melt the remaining 1 tablespoon butter in a small saucepan over medium heat. Stir in the flour and cook for 1 minute. Add the milk, stock, and chili. Whisk until smooth, then bring to a boil and cook for 3 minutes. Remove and discard the chili. Stir in the fish sauce, reserved 1/2 cup mushroom liquid, pepper, and cilantro. Pour the sauce over the soba and mushrooms. Stir to mix well and coat the pasta.

Spoon the mixture into the buttered baking dish. Sprinkle the cheese on top and bake in the preheated oven until bubbling and set, about 20 minutes.

Makes 6 first-course or 3 main-dish servings.

Chicken and Cucumbers with Soba

I created this dish one night when I was looking for something interesting to do with leftover chicken. The results were so good that now I cook extra chicken on purpose. The dish can stand as a meal in itself, served with a salad or after a bowl of Clam Chowder, page 56, or Hearty Vegetable Soup, page 52.

3/4 POUND SOBA

1/4 CUP DIJON MUSTARD

2 TABLESPOONS SOY SAUCE

2 TABLESPOONS RICE WINE VINEGAR

3 TABLESPOONS VEGETABLE OIL

1 TABLESPOON MINCED FRESH GINGERROOT

4 GREEN ONIONS, SLICED

2 CUCUMBERS, PEELED, SEEDED, CUT INTO 1/4- BY 3-INCH STRIPS

2 CUPS COOKED CHICKEN STRIPS, 1/4 INCH WIDE, UP TO 3 INCHES LONG

■ Bring a large pot of salted water to a boil. Add the soba, return to a boil, and cook until barely tender, about 7 minutes. Drain well and set aside.

In a small bowl, mix together the mustard, soy sauce, and vinegar. Set aside.

Heat the oil in a wok over high heat. Add the gingerroot and cook, stirring, for 10 seconds. Add the green onions and cook for 10 seconds longer. Toss in the cucumbers and chicken. Cook for 15 seconds longer, then add the mustard mixture.

Simmer for about 30 seconds. Add the soba; toss and cook for 1 minute longer. Serve hot.

Makes 6 first-course or 3 main-dish servings.

Soba and Tuna Salad

Cold pasta salads are ideal for lunch or summer suppers, or as part of a picnic or buffet. This colorful mixture of soba, vegetables and tuna is a meal in one bowl. Serve with whole-grain bread and an aged Cheddar.

1/2 POUND SOBA

3 TABLESPOONS RICE WINE VINEGAR

1 TABLESPOON SAKE

2 TABLESPOONS SOY SAUCE

3 TABLESPOONS SESAME OIL

1 (6-1/2-OUNCE) CAN TUNA, DRAINED, FLAKED

1/4 CUP PITTED KALAMATA OLIVES, CHOPPED

1 GREEN ONION, CHOPPED

1 RED BELL PEPPER, CORED, SEEDED, CUT INTO 1/2-INCH SQUARES

1 GREEN BELL PEPPER, CORED, SEEDED, CUT INTO 1/2-INCH SQUARES

1/4 CUP THINLY SLICED RADISHES

Bring a large pot of salted water to a boil. Add the soba, return to a boil, and cook until barely tender, about 7 minutes. Drain well, rinse under cold water, and drain again. Set aside. In a small bowl, mix together the vinegar, sake, soy sauce, and sesame oil. In a separate bowl, combine the tuna, olives, green onion, red and green bell peppers, and radishes. Toss with about 1/4 cup of the sesame dressing.

Toss the soba with the remaining dressing, then arrange in a bowl or on a deep-rimmed plate. Spoon the tuna mixture on top.

Makes 3 or 4 main-dish (lunch or supper) servings.

Even before beans became such a popular source of fiber, I started cooking them for their range of flavors and colors—and their low price. They make wonderful side dishes, as these recipes show. Most types do take a while to cook, but they're simple to reheat, and they'll last for a few days in room-temperature salads. Make one for your next picnic or buffet and see how easily it goes together.

This chapter also includes some unusual breads, fragrant Sesame Crêpes, and Polenta, a European cornmeal dish that is a perfect foil for certain rich Oriental sauces.

Scallion Bread, page 177, or Focaccia with Chinese Sausage, page 178, are ideal accompaniments to soups or green salads.

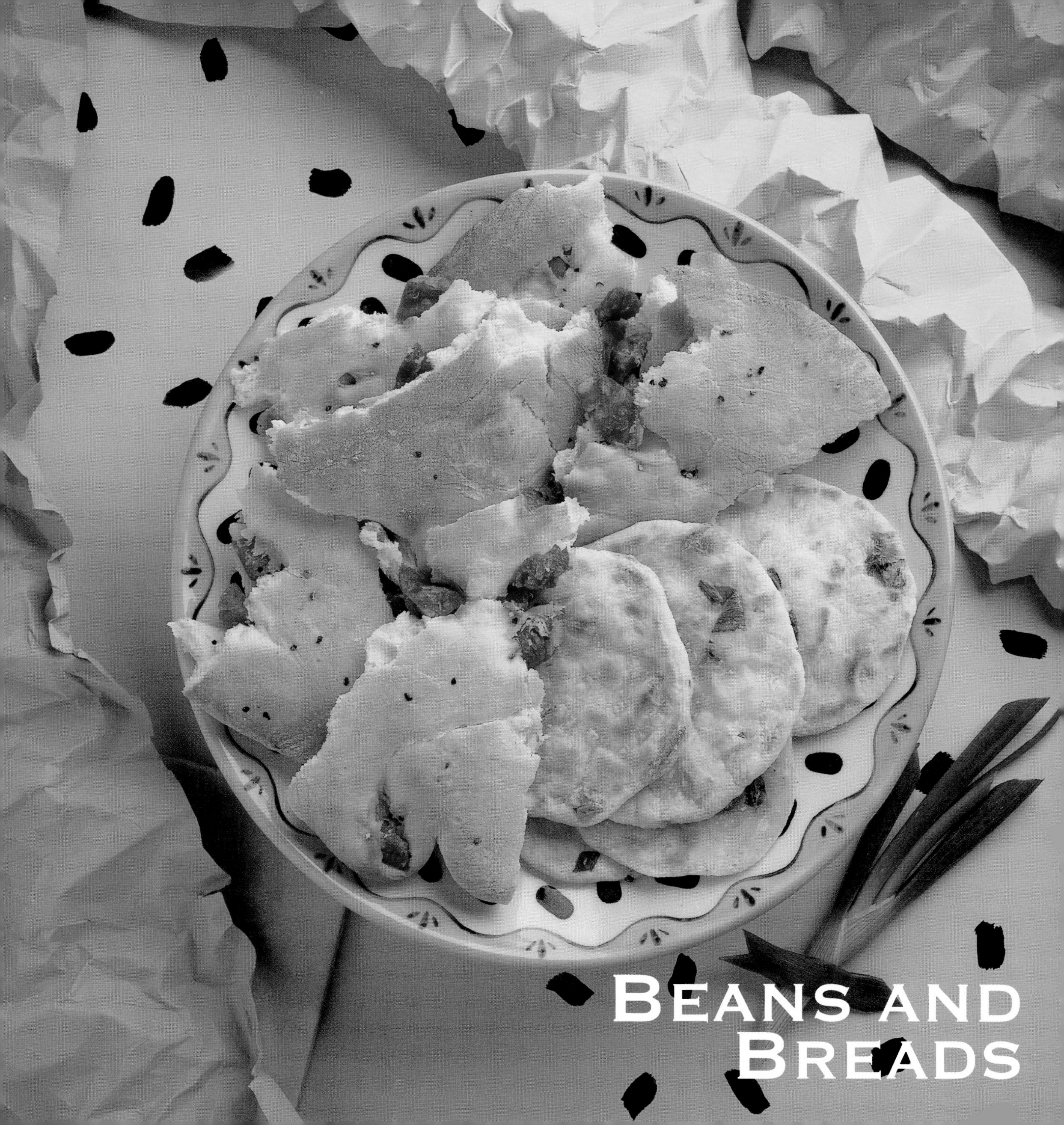

Beans and Breads

Curried Black-Eyed Peas

Like most Americans, I always assumed that the black-eyed peas so beloved of Southern cooks were native to this continent. A little research proved me wrong. Although I've never seen them in a Chinese restaurant or in any Chinese cookbooks, these black-tipped beans are actually native to China. That bit of knowledge aside, I still consider this recipe a cross-cultural one: the use of beans as a side dish is common to the West, but the seasonings here are definitely Eastern.

These beans are quite spicy, perfect with roast chicken, grilled fish, or any lightly seasoned stew.

1 CUP (ABOUT 5 OUNCES) DRIED BLACK-EYED PEAS, SOAKED IN COLD WATER OVERNIGHT

2 CUPS PLUS 2 TABLESPOONS WATER

5 DRIED CHILIES

4 GARLIC CLOVES

1 TEASPOON KOSHER SALT

1 TEASPOON DRIED SLICED LEMON GRASS

1 TEASPOON CORIANDER SEEDS

1 TEASPOON CUMIN SEEDS

1/2 TEASPOON WHOLE BLACK PEPPERCORNS

1 TEASPOON POWDERED GALANGAL (LAOS)

1 TEASPOON GROUND TURMERIC

1/4 TEASPOON GROUND CINNAMON

2 TABLESPOONS OLIVE OIL

1/2 CUP CHOPPED ONION

1 TEASPOON SHRIMP PASTE

Drain the peas and place in a 2-quart saucepan with 2 cups water, 2 chilies, and 2 whole garlic cloves. Bring to a boil; reduce the heat, partially cover the pan, and simmer for 30 minutes. Stir in the salt and continue to cook until the peas are soft but not mushy, about 30 minutes longer. Drain off any unabsorbed liquid. Discard the chilies. The garlic cloves will be soft; mash them with a spoon and stir thorough the peas.

In a spice grinder, grind the remaining 3 chilies, the lemon grass, coriander seeds, cumin seeds, and peppercorns to a powder. Mix the powder with the galangal, turmeric, and cinnamon. Set aside.

Mince the remaining 2 garlic cloves. Heat the oil in a large skillet over high heat. Add the minced garlic and onion and cook for 1 minute. Add the shrimp paste and stir vigorously to mix it into the onion, about 1 minute. Stir in the spice mixture until completely blended. Cook for about 1 minute longer. Add the remaining 2 tablespoons water to make a sauce, then stir in the cooked peas. Cook to blend and heat through, about 3 minutes longer.

Makes about 3 cups (6 servings).

Braised Lentils

I love the flavor of lentils in soups and salads. In this dish, miso paste gives them a mellow taste; chopped water chestnuts add crunch.

Serve the lentils with Spicy Grilled Flank Steak, page 88, or spoon them onto a ham sandwich.

2 TABLESPOONS VEGETABLE OIL

1 TABLESPOON MINCED GARLIC

1 TABLESPOON MINCED FRESH
    GINGERROOT

1/2 CUP CHOPPED ONION

1/2 CUP DICED CARROT (1/8-INCH
    DICE)

1/4 CUP DICED WATER CHESTNUTS
    (1/8-INCH DICE)

1 CUP (ABOUT 6-1/2 OUNCES)
    DRIED LENTILS, WASHED

1/4 CUP MISO

3 CUPS WATER

2 TABLESPOONS RICE WINE
    VINEGAR

FRESHLY GROUND BLACK PEPPER
    TO TASTE

2 TABLESPOONS CHOPPED FRESH
    CILANTRO LEAVES

▬ Heat the oil in a 2-quart pot over high heat. Add the garlic and gingerroot and cook for 30 seconds. Add the onion and cook for 1 minute longer. Add the carrot and water chestnuts; cook for 30 seconds. Add the lentils and toss to mix, then stir in the miso. Stir in the water and bring to a boil. Reduce the heat, partially cover the pot, and simmer for 30 minutes.

Uncover the pot and add the vinegar. Simmer until the lentils are soft but not mushy, about 15 minutes longer. Almost all the liquid should be absorbed. Season with pepper and stir in the cilantro. Serve warm or at room temperature.

Makes 3-1/2 cups.

Adzuki Beans

In Japan, tiny red adzuki beans are commonly served with rice (often glutinous) or mashed into a sweet paste. Their particularly nice flavor adds interest to mixed green salads and hearty soups. They're also good in Three-Bean Salad, page 174, and Refried Adzuki Beans, page 172.

6 OUNCES (1 SCANT CUP) DRIED
    ADZUKI BEANS

2-1/2 CUPS WATER

1/2 TEASPOON KOSHER SALT

▬ Rinse and sort through the beans, removing any small stones that may be mixed in with them. Place the beans and water in a 2-quart pot and bring to a boil. Reduce the heat, partially cover the pot, and simmer for 1 hour. Add the salt and continue to cook until the beans are soft, about 30 minutes longer.

Makes about 2-1/2 cups.

Refried Adzuki Beans

Mexican cooks mash pinto beans and cook them in fat to make refried beans, a side dish that's a staple of most Tex-Mex restaurants. Using flavorful adzuki beans instead of pintos makes for an unusual variation. Try this at your next Mexican meal or with Stir-Fried Chicken Enchiladas, page 60.

2 TABLESPOONS OLIVE OIL

1 TEASPOON MINCED GARLIC

1/2 CUP CHOPPED ONION

1 RECIPE COOKED ADZUKI BEANS,
    PAGE 171

ABOUT 1/4 CUP WATER

1/2 TEASPOON KOSHER SALT

1 TEASPOON SESAME OIL

■ Heat the olive oil in a large skillet over high heat, add the garlic and onion, and cook until soft, about 3 minutes. Add 1/2 cup beans, crushing and stirring them with a wooden spoon or a Mexican bean masher until fairly smooth. Add another 1/2 cup beans; cook and stir in the same way. When the mixture gets very dry, thin it a bit with some of the water; it should be thick but moist. Add the remaining beans, 1/2 cup at a time, crushing and stirring each addition and thinning with water as needed. Stir in the salt and sesame oil. Continue to cook, turning the mixture often, until it is smooth and thick, about 5 minutes. Serve hot. The beans dry out as they stand.

Makes 4 to 6 servings.

Black Beans

Of all dried beans, black beans are my favorite, partly for flavor and partly for color. Most familiar to Westerners are *frijoles negros*, commonly used in Central and South America. The rounder, smaller black soybeans are sold here as fermented black beans; quite salty, they are a wonderful seasoning for sauces and other foods.

Combining dried and fermented black beans, this simple dish is good with steamed chicken or in place of ordinary beans at a Mexican dinner. You might add a little chopped tomato and cilantro for an excellent salad.

1/2 POUND (ABOUT 1-1/4 CUPS) DRIED BLACK BEANS

4 TO 6 CUPS WATER

2 GARLIC CLOVES

1 (1/2-INCH) CUBE FRESH GINGERROOT, HALVED

1 SMALL (2-OUNCE) ONION, CHOPPED

1/4 CUP FERMENTED BLACK BEANS, RINSED BRIEFLY, ROUGHLY CHOPPED

1/2 TEASPOON SAMBAL OELEK

1 TEASPOON SOY SAUCE

■ Rinse and sort through the dried beans, removing any small stones that may be mixed in with them. Place the beans and 4 cups water in a 3-quart pot. Add the garlic, gingerroot, and onion. Bring to a boil; reduce the heat, partially cover the pot, and simmer for 1 hour. Add the fermented black beans, sambal, and soy sauce. Continue to cook until the dried beans are soft enough to mash with a spoon, 1 to 2 hours, adding more water as needed (the amount of water varies with the age of the beans). The garlic cloves will be soft; mash them with a spoon and stir through the beans.

Makes about 3 cups.

Black Bean Cakes

Given the trend toward meals with less meat, beans are becoming increasingly popular in America. These savory cakes, made with black beans, are delicious alongside Roast Chicken with Cilantro and Lime, page 72, or even as a meal in themselves, topped with Tomato Sauce, page 190.

1 CUP COOKED BLACK BEANS, ABOVE

2 TABLESPOONS CHOPPED FRESH CILANTRO LEAVES

1 LARGE EGG

1/4 TEASPOON RED CURRY PASTE, PAGE 189

1/4 TEASPOON KOSHER SALT

1 OUNCE MOZZARELLA CHEESE, CUT INTO SMALL PIECES

FINE DRY BREAD CRUMBS

2 TABLESPOONS VEGETABLE OIL

■ Place the beans and cilantro in a food processor and process until finely chopped. Add the egg, Red Curry Paste, and salt. Process to form a paste; then transfer the paste to a bowl and stir in the cheese.

Divide the bean paste into fourths. Shape each portion into a cake about 1/3 inch thick. Coat the cakes completely with the bread crumbs, pressing the crumbs into the cakes to make them stick.

Heat the oil in an 8-inch skillet over medium-high heat. Add the bean cakes and cook until browned, about 1 minute on each side.

Makes 4 bean cakes (4 side-dish or 2 main-dish servings).

Three-Bean Salad

This salad might better be called *four*-bean salad—the black beans are cooked with fermented black beans. By any name, it's a pretty dish: the pale navy beans contrast in flavor and color with the dark adzuki and black beans, bright tomatoes, and red onion. The dressing is full of the perfume of sesame oil.

This is excellent picnic fare. Try it with grilled hamburgers and hot dogs or smoked chicken sandwiches on rye. I also like it with poached fish.

6 OUNCES (1 SCANT CUP) DRIED NAVY BEANS

3 TO 4 CUPS WATER

1 TEASPOON KOSHER SALT

1 CUP COOKED BLACK BEANS, PAGE 173

1 CUP COOKED ADZUKI BEANS, PAGE 171

1/2 CUP CHOPPED RED ONION

1 CUP CHOPPED TOMATOES

2 TABLESPOONS RICE WINE VINEGAR

2 TABLESPOONS SESAME OIL

2 TABLESPOONS OLIVE OIL

1 TEASPOON DIJON MUSTARD

1/4 TEASPOON FRESHLY GROUND BLACK PEPPER

■■■ Rinse and sort through the navy beans, removing any small stones that may be mixed in with them. Then place the navy beans in a 2-quart pot with 3 cups water. Bring to a boil; reduce the heat, partially cover the pot, and simmer for 1 hour. Add the salt and simmer until the beans are soft, 30 minutes to 1 hour longer. Add more water as necessary. When the beans are done, drain them; then place in a bowl and add the Black Beans, Adzuki Beans, onion, and tomatoes. In a separate bowl, whisk together the vinegar, sesame oil, olive oil, mustard, and pepper. Pour the dressing over the beans and stir to blend completely. Serve at room temperature.

Makes about 5 cups.

Polenta

Cornmeal mush is popular in Italy and Eastern Europe. In Rumania, it's called *mamaliga* and served with cheese. Northern Italians like to top it with rich sauces or cool it until firm, then slice and sauté it. I love it with Braised Spareribs, page 97, and spicy stir-fried meats. The bright yellow color is a nice change from white or brown rice.

Though it's not difficult to make, polenta does require constant attention and fairly vigorous stirring. The goal is to get it very smooth, without a single lump. I find this easiest to achieve if the water is just simmering—definitely not boiling. Then I pour the cornmeal in slowly, whisking vigorously all the time. Once all the cornmeal has been mixed in, I switch to a wooden spoon. If I end up with lumps anyway, I press the finished polenta through a sieve to eliminate them.

6 CUPS WATER

1 TABLESPOON KOSHER SALT

2 CUPS YELLOW CORNMEAL

■ Bring the water to a boil in a large pot. Add the salt and reduce the heat so the water is not quite boiling. Slowly whisk in the cornmeal, stirring constantly. When all the cornmeal has been added, increase the heat slightly and continue to cook, stirring, until the mixture is thick enough to hold its shape, about 15 minutes.

Makes about 6 cups.

Vegetable Pancakes

I'm a sucker for crispy potato pancakes, but I like this Oriental vegetable version even better. Though the cakes taste best if the vegetables are grated by hand, for a large group I use the coarse grating disk of a food processor.

Serve these with any simple meat or fish dish or with barely-set omelets.

4 CARROTS, GRATED

1/2 POUND DAIKON, PEELED, GRATED

1 POUND POTATOES, PEELED, GRATED

1 CUP CHOPPED GREEN ONIONS

2 TEASPOONS GRATED FRESH GINGERROOT

2 LARGE EGGS

6 TABLESPOONS ALL-PURPOSE FLOUR

3 TABLESPOONS SESAME OIL

6 TABLESPOONS VEGETABLE OIL

KOSHER SALT AND FRESHLY GROUND BLACK PEPPER TO TASTE

■ Place the carrots, daikon, and potatoes in a bowl. Squeeze to release as much liquid as possible from the vegetables; pour off and discard the liquid. (Processor-grated vegetables will release more liquid.) Stir in the green onions, gingerroot, eggs, and flour. Mix well.

Pour the sesame oil and vegetable oil into a heavy 10-inch skillet. The oil should be about 1/8 inch deep. If you use a smaller skillet, adjust the quantity of oil, keeping the ratio of 2 parts vegetable oil to 1 part sesame oil.

Heat the oil. Pile about 1/3 cup of the vegetable mixture into the skillet, then press down on the top of the pile to flatten it a bit. You should be able to cook about 3 pancakes at a time. Cook until browned on the bottom, about 5 minutes. Turn and cook until browned on the other side, about 3 minutes longer. Place the finished pancakes on a plate lined with paper towels and keep warm in a low oven until ready to serve.

Season the pancakes with salt and pepper.

Makes about 16 (4-inch) pancakes (enough for 6 to 8 servings).

Scallion Bread

Although rice is the staple Asian grain, bread is also popular. A favorite Chinese snack is browned scallion bread, an ideal accompaniment to simple dinners of salad and soup or more elaborate meals of chicken and fish. In fact, I could eat this bread just about any time except at a formal dinner—I like to pick it up with my hands, and it is a little greasy.

The directions here tell you how to make two 6-inch breads. If you prefer smaller breads, divide the dough into four or more pieces and shape them as directed, using proportionately less sesame oil, salt, and green onion for each.

2 CUPS ALL-PURPOSE FLOUR
3/4 CUP BOILING WATER
2 TEASPOONS SESAME OIL
1 TEASPOON KOSHER SALT
1/2 CUP CHOPPED GREEN ONIONS
(SEE NOTE BELOW)
VEGETABLE OIL FOR FRYING

■ Place the flour in a food processor. With the machine running, pour the boiling water through the feed tube and process just until the dough holds together (do not overprocess). Turn out the dough onto a very lightly floured work surface and knead until silky smooth. Place the dough in a lightly oiled bowl and turn over to oil the top. Cover and let rest for 30 minutes.

Divide the dough into 2 equal parts and cover 1 part. Place the other part on a lightly floured surface. Roll into an 8- by 12-inch rectangle. Brush 1 teaspoon sesame oil over the rectangle, then sprinkle half the salt and green onions evenly on top. Starting at a 12-inch side, roll up the dough jelly-roll style. Pinch the open edges to seal and press down slightly with your hand to flatten the dough. Holding 1 end of the dough stationary, coil the dough around itself in a spiral (like a coiled rug). Push the loose end under and press to seal. With a rolling pin, gently roll the dough out into a circle about 6-1/2 inches in diameter.

Repeat with the remaining dough, sesame oil, salt, and green onions to make a second bread.

In a heavy 8-inch skillet, heat 1/4 inch of vegetable oil over medium-high heat. Add 1 bread, cover the skillet, and cook until the bread is well browned on the bottom, about 5 minutes. Turn the bread over and cook until browned on the other side, about 5 minutes longer. Drain on paper towels, then cut into 6 wedges. Repeat to cook the second bread.

Makes 2 (6-inch) breads.

NOTE: "Scallion" and "green onion" are synonymous. Both refer to onions pulled when still very small, with tiny bulbs and long, green shoots. In New York, where I live, these young onions are always called "scallions"—but since "green onion" seems to be the commoner name in most of the country, I've used that term in the other recipes in this book. However, I've never heard of Green Onion Bread, so to avoid confusion (while perhaps causing it in other ways), I've called this recipe Scallion Bread.

Focaccia with Chinese Sausage

Focaccia is a round, flat, crusty Italian bread served warm as a snack. The simplest versions are topped with just a sprinkling of coarse salt, while others are flavored with sausage or herbs. This one, bowing to the Orient, uses sweet Chinese sausage and sesame oil. Serve it warm with drinks or a mixed green salad.

1 (1/4-OUNCE) PACKAGE ACTIVE DRY YEAST

1 CUP WARM WATER

3 CUPS ALL-PURPOSE FLOUR

1 TEASPOON KOSHER SALT

1/4 TEASPOON FRESHLY GROUND BLACK PEPPER

1/4 CUP SESAME OIL

2 CHINESE-STYLE PORK SAUSAGES (ABOUT 1/4 POUND *TOTAL*)

Dissolve the yeast in the warm water. Set aside for 5 minutes.

Place the flour, salt, and pepper in a food processor. Process briefly to mix. With the machine running, pour the dissolved yeast and the sesame oil through the feed tube. Process until the mixture begins to hold together.

Turn out the dough onto a lightly floured work surface and knead until very smooth. Place the dough in an oiled bowl, turn over to oil the top, cover, and let rise in a warm place until doubled in bulk, 45 minutes to 1 hour.

While the dough is rising, bring water to a boil in the bottom of a steamer or wok. Reduce the heat so the water simmers. Place the sausages on a steamer rack. Set the rack in place over the simmering water, cover, and steam until the sausages are softened and the fat becomes translucent, about 15 minutes. Let the sausages cool slightly, then quarter them lengthwise and cut crosswise into 1/2-inch pieces.

Punch down the dough and return it to the floured work surface. Knead all the sausage into the dough (some bits will stick out; that's OK). Return the dough to the bowl, cover again, and let rise 30 minutes longer.

Punch down the dough again and knead into a ball. Flatten the ball, then roll into a 12-inch circle. Place the circle on an ungreased baking sheet, cover, and let rest for 15 minutes. Meanwhile, preheat the oven to 425F (220C). Bake the focaccia in the preheated oven until lightly browned and cooked through, 20 to 30 minutes. Serve warm.

Makes 1 (12-inch) focaccia.

Sesame Crêpes

Thin pancakes are common throughout the world, be they the delicate crêpes of France or the firmer pancakes of China. This recipe follows the basic French technique, but the batter is made with water instead of milk, and the finished crêpes have the wonderful flavor and aroma of sesame oil. I first made them to serve with stir-fried pork, but they also make nice wrappers for Mo-Shu Vegetables, page 124, and other fairly "dry" stir-fries (overly saucy foods will make the crêpes soggy). You can also serve them on the side, as you would tortillas or rolls.

3 LARGE EGGS
1 CUP ALL-PURPOSE FLOUR
1-1/2 CUPS WATER
1/2 TEASPOON KOSHER SALT
1 TABLESPOON SESAME OIL
VEGETABLE OIL FOR COOKING

▬ Place the eggs, flour, water, salt, and sesame oil in a blender or food processor and process until very smooth. (You can also beat by hand or with an electric mixer.) Cover and refrigerate for at least 1 hour.

Lightly brush a 7-inch crêpe or omelet pan with vegetable oil. Heat the pan over high heat. Stir the batter, then pour a scant 1/4 cup into the pan. Rotate to make sure the batter is evenly distributed. Cook until the edges curl and the crêpe is lightly browned on the bottom, 1 to 1-1/2 minutes. Loosen the crêpe carefully with a spatula and your fingers; turn the crêpe over and cook until spotted with brown on the other side, about 15 seconds longer. Remove to a plate. Cook the remaining batter in the same way, adjusting the heat as needed. Brush the pan with oil from time to time.

Makes about 12 (6-1/2-inch) crêpes.

Cornbread Stuffing

Cornbread stuffings have lately shown a Southwestern influence, often seasoned with a hint of jalapeño chili. This one, flavored with Chinese sausage and peanuts, is a fabulous variation—a little different, but not so exotic that it won't be accepted at most Thanksgiving dinners. If your family insists on tradition, save this for another time and serve it with roast chicken.

- 1 POUND CHINESE-STYLE PORK SAUSAGES
- 1/4 CUP VEGETABLE OIL
- 2 GARLIC CLOVES, MINCED
- 1-1/2 CUPS CHOPPED GREEN ONIONS
- 1 RECIPE SZECHUAN CORNBREAD, BELOW, COOLED, CUT INTO 1/2-INCH CUBES
- 1 CUP CHOPPED ROASTED UNSALTED PEANUTS
- 1/2 CUP CHOPPED FRESH CILANTRO LEAVES
- 1 CUP CHICKEN STOCK

■ Bring water to a boil in the bottom of a steamer or wok. Reduce the heat so the water simmers. Place the sausages on a steamer rack. Set the rack in place over the simmering water, cover, and steam until the sausages are softened and the fat becomes translucent, about 15 minutes. Let the sausages cool briefly. Cut each one lengthwise into 4 pieces, then crosswise into 1/4-inch slices. Place in a large bowl.

Heat the oil in a large skillet over medium-high heat. Add the garlic and green onions and cook until soft, about 2 minutes. Add the green onion mixture to the sausages along with the cornbread, peanuts, and cilantro. Stir to mix. Don't worry if the cornbread crumbles a bit. Add the stock and stir again.

You can stuff a 22-pound turkey with all the stuffing or a smaller bird with some of the stuffing. Place any leftover stuffing (or all of it, if you prefer) in a baking dish and bake in a 350F (175C) oven for 1 hour.

Makes 12 cups.

Szechuan Cornbread

Cornbread is the traditional bread of the American South and Southwest. Many typical versions are sweet and cakelike, but this one is a spicier bread. It's firm enough to cube for stuffing but tender enough to eat on its own, perhaps with Soy-Roasted Chicken, page 63, or Lamb Kabobs with Hoisin, page 78.

- 1 TABLESPOON SZECHUAN PEPPERCORNS
- 3 TABLESPOONS UNSALTED BUTTER
- 1 TABLESPOON MINCED FRESH GINGERROOT
- 1 CUP YELLOW CORNMEAL
- 1 CUP ALL-PURPOSE FLOUR
- 1 TABLESPOON SUGAR
- 1 TABLESPOON BAKING POWDER
- 1 TEASPOON KOSHER SALT
- 1 LARGE EGG
- 1 CUP MILK

■ Preheat the oven to 425F (220C). Grease a 9-inch-square baking pan; set aside.

Toast the peppercorns in a dry skillet over medium heat until they begin to smoke, about 1 minute. Grind to a powder, using a spice grinder, suribachi, or mortar and pestle. Set aside. Melt the butter in a small skillet over medium heat; add the gingerroot and cook for 1 minute. In a bowl, combine the cornmeal, flour, sugar, baking powder, salt, and ground peppercorns. Stir to mix. Beat the egg with the milk and pour into the center of the flour mixture along with the gingerroot and butter. Stir just to mix, then pour into the greased pan. Bake in the preheated oven until lightly browned on top, 20 to 25 minutes.

Makes 9 (3-inch) squares of cornbread

Turn to this chapter when you want a different salad dressing or something to perk up a broiled steak or grilled or poached fish. You'll also find some great sauces for carrots, eggplant, and other vegetables. In keeping with the Oriental style, most of these recipes, even those that are Western in inspiration, are very quick to make. Many are just whisked together, needing no cooking at all.

Try green Wasabi-Ginger Butter, page 186, on grilled fish or meat. Curried Mayonnaise, page 186, is delicious on sandwiches. Serve spicy Red Pepper Salsa, page 181, with corn chips.

SAUCES

Tomato Salsa

A spicy uncooked tomato sauce like this one is a standard on the tables of many Mexican families. I much prefer it to ketchup on my hamburgers and French fries. It's excellent with Fried Won Tons, page 26, Cheese Roulade, page 126, Tortillas with Oriental Beef and Black Beans, page 82, and tortilla chips.

This quick sauce is best made just before using, although it will last a day or two in the refrigerator. If you can't find fresh jalapeños or other chilies, use a few drops of hot-pepper sauce to add bite.

2 FRESH JALAPEÑO CHILIES, CORED, SEEDED, DERIBBED, MINCED

1/4 CUP MINCED ONION

1/2 POUND TOMATOES, CORED, DICED

2 TABLESPOONS MINCED FRESH CILANTRO LEAVES

1/2 TEASPOON KOSHER SALT

1 TABLESPOON WATER

In a small bowl, combine all the ingredients and stir to mix well.

Makes about 1 cup.

Red Pepper Salsa

Although related to Tomato Salsa (above) and used in the same ways, this sauce has sweet bell peppers added for crunch. The spicy flavor comes from sambal, an Indonesian chili sauce. Try Red Pepper Salsa with chicken, beef, or blue corn tortilla chips.

3/4 CUP FINELY CHOPPED RED BELL PEPPER

1-1/2 CUPS CHOPPED SEEDED TOMATOES

1/2 TO 1 TEASPOON SAMBAL OELEK

2 TABLESPOONS MINCED ONION

2 TABLESPOONS OLIVE OIL

In a small bowl, combine all the ingredients and stir to mix well.

Makes about 2 cups.

Soy Vinaigrette

I use this standard vinaigrette on most salads—assortments of greens and herbs, chunks of tomato and red onion in season, heartier dishes with meat and cheese. The soy sauce is an excellent replacement for salt, and the sesame oil adds a distinctive accent. I do vary the vinegar from time to time, using balsamic or red wine varieties instead of rice wine vinegar.

1 TABLESPOON RICE WINE VINEGAR

2 TEASPOONS SOY SAUCE

1 TEASPOON DIJON MUSTARD

2 TABLESPOONS OLIVE OIL

1 TEASPOON SESAME OIL

■ In a small bowl, whisk together the vinegar, soy sauce, and mustard. Whisk in the olive oil and sesame oil.

Makes about 1/4 cup.

Ginger Vinaigrette

Ginger adds an exotic touch to this sauce, an excellent dressing for Chicken and Sun-Dried Tomato Salad, page 66, or other hearty salads with fish, beef, or lots of vegetables.

Like all vinaigrettes, this can be made ahead, but it must be stirred right before using.

1 TABLESPOON MINCED FRESH
   GINGERROOT

2 TABLESPOONS MINCED SHALLOT

1 TABLESPOON RICE WINE VINEGAR

2 TABLESPOONS LIME JUICE

2 TEASPOONS SOY SAUCE

1/4 CUP OLIVE OIL

1/2 TEASPOON SESAME OIL

FRESHLY GROUND BLACK PEPPER
   TO TASTE

■ In a small bowl, combine all the ingredients and whisk to mix well.

Makes about 1/2 cup.

Spicy Peanut Vinaigrette

I like the texture this sauce gets from the chopped peanuts. Spoon it over a salad of mixed greens with chunks of tuna and green onion, or serve it with grilled pork kabobs.

3 TABLESPOONS RICE WINE
   VINEGAR

2 TEASPOONS SOY SAUCE

2 TEASPOONS HOT SESAME (CHILI)
   OIL

1/4 CUP PEANUT OIL

1/4 TEASPOON HOT-PEPPER SAUCE

1/4 CUP CHOPPED ROASTED
   UNSALTED PEANUTS

■ In a small bowl, combine the vinegar and soy sauce. Whisk in the hot sesame oil, peanut oil, and hot-pepper sauce. Stir in the peanuts.
  Makes about 1/2 cup.

Fermented Black Bean and Tomato Sauce

The saltiness of fermented black beans marries well with the acidity of tomatoes. I usually serve this sauce with salmon or salmon trout, since the colors are particularly pretty together. It's almost a salad by itself, but I've tossed it with Boston or Bibb lettuce to make an intriguing first course or side dish.

1/4 CUP OLIVE OIL

2 TABLESPOONS CHINESE BLACK
   VINEGAR

1/2 POUND TOMATOES, CORED,
   SEEDED, CUT INTO THIN STRIPS

2 TABLESPOONS FERMENTED BLACK
   BEANS, RINSED, ROUGHLY
   CHOPPED

1 TABLESPOON MINCED FRESH
   GINGERROOT

■ In a small bowl, whisk together the oil and vinegar. Add the tomatoes, black beans, and gingerroot. Stir to mix. If possible, let stand for at least 30 minutes to develop the flavors.
  Makes about 1 cup.

Cilantro-Miso Sauce

This bright green sauce, refreshingly tangy with lime, adds a splash of contrasting color to grilled pork or beef. It's also good over grilled fish or in a salad of radicchio, watercress, and chicken. In a covered container, it will keep in the refrigerator for a few days.

1/2 CUP FRESH CILANTRO LEAVES

JUICE OF 1 LIME

3 TABLESPOONS LIGHT-COLORED MISO

1 TABLESPOON OLIVE OIL

1/4 TEASPOON FRESHLY GROUND BLACK PEPPER

1 TABLESPOON MIRIN

■ Place the cilantro in a food processor and process until well chopped. Add the lime juice, miso, oil, pepper, and mirin. Process until smooth, stopping to scrape down the sides of the bowl as necessary.

Makes about 1/2 cup.

Creamy Miso Dressing

Miso adds a special flavor to this mayonnaise dressing. Because it's thick, it's especially good on chef and chunky chicken salads.

1/4 CUP MAYONNAISE

2 TABLESPOONS LIGHT-COLORED MISO

1 TABLESPOON LEMON JUICE

1 TABLESPOON MINCED ONION

■ In a small bowl, combine all the ingredients and whisk to mix well.

Makes about 1/3 cup.

Wasabi-Ginger Butter

This is a very quick sauce for grilled fish or beef. Pale green in color, it's very pretty over pink salmon.

1 TABLESPOON WASABI POWDER

1-1/2 TEASPOONS WATER

1 (1/2-INCH) CUBE FRESH GINGERROOT

1/4 CUP (4 TABLESPOONS) UNSALTED BUTTER, AT ROOM TEMPERATURE

1 TABLESPOON LEMON JUICE

1 TEASPOON KOSHER SALT

━ In a small bowl, mix together the wasabi powder and water. Cover and let stand for 5 minutes to develop the wasabi's flavor.

Place the gingerroot in a food processor and process until minced. Add the butter and process until creamy. Add the wasabi paste, lemon juice, and salt; process until smooth. Scrape the butter mixture onto a sheet of wax paper. Use the paper to shape the mixture into a log about 2 inches long. Refrigerate until firm. When ready to serve, cut into 1/4-inch slices and melt over hot fish or beef.

Makes about 1/4 cup (enough for 8 servings).

Curried Mayonnaise

I made this sauce to serve with Oriental Bouillabaisse, page 115, as a substitute for the traditional garlicky aïoli. It also adds spice to ham sandwiches and tuna salad and gives a lift to turkey the day after Thanksgiving.

1 CUP MAYONNAISE

1 TABLESPOON RED CURRY PASTE, PAGE 189

2 TEASPOONS LIME JUICE

1/4 TEASPOON CRUMBLED SAFFRON THREADS MIXED WITH 1/4 TEASPOON WATER

━ Combine all the ingredients in a food processor. Process until smooth.

Makes about 1 cup.

Sweet Mustard Sauce

Mirin adds a touch of sweetness to this versatile, quick-to-make sauce. It goes with Sesame Chicken in Phyllo, page 39, as well as poached salmon or cod or grilled flank steak. It's also a flavorful dressing for salads made with assorted greens, grated Swiss cheese, and smoked ham.

1/4 CUP DIJON MUSTARD

2 TABLESPOONS RICE WINE VINEGAR

2 TABLESPOONS MIRIN

1/4 CUP VEGETABLE OIL

▬ Place the mustard in a small bowl. Gradually whisk in the vinegar, then the mirin and oil. The sauce should be smooth.
Makes about 2/3 cup.

Mustard Dipping Sauce

Thinner than Sweet Mustard Sauce, this one is meant for dipping Pearl Balls, page 29, or egg rolls. It goes nicely with *zarusoba*, a Japanese dish of cold soba served in a bamboo basket. Each mouthful of noodles is dipped in the soy-based sauce before eating.

2 TABLESPOONS SOY SAUCE

2 TABLESPOONS SAKE

1 TABLESPOON DIJON MUSTARD

1/4 TEASPOON HOT-PEPPER SAUCE

▬ In a small bowl, combine all the ingredients and whisk to mix well.
Makes about 1/3 cup.

Peanut Sauce

This sauce is excellent with Pork and Crab Terrine, page 41. It also makes a nice dipping sauce for somen.

1/4 CUP LIME JUICE

2 TABLESPOONS FISH SAUCE

2 TABLESPOONS CHOPPED ROASTED UNSALTED PEANUTS

2 TEASPOONS SUGAR

▬ In a small bowl, combine all the ingredients and stir to mix well.
Makes about 1/2 cup.

Nuoc Cham

In Vietnamese homes, *nuoc cham* is always on the table. It is delicious poured over everything from vegetables to hamburgers. To better suit Western palates, I've toned down the spiciness, but feel free to add more red pepper if you like.

1 GARLIC CLOVE, MINCED

1 TEASPOON MINCED LIME PEEL

1/4 TEASPOON CRUSHED RED PEPPER FLAKES

2 TEASPOONS LIME JUICE

2 TABLESPOONS FISH SAUCE

3 TABLESPOONS WATER

2 TEASPOONS SUGAR

■ In a small bowl, combine the garlic, lime peel, and red pepper flakes. Add the lime juice, fish sauce, water, and sugar. Whisk until all ingredients are well blended and the sugar is dissolved.

Makes about 1/3 cup.

Sesame Steak Sauce

Much lighter than traditional Western steak sauces, this one is good on thin slices of grilled or broiled flank steak or London broil.

1 TABLESPOON SESAME SEEDS, TOASTED IN A DRY SKILLET

3 TABLESPOONS SOY SAUCE

1 TABLESPOON SESAME OIL

2 TABLESPOONS CHOPPED GREEN ONION

1/4 TEASPOON CHILI POWDER

2 TEASPOONS RICE WINE VINEGAR

1/2 TEASPOON SUGAR

■ Crush the sesame seeds until most of them are powdery, using a mortar and pestle, a suribachi, or a spice grinder. Place in a bowl with the remaining ingredients. Stir until well mixed.

Makes about 1/3 cup.

Ginger-Tamarind Sauce

Tamarind has a tart, citrusy flavor. This sauce is easy to make ahead and excellent on steamed or grilled fish fillets.

2 TABLESPOONS TAMARIND PULP
1/4 CUP HOT WATER
1-1/2 TABLESPOONS MINCED GARLIC
3 TABLESPOONS WATER
2 TABLESPOONS SHREDDED FRESH
  GINGERROOT
1 TEASPOON SUGAR

■ Place the tamarind pulp in a bowl and add 1/4 cup hot water. Let soak for 20 minutes, stirring occasionally to help the pulp dissolve. Then press the mixture through a strainer to eliminate the seeds and undissolved pulp. You need 3 tablespoons of tamarind liquid.

Place the tamarind liquid in a bowl and add the garlic, 3 tablespoons water, gingerroot, and sugar. Stir to blend.

Makes about 1/2 cup.

Red Curry Paste

Most of us think of curries as yellow sauces from India, but in Thailand they're usually red or green—depending on the color of the basic chili—and much spicier than most Indian versions. Many Thai cooks make curry paste in quantity to keep on hand in a covered jar in the refrigerator, while others turn to commercial products. If you have the time and can get the ingredients, try the homemade version; otherwise, buy some. It's handy to have around for flavoring sauces and marinades for fish, chicken, and pasta. It also transforms mixed vegetables, as in Curried Vegetables, page 126.

1 TABLESPOON VEGETABLE OIL
1/2 CUP CHOPPED ONION
1 TABLESPOON MINCED GARLIC
2 TEASPOONS SHRIMP PASTE
3 DRIED CHILIES, SEEDS REMOVED,
  CRUMBLED
2 TEASPOONS CUMIN SEEDS
1 TABLESPOON CORIANDER SEEDS
1 TEASPOON DRIED SLICED LEMON
  GRASS OR POWDERED LEMON
  GRASS (SEREH)
1 TEASPOON POWDERED GALANGAL
  (LAOS)
2 TEASPOONS MINCED LEMON PEEL
2 TABLESPOONS CHOPPED FRESH
  CILANTRO LEAVES
1 TEASPOON KOSHER SALT
1 TEASPOON GROUND TURMERIC
2 TEASPOONS PAPRIKA

■ Heat the oil in a small skillet over medium-high heat. Add the onion and garlic and cook until soft and beginning to brown, about 5 minutes. Add the shrimp paste and stir to mix well, pressing against the paste to make it blend into the other ingredients. Cook about 3 minutes longer. Remove from the heat.

Place the chilies, cumin seeds, coriander seeds, and lemon grass in a spice grinder and grind until powdery. Set aside.

Place the onion mixture in a food processor or blender and process until fairly smooth. Add the ground spices, galangal, lemon peel, cilantro, salt, turmeric, and paprika. Process until the mixture is a smooth paste.

Makes about 1/4 cup.

Tomato Sauce

This classic tomato sauce has a hint of the East in the seasoning. Try it with Stuffed Cabbage Rolls, page 148, and Poblano Chilies Stuffed with Glutinous Rice, page 146, as well as with spaghetti or steamed fish. If you prefer a milder sauce, leave out the sambal.

2 TABLESPOONS OLIVE OIL

2 TEASPOONS MINCED GARLIC

1 TEASPOON MINCED FRESH GINGERROOT

1 CUP CHOPPED ONION

1 (28-OUNCE) CAN WHOLE TOMATOES WITH PUREE

1 TEASPOON SAMBAL OELEK

1 TEASPOON SOY SAUCE

Heat the oil in a 2-quart saucepan over high heat. Add the garlic and gingerroot and cook for 30 seconds. Add the onion and cook until soft, about 3 minutes. Add the tomatoes along with their puree, breaking up the tomatoes with a wooden spoon. Reduce the heat and simmer for 15 minutes. Add the sambal and soy sauce and simmer for 15 minutes longer. Put the sauce through the coarse blade of a food mill. Reheat before serving, adjusting the seasonings to taste.

Makes 2-3/4 cups.

NOTE: You may puree this sauce in a food processor if you like. I prefer to use a food mill, since it removes most of the seeds from the sauce.

SAUCES

Red Pepper Puree

Red bell peppers are a versatile vegetable. In this smooth sauce, a touch of hot chili provides a nice counterpoint to the sweetness of the peppers. Use the sauce for Stir-Fried Chicken Enchiladas, page 60, steamed chicken or fish, or baked pasta shells stuffed with ricotta.

2 TABLESPOONS OLIVE OIL

2 CUPS CHOPPED ONIONS

2 GARLIC CLOVES, MINCED

1 POUND RED BELL PEPPERS, CORED, SEEDED, CHOPPED

2 CUPS CHICKEN STOCK

1 TEASPOON SZECHUAN CHILI SAUCE

Heat the oil in a 2-quart saucepan over high heat. Add the onions, garlic, and bell peppers. Sauté for 10 minutes. Add the stock and chili sauce. Bring to a boil; reduce the heat, cover, and simmer until the vegetables are very soft, about 15 minutes longer. Let cool; pour into a food processor and process until pureed.

Makes about 3-1/2 cups.

Indonesian-Style Peanut Sauce

This recipe takes peanut butter a step farther, turning it into a very flavorful spread. The interesting crunch comes from crisp onions and garlic, often used as garnishes in Indonesia. Indonesians spoon peanut sauce over cold cooked vegetables to make the popular dish called *gado-gado*, but it's also an excellent dip for raw vegetables (if thinned with a bit of water) and a tasty sauce for pasta. You might also try it on toast with or without jelly for an adult version of that childhood favorite. Keep it in a jar in the refrigerator, ready for unexpected company.

1/4 CUP VEGETABLE OIL

4 GARLIC CLOVES, THINLY SLICED

1 MEDIUM (1/4-POUND) ONION, THINLY SLICED

1 TEASPOON CRUSHED RED PEPPER FLAKES

1 TEASPOON SHRIMP PASTE

1 TABLESPOON SOY SAUCE

1 TABLESPOON LEMON JUICE

1 CUP CHUNKY PEANUT BUTTER

1 TEASPOON SUGAR

■ Heat the oil in an 8-inch skillet over high heat. Add the garlic and onion; cook until golden, about 5 minutes. Add the red pepper flakes and cook until the onion is nicely browned, about 4 minutes longer. With a slotted spoon, remove the onions and garlic to a bowl, leaving the oil in the skillet.

Return the skillet to the heat and add the shrimp paste, pressing down on it with a wooden spoon to make it dissolve. Stir in the soy sauce and lemon juice; cook just until the mixture is smooth. Remove the skillet from the heat and stir in the peanut butter until well blended. Add the peanut butter mixture and sugar to the onion and garlic. Stir to blend completely.

Makes about 1-1/4 cups.

Orange Barbecue Sauce

There are dozens of popular American barbecue sauces, varying from the simple vinegar sauces of North Carolina to the rich molasses ones of Kansas to the incredibly hot chili sauces of Texas. This one marries the fruitiness of Polynesian sauces with molasses and chili. It's rich and not very hot. Use it for Barbecued Ribs, page 98, or with roast chicken or beef.

1/2 CUP BOTTLED TOMATO-BASED CHILI SAUCE

1/4 CUP ORANGE JUICE

1/4 CUP SOY SAUCE

1/4 CUP MOLASSES

2 TABLESPOONS CHINESE BLACK VINEGAR

2 TABLESPOONS GRATED ONION

1/2 TEASPOON GRATED FRESH GINGERROOT

2 TEASPOONS HOT-PEPPER SAUCE

■ Place all the ingredients in a 2-quart saucepan. Stir to blend, then bring to a full boil. Let cool.

Makes about 1-1/4 cups.

Eating rich desserts after a meal is a typically American custom. In other countries, meals often end with some fresh fruit and perhaps a cookie or two; the creamy, gooey treats are usually served alone with afternoon tea or coffee. This is really the most sensible way to eat, and nearly all the desserts I serve —except on birthdays, which require an iced cake and candles—are fruit desserts, sorbets, tarts, or light puddings. Most of the recipes that follow, usually Western dishes with an Oriental twist, fit in that category and can be served nicely after dinner. The exceptions are probably the rice and noodle puddings, which I can happily eat as meals in themselves.

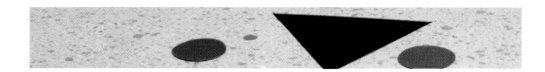

Luscious Coconut Bavarian Cream, page 200, is delicious with any seasonal fruit.

DESSERTS

Jasmine Tea Sorbet

Sorbets are wonderfully refreshing after a meal or as a pick-me-up during the day. This one, made with fragrant jasmine tea, has a pale, pretty, creamy color.

2 TABLESPOONS JASMINE TEA
    LEAVES
1 CUP BOILING WATER
1/2 CUP SUGAR
1/2 CUP WATER
1 TEASPOON LEMON JUICE

Place the tea leaves in a bowl. Pour 1 cup boiling water over the leaves, cover, and let steep for 10 minutes. Strain the liquid into another bowl; discard the leaves.

In a saucepan, heat the sugar and 1/2 cup water until the sugar is dissolved, stirring occasionally. Then bring to a boil and cook for 1 minute. Add the hot sugar syrup to the strained tea. Stir in the lemon juice, cover, and refrigerate until cold.

Freeze the mixture in an ice cream maker according to the manufacturer's directions.

Makes about 1-1/2 cups.

Plum Wine Sorbet

Plum wine, a refreshing change from heavier liqueurs, is fruity and fragrant, a lovely base for this sorbet. Serve with chunks of purple or red plums.

1 CUP SUGAR
1 CUP WATER
1 CUP PLUM WINE
1/4 CUP LEMON JUICE

In a saucepan, heat the sugar and water until the sugar is dissolved, stirring occasionally. Then bring to a boil and cook for 1 minute. Let the sugar syrup cool to room temperature, then mix it with the wine and lemon juice. Cover and refrigerate until cold. Freeze the mixture in an ice cream maker according to the manufacturer's directions.

Makes about 3 cups.

Ginger Ice Cream

Ginger preserves give this rich custard-based ice cream its light, tangy flavor. Spoon it over bowls of blueberries, strawberries, and blackberries in summer, over hot apple pie in the fall.

1/3 CUP SUGAR

1 CUP MILK

1 CUP WHIPPING CREAM

2 LARGE EGG YOLKS, AT ROOM
    TEMPERATURE

1/2 CUP GINGER PRESERVES

▰ Place the sugar, milk, and cream in a 2-quart saucepan. Bring to a boil over low heat, stirring occasionally to make sure the sugar is dissolved. Meanwhile, whisk the egg yolks together in a bowl.

When the cream mixture comes to a boil, remove it from the heat. Slowly begin whisking the hot cream mixture into the yolks to raise their temperature gradually. When you have added at least half the cream mixture to the yolks and the mixture in the bowl is steaming, slowly pour it back into the saucepan, whisking constantly.

Place the pan over low heat and cook, stirring constantly with a wooden spoon, until the custard is thick enough to coat the spoon, about 5 minutes. Pour the custard through a strainer into a clean metal bowl. Stir in the ginger preserves, cover, and refrigerate until cold.

Freeze the custard in an ice cream maker according to the manufacturer's directions.

Makes about 2 cups.

Poached Pears with Kumquats

Kumquats add tartness and a splash of color to this simple dessert. The pears can be cooked ahead and refrigerated for several days.

1-1/2 CUPS SUGAR

1-1/2 CUPS WATER

1/4 POUND KUMQUATS, CUT CROSSWISE INTO THIN ROUNDS, SEEDS REMOVED

3 LARGE, FIRM PEARS, PEELED, HALVED, CORED

In an 8-inch skillet, heat the sugar and water until the sugar is dissolved, stirring occasionally. Bring to a boil; reduce the heat and cook slowly until the syrup is clear. Add the kumquats and simmer for 5 minutes. Add the pear halves, cut side down, in a single layer. Cover the skillet and simmer for 15 minutes; turn the pear halves over and cook until they are easy to pierce with a wooden pick, about 15 minutes longer. Turn off the heat and let the fruit cool in the syrup.

With a slotted spoon, remove the pear halves to a cutting board. Working from the stem end of the pear toward the blossom end, make several long, even cuts through each pear half, leaving the slices attached at the stem end. Place each pear half on a plate, cut side down, so the slices fan out. Spoon the kumquats with some of the poaching syrup over the pears.

Makes 6 servings.

Baked Asian Pears

Smooth, round, and crisp like apples but with a pearlike flavor, Asian pears make interesting substitutes for other fruits. In this case, I've used them in a traditional baked apple recipe with maple syrup and walnuts. It's quick to prepare (although slow to bake) and makes a satisfying end to most meals. The pears never get as soft as apples do—an advantage for the cook, since the flesh won't turn to mush—but they soften enough to make eating them with a spoon a delight.

4 LARGE (ABOUT 3/4-POUND) ASIAN PEARS
1 TABLESPOON CHOPPED PECANS
8 TEASPOONS MAPLE SYRUP
4 TEASPOONS ORANGE JUICE
WHIPPING CREAM OR VANILLA ICE CREAM, IF DESIRED

Preheat the oven to 350F (175C).

Core the pears with an apple corer, leaving the bottom 1/2 inch intact. Remove all the seeds with a small knife or spoon and make the hole a little larger. Place the pears, cored ends up, in a baking dish just large enough to hold them. Sprinkle 1/4 of the pecans into the cavity of each pear, then pour 2 teaspoons maple syrup and 1 teaspoon orange juice into each. Add enough water to the dish to come about 1/2 inch up the sides. Cover the dish with foil and bake in the preheated oven until the pears are soft enough to pierce easily with a skewer, about 1 hour.

Serve hot with a bit of the pan juices, plain or with whipping cream or ice cream.

Makes 4 servings.

Apricot Sauce

Made with dried apricots and tangy ginger preserves, this is a wonderful sauce with Asian Pear Soufflé, page 204. If you like, double the recipe and keep leftovers in the refrigerator, ready to warm up and spoon over ice cream or poached pears.

1/2 CUP (ABOUT 3 OUNCES) DRIED APRICOTS
3/4 CUP WATER
1/4 CUP SUGAR
1/4 CUP GINGER PRESERVES
2 TEASPOONS COINTREAU

Place the apricots in a 1-quart pot with 1/2 cup water. Bring to a boil, reduce the heat, and simmer until the apricots are very soft, about 30 minutes. Let cool a bit, then process the apricots with their liquid in a food processor until pureed.

In a separate small pot, combine the sugar and remaining 1/4 cup water. Bring to a boil; boil, stirring occasionally, just until the sugar is dissolved. Stir the sugar syrup into the apricot puree along with the ginger preserves and Cointreau.

Reheat gently before serving.

Makes about 3/4 cup.

Almond Paste Buns

Puffy yeast buns filled with sweet bean paste are a popular Chinese snack that sounds and tastes strange to many Americans, especially those who bite into the brown paste expecting chocolate. In this recipe, the buns are filled with almond paste, and the result is terrific. Except for the orange flower water, the dough is a classic Chinese one that could also be filled with barbecued pork or cooked vegetables for a snack. Unlike most yeast doughs, it contains baking powder for extra leavening.

The buns are best served warm. Keep extras in the freezer. To serve, steam them for about 15 minutes to defrost and heat.

DESSERTS

1/2 (1/4-OUNCE) PACKAGE ACTIVE DRY YEAST (ABOUT 1 TEASPOON)

1/2 CUP PLUS 1 TABLESPOON SUGAR

1 CUP WARM WATER

2-1/2 TO 3 CUPS ALL-PURPOSE FLOUR

1 TABLESPOON VEGETABLE OIL

1 TEASPOON ORANGE FLOWER WATER, IF DESIRED

8 OUNCES (ABOUT 1 CUP) ALMOND PASTE

GRATED PEEL OF 1 LEMON

1 LARGE EGG WHITE

1 TEASPOON BAKING POWDER

Dissolve the yeast and 1 tablespoon sugar in the warm water. Set aside for about 5 minutes to let the yeast start growing.

Place 2-1/2 cups flour in the bowl of an electric mixer fitted with a dough hook. Add the yeast mixture, oil, and orange flower water, if desired. Knead with the mixer until smooth, then turn out onto a work surface sprinkled with flour. Continue to knead the dough, working in up to 1/2 cup more flour as needed, until it is very smooth but still soft, about 5 minutes. Do not add too much flour or the dough will be heavy.

Place the dough in an oiled bowl and turn it over to oil the top. Cover and let rise in a warm place for 3 hours. The dough will have more than doubled in bulk and will be very soft and spongy.

While the dough is rising, place the almond paste, the remaining 1/2 cup sugar, and the lemon peel in a food processor. Process for 10 seconds to blend. Add the egg white and process until the mixture is smooth and comes together in a ball. Set aside. Also line the bottoms of 2 steamer trays with dampened cheesecloth; set aside.

When the dough has finished rising, turn it out onto a very lightly floured board. Sprinkle the baking powder on top of the dough and knead briefly to distribute it evenly through the dough. Shape the dough into a roll and divide it into 12 equal pieces.

Roll 1 piece of dough into a smooth ball. Flatten it into a disk about 4 inches in diameter. Roll about 2 tablespoons of the almond paste mixture into a ball and place it in the center of the dough; bring up the edges of the dough and pinch to seal. Place the finished bun, seam side down, in a steamer tray. Repeat to use the remaining dough and almond paste mixture, making 11 more buns. Space the buns at least 1/2 inch apart in the steamer trays.

Cover the buns and let rest for about 15 minutes. Meanwhile, bring water to a boil in the bottom of a steamer. Reduce the heat so the water simmers. Set the trays in place over the simmering water, cover, and steam until the buns are firm to the touch, about 20 minutes. The buns will puff up considerably. Let cool slightly, but serve warm.

If you make the buns ahead, resteam them for about 5 minutes before serving.

Makes 12 buns.

Ginger Rice Pudding

This rich rice pudding gets its unctuous texture from glutinous rice and its bite from stem ginger. My family can't get enough of it. Stirring the mixture as it bakes keeps the rice from settling to the bottom.

3/4 CUP UNCOOKED GLUTINOUS
    RICE

2 LARGE EGGS

2 CUPS MILK

1/2 CUP WHIPPING CREAM

1/3 CUP SUGAR

1/2 CUP CHOPPED STEM GINGER
    PACKED IN SYRUP

1 TABLESPOON STEM GINGER SYRUP

1 TEASPOON MINCED ORANGE PEEL

▬ Rinse the rice in several changes of cold water until the water runs clear. Place the rice in a bowl, cover generously with cold water, and let soak for 1 hour.

Preheat the oven to 350F (175C). Grease a 2-quart casserole and set aside.

In a large bowl, whisk the eggs just to blend the yolks and whites. Stir in the milk, cream, and sugar. Drain the rice and add it to the bowl with the ginger, ginger syrup, and orange peel. Stir to mix. Pour the rice mixture into the greased casserole and bake in the preheated oven for 15 minutes. Stir the mixture and bake for 45 to 50 minutes longer, stirring every 15 minutes. The pudding should be set, but it may be a little runny on top. Let cool slightly, but serve warm.

Makes 6 to 8 servings.

Somen Noodle Pudding

In many ways like a rice pudding, this delicate dessert is made with thin somen noodles, raisins, coconut milk, and New England maple syrup. It's not too sweet, with a hint of coconut flavor. If you leave it unattended in the kitchen, you'll be amazed how quickly it disappears as everyone who passes takes just a spoonful or two—and keeps coming back. More a family dessert than a fancy sweet, it is good any time except after a particularly heavy meal.

1/2 POUND SOMEN
2 CUPS COCONUT MILK
3 LARGE EGGS
1/2 CUP MAPLE SYRUP
1/4 CUP SUGAR
1/2 TEASPOON GROUND CARDAMOM
1/2 TEASPOON GROUND CINNAMON
1/2 CUP RAISINS

Preheat the oven to 375F (190C).

Bring a large pot of water to a boil. Add the somen, return to a boil, and cook until barely tender, about 3 minutes. Drain well, rinse under cold water, and drain again.

In a large bowl, whisk together the coconut milk and eggs. Stir in the maple syrup, sugar, cardamom, and cinnamon. Add the drained noodles and stir to mix well. Add the raisins and stir to distribute them evenly. Pour the mixture into a deep 6-cup baking dish and bake in the preheated oven until set, about 1 hour. Serve hot, warm, or at room temperature.

Makes 6 to 8 servings.

Coconut Bavarian Cream

Combining custard, whipped cream, and beaten egg whites, this luscious dessert is an impressive ending for any meal. What makes the recipe unusual is the use of coconut rather than dairy milk, resulting in a full coconut flavor that's further emphasized by bits of toasted coconut. You can chill the Bavarian in any bowl or form; it is particularly attractive when made in a ring mold, then unmolded and filled with blue and red berries.

1/2 CUP COLD WATER
1 (1/4-OUNCE) PACKAGE UNFLAVORED GELATIN
1 CUP COCONUT MILK
2/3 CUP PLUS 1 TABLESPOON SUGAR
4 LARGE EGGS, SEPARATED
1 LARGE EGG YOLK
1/3 CUP TOASTED FLAKED COCONUT, PREFERABLY UNSWEETENED
1 TEASPOON VANILLA EXTRACT
1/2 CUP WHIPPING CREAM
MIXED BERRIES, SUCH AS BLUEBERRIES, STRAWBERRIES, AND RASPBERRIES

Place the cold water in a small metal bowl or pot. Sprinkle the gelatin on top. Let stand for a few minutes, just until all the gelatin is absorbed. Place the bowl or pot over very low heat (preferably with a flame tamer) and cook, stirring, until the gelatin is completely dissolved and the liquid is clear. Set aside, but keep warm and liquid.

Place the coconut milk and 2/3 cup sugar in a 2-quart saucepan and bring to a boil, stirring to make sure the sugar is dissolved. Remove from the heat.

Place all 5 of the egg yolks in a bowl and whisk until blended. Beating constantly, slowly ladle the hot coconut milk mixture into the yolks to raise their temperature. When most of the coconut milk mixture has been added, pour the contents of the bowl back into the saucepan. Return the pan to medium heat and cook, stirring constantly with a wooden spoon, until the mixture is thick enough to coat the bottom of the pan. This takes 10 to 15 minutes, depending on the intensity of the heat. To prevent the custard from curdling, it is better to use a slightly lower heat and take the extra time.

Pour the thickened custard through a strainer into a clean metal bowl. Stir in the dissolved gelatin. Place the bowl over another bowl filled with ice and water. Stir often until the mixture begins to thicken. Add the coconut and vanilla, stirring to mix.

In a clean bowl, beat the egg whites until frothy. Add the remaining 1 tablespoon sugar and continue to beat until the whites are stiff but not dry. Carefully and swiftly fold them into the custard base. Refrigerate while you whip the cream.

In a separate bowl, beat the cream until thick enough to hold soft peaks. Fold the cream into the custard.

Rinse a 6-cup ring mold (preferably metal, if you plan to unmold the Bavarian) with cold water. Shake out the excess water, but do not dry the mold. Spoon the custard mixture into the mold and smooth the top. Cover and refrigerate until set, about 4 hours. You can chill it longer.

When ready to serve, dip the mold into a sink filled with hot water or hold a hot towel around the mold to loosen the custard slightly. Invert a platter over the mold; holding the platter and the mold together, turn both over so the mold is upside down. If the custard does not come free immediately, shake the mold and platter firmly together. If it is still stuck, wrap the mold briefly again with a hot towel.

Lift off the mold. Fill the center of the custard with some of the berries; spoon the rest around the outside or serve them on the side.

Makes about 8 servings.

Pastry Shell

This basic crust is good for all kinds of pies, tarts, and quiches. For dessert tarts, I usually add a little sugar. For savory dishes, I leave it out. You can line a tart or pie pan with the raw dough and freeze it for a few weeks until ready to use.

1-1/2 CUPS ALL-PURPOSE FLOUR

1 TABLESPOON SUGAR (FOR DESSERT TARTS)

PINCH OF SALT

1/2 CUP (1/4 POUND) UNSALTED BUTTER, CUT INTO 16 PIECES

4 TO 5 TABLESPOONS ICE WATER

Place the flour, sugar (if used), and salt in a food processor or in the bowl of an electric mixer. Add the butter and process or mix until the butter is broken into pieces about the size of small peas. The mixture will be crumbly. Slowly pour in the ice water, mixing just until it is absorbed and the dough begins to hold together. Dump the dough onto a sheet of wax paper and press off pieces with the palm of your hand to finish blending the ingredients. Shape into a ball, flatten into a disk, cover, and refrigerate for at least 1 hour.

On a floured board or between sheets of wax paper, roll the dough into a 12-inch circle. Fit the circle into a 10-inch tart pan with a removable bottom; trim and crimp the edges. Freeze for at least 1 hour.

Preheat the oven to 400F (205C). Line the pastry shell with foil and weight it with dried beans, uncooked rice, or aluminum scraps. Bake for 10 minutes. Remove the foil and weights. Prick the bottom of the shell with a fork and return to the oven. For a partially baked crust, bake until beginning to brown all over, about 7 minutes longer. For a fully baked crust, bake until lightly browned all over, about 15 minutes longer.

Makes 1 (10-inch) crust.

Pastry Cream

This is a standard pastry cream used to fill tarts made with raw fruit. It takes a little time to make but can be prepared in advance.

1-1/4 CUPS MILK
4 LARGE EGG YOLKS
2/3 CUP SUGAR
1/2 CUP ALL-PURPOSE FLOUR
1 TABLESPOON UNSALTED BUTTER
1 TEASPOON VANILLA EXTRACT
1 TABLESPOON COINTREAU

In a small saucepan, bring the milk to a boil.

Meanwhile, place the egg yolks in a 2-quart saucepan and whisk until smooth. Whisk in the sugar, then beat until the mixture is thick and pale in color. Slowly beat in the flour. Slowly whisk in the boiling milk, then place the saucepan over medium-high heat. Cook, stirring or whisking often, until the mixture thickens and comes to a boil. As you stir, be sure to get into the corners of the pan and across the bottom. Reduce the heat slightly and cook for about 2 minutes longer. Remove from the heat; if the mixture is lumpy, press it through a strainer.

Stir in the butter, vanilla, and Cointreau. If not using immediately, cover with buttered wax paper and refrigerate.

Makes about 1-1/2 cups.

Mandarin Orange Tart

Mandarin oranges, a type of tangerine, are petite and delicious. By cutting the sections almost in half, you can get vibrant rounds that make an attractive topping for tarts. This one makes a satisfying finale to a special meal.

3 OR 4 MANDARIN ORANGES
1 RECIPE PASTRY CREAM, ABOVE
1 (10-INCH) FULLY BAKED PASTRY SHELL, PAGE 202
1/4 CUP APRICOT PRESERVES, SIEVED
2 TABLESPOONS COINTREAU

Peel the oranges and remove all the strings of white pith. Separate the oranges into sections. With a small, sharp knife, cut through the wide back of each section almost through to the center. Open each cut section to make a round. Set aside.

Spread the Pastry Cream evenly in the baked Pastry Shell. Beginning at the outside edge, make concentric circles of the orange rounds, letting each round slightly overlap its neighbor. The Pastry Cream should be almost completely hidden by the oranges.

In a small pan, combine the apricot preserves and Cointreau. Bring to a boil, stirring. With a pastry brush, spread the mixture over the orange sections. Refrigerate until ready to serve. This tart is best eaten the day it's made.

Makes 8 to 10 servings.

METRIC CHART

Comparison to Metric Measure

When You Know	Symbol	Multiply By	To Find	Symbol
teaspoons	tsp	5.0	milliliters	ml
tablespoons	tbsp	15.0	milliliters	ml
fluid ounces	fl. oz.	30.0	milliliters	ml
cups	c	0.24	liters	l
pints	pt.	0.47	liters	l
quarts	qt.	0.95	liters	l
ounces	oz.	28.0	grams	g
pounds	lb.	0.45	kilograms	kg
Fahrenheit	F	5/9 (after subtracting 32)	Celsius	C

Liquid Measure to Milliliters

1/4 teaspoon	=	1.25 milliliters
1/2 teaspoon	=	2.5 milliliters
3/4 teaspoon	=	3.75 milliliters
1 teaspoon	=	5.0 milliliters
1-1/4 teaspoons	=	6.25 milliliters
1-1/2 teaspoons	=	7.5 milliliters
1-3/4 teaspoons	=	8.75 milliliters
2 teaspoons	=	10.0 milliliters
1 tablespoon	=	15.0 milliliters
2 tablespoons	=	30.0 milliliters

Liquid Measure to Liters

1/4 cup	=	0.06 liters
1/2 cup	=	0.12 liters
3/4 cup	=	0.18 liters
1 cup	=	0.24 liters
1-1/4 cups	=	0.3 liters
1-1/2 cups	=	0.36 liters
2 cups	=	0.48 liters
2-1/2 cups	=	0.6 liters
3 cups	=	0.72 liters
3-1/2 cups	=	0.84 liters
4 cups	=	0.96 liters
4-1/2 cups	=	1.08 liters
5 cups	=	1.2 liters
5-1/2 cups	=	1.32 liters

Fahrenheit to Celsius

F	C
200—205	95
220—225	105
245—250	120
275	135
300—305	150
325—330	165
345—350	175
370—375	190
400—405	205
425—430	220
445—450	230
470—475	245
500	260

Mail-Order Sources

If you can't find some of the ingredients needed for recipes in this book at local supermarkets, Oriental markets, or health food stores, you should be able to get most of them through mail-order sources. The following list isn't long, but the stores mentioned should be able to provide everything you need. Not all of them have complete listings of their merchandise, so you may find it easiest to make a list of what you want and send it along with your request for a catalogue.

Anzen Pacific Corporation
7750 N.E. 17th Avenue
P.O. Box 11407
Portland, OR 97211
(503) 283-1284
　A very full range of Japanese and Chinese items as well as lemon grass and other Thai ingredients; Oriental vegetable seeds, including daikon and Chinese cabbage.

De Wildt Imports, Inc.
R.D. 3
Bangor, PA 18013
(215) 588-1042
　Almost all the spices and other Thai, Filipino, and Indonesian ingredients you might need, including shrimp paste, coconut milk, tamarind pulp, fish sauce, and curry paste; utensils such as woks and steamers. Detailed catalogue available.

Katagiri & Co., Inc.
224 East 59th Street
New York, NY 10022
(212) 755-3566
　Just about every Japanese ingredient you can think of, plus a full line of Japanese equipment. Detailed catalogue available.

Star Market, Inc.
3349 North Clark Street
Chicago, IL 60657
(312) 472-2184 or 472-0599
　A wide range of Japanese and Chinese sauces, noodles, sea vegetation, rices, and seasonings. Detailed list of items with brand names available.

Uwajimaya Inc.
519 Sixth Avenue South
Seattle, WA 98104
(206) 624-6248
　Assorted Japanese and Chinese ingredients. Printed listing available.

Vietnam House
242 Farmington Avenue
Hartford, CT 06105
(203) 524-0010
　Vietnamese and other Oriental ingredients and equipment. No catalogue available.

INDEX